As one of the world's longest established and best-known travel brands, Thomas Cook are the experts in travel.

For more than 135 years our guidebooks have unlocked the secrets of destinations around the world, sharing with travellers a wealth of experience and a passion for travel.

**Rely on Thomas Cook as your travelling companion on your next trip and benefit from our unique heritage.**

Thomas Cook **driving** guides

# LANGUEDOC &
## SOUTHWEST FRANCE

### Gillian Thomas and John Harrison

**Written and updated by Gillian Thomas and John Harrison**
Original photography by Image Select International/Chris Fairclough Colour Library

**Published by Thomas Cook Publishing**
A division of Thomas Cook Tour Operations Limited
Company registration no. 3772199 England
The Thomas Cook Business Park, Unit 9, Coningsby Road,
Peterborough PE3 8SB, United Kingdom
Email: books@thomascook.com, Tel: +44 (0) 1733 416477
www.thomascookpublishing.com

**Produced by Cambridge Publishing Management Limited**
Burr Elm Court, Main Street, Caldecote CB23 7NU
www.cambridgepm.co.uk

ISBN: 978-1-84848-358-3

© 2005, 2007, 2009 Thomas Cook Publishing
This fourth edition © 2011
Text © Thomas Cook Publishing
Maps © Thomas Cook Publishing/PCGraphics (UK) Limited

Series Editor: Karen Beaulah
Production/DTP: Steven Collins

Printed and bound in India by Replika Press Pvt Ltd

Cover photography © SuperStock

Although every care has been taken in compiling this publication, and the contents are
believed to be correct at the time of printing, Thomas Cook Tour Operations Limited
cannot accept any responsibility for errors or omissions, however caused, or for changes in
details given in the guidebook, or for the consequences of any reliance on the information
provided. Descriptions and assessments are based on the authors' views and experiences when
writing and do not necessarily represent those of Thomas Cook Tour Operations Limited.

# About the authors

**Gillian Thomas** and **John Harrison**, husband-and-wife authors of this book, are both members of the British Guild of Travel Writers. They live in Ealing, West London.

After graduating in French and German at Birmingham University, Gillian joined the BBC. She first combined travel with writing while working in the Paris news office. Returning to the UK, she became a freelance journalist, mainly covering women's and educational topics. Later she moved into travel writing, initially by describing family holidays in France with their three young children.

John's first steps in journalism were on *Cherwell*, the undergraduate newspaper at Oxford which he edited. He then spent 31 years with the BBC where his jobs ranged from radio announcer to TV science programmes organiser; he also set up the British Forces TV service in Germany. Having spent many hours as his wife's unpaid assistant, he joined her in full-time travel writing when he left the BBC.

**Below**
Château de Peyrepertuse

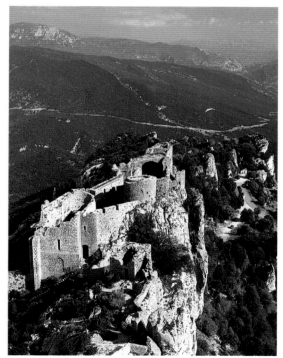

They have been visiting the Languedoc on holiday for many years, attracted initially by its long sandy beaches. Both had happy memories of their own childhood holidays in England but wanted to be sure of sunshine and warm sea for their small children as well as good sand for buckets and spades.

With the bonus of French food and wine and the area's wide choice of campsites, it proved an ideal formula. They all enjoyed the area's colourful markets, driving through its dramatic gorges, trips on its scenic railways, clambering around lofty rugged castles and venturing into the awe-inspiring caves. The scenery was a continuous delight too, embellished at dusk by magnificent sunsets.

Gillian and John would like to thank Ann Noon and Marie-Thérèse Smith of the French Tourist Office in London, Peter Mills of Rail Europe in London and Patricia de Pouzilhac of the Languedoc-Roussillon CRT for the help they gave them during their research for this book.

# Contents

# About driving guides

Thomas Cook's driving guides are designed to provide you with a comprehensive but flexible reference source to guide you as you tour a country or region by car. This guide divides the Languedoc and Southwest France into touring areas – one per chapter. Major cultural centres or cities form chapters in their own right. Each chapter contains enough attractions to provide at least a day's worth of activities – often more.

## Ratings

To make it easier for you to plan your time and decide what to see, every area is rated according to its attractions in categories such as Architecture, Entertainment and Children.

## Chapter contents

Every chapter has an introduction summing up the main attractions of the area, and a ratings box, which will highlight the area's strengths and weaknesses – some areas may be more attractive to families travelling with children, others to wine lovers or people interested in finding castles, churches or good beaches.

Each chapter is then divided into an alphabetical gazetteer, and a suggested tour. You can select whether you just want to visit a particular sight or attraction, choosing from those described in the gazetteer, or whether you want to tour the area comprehensively. If the latter, you can construct your own itinerary, or follow the authors' suggested tour, which comes at the end of every area chapter.

## The gazetteer

The gazetteer section describes all the major attractions in the area – the villages, towns, historic sites, nature reserves, parks or museums that you are most likely to want to see. Maps of the area highlight all the places mentioned in the text. Using this comprehensive overview of the area, you may choose just to visit one or two sights.

One way to use the guide is simply to find individual sights that interest you, using the index or overview map, and read what our authors have to say about them. This will help you decide whether to visit the sight. If you do, you will find plenty of practical information, such as the address, the telephone number and opening times.

Alternatively, you can choose a hotel, perhaps with the help of the accommodation recommendations contained in this guide. You can then turn to the overall map on page 8 to help you work out which chapters in the book describe those cities and regions that lie closest to your chosen touring base.

## Symbol Key

- **❶** Tourist Information Centre
- **❷** Advice on arriving or departing
- **❷** Parking locations
- **❷** Advice on getting around
- **❷** Directions
- **❶** Sights and attractions
- **❶** Accommodation
- **❶** Eating
- **⬤** Shopping
- **❷** Sport
- **❷** Entertainment

## Practical information

The practical information in the page margins, or sidebars, will help you locate the services you need as an independent traveller – including the tourist information centre, car parks and public transport facilities. You will also find the opening times of sights, museums, churches and other attractions, as well as useful tips on shopping, market days, cultural events, entertainment, festivals and sports facilities.

## Driving tours

The suggested tour is just that – a suggestion, with plenty of optional detours and one or two ideas for making your own discoveries, under the heading *Also worth exploring*. The routes are designed to link the attractions described in the gazetteer section, and to cover outstandingly scenic coastal, mountain and rural landscapes. The total distance is given for each tour, as is the time it will take you to drive the complete route, but bear in mind that this indication is just for the driving time: you will need to add on extra time for visiting attractions along the way.

Many of the routes are circular, so that you can join them at any point. Where the nature of the terrain dictates that the route has to be linear, the route can either be followed out and back, or you can use it as a link route, to get from one area in the book to another.

As you follow the route descriptions, you will find names picked out in bold capital letters – this means that the place is described fully in the gazetteer. Other names picked out in bold indicate additional villages or attractions worth a brief stop along the route.

## Accommodation and food

In every chapter you will find lodging and eating recommendations for individual towns, or for the area as a whole. These are designed to cover a range of price brackets and concentrate on more characterful small or individualistic hotels and restaurants. In addition, you will find information in the *Travel facts* chapter on chain hotels, with an address to which you can write for a guide, map or directory. The price indications used in the guide have the following meanings:

€        budget level
€€       typical/average prices
€€€      de luxe

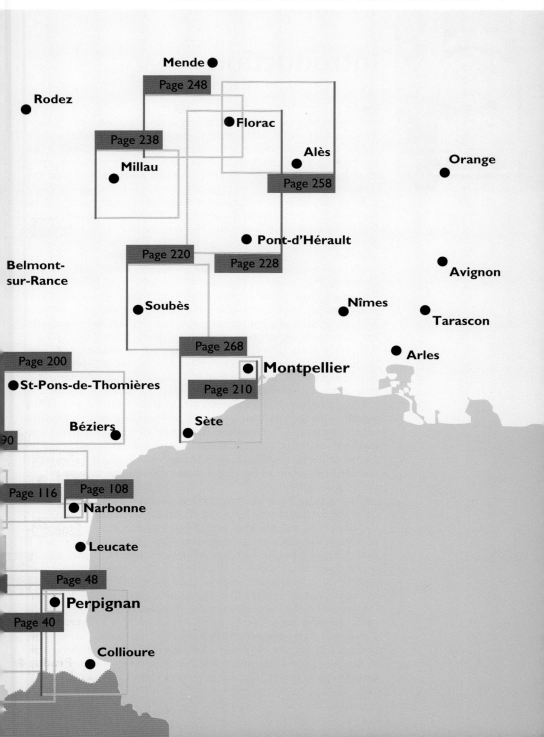

Mende

Page 248

Rodez

Page 238

Florac

Millau

Alès

Page 258

Orange

Pont-d'Hérault

Page 220

Page 228

Belmont-
sur-Rance

Avignon

Soubès

Nîmes

Tarascon

Page 268

Arles

Page 200

Montpellier

St-Pons-de-Thomières

Page 210

90

Sète

Béziers

Page 116    Page 108

Narbonne

Leucate

Page 48

Perpignan

Page 40

Collioure

# Introduction

The area covered by this book is one of the most varied in France. Glossy coastal resorts, wild remote plateaux, towering mountains, deep gorges, forests and caves – it has them all in abundance. Add a rich history, castles, cathedrals and an exceptionally wide variety of museums and it provides plenty to interest every visitor, whatever their particular taste.

All five *départements* of Languedoc-Roussillon (one of the 22 regions into which France is divided) are covered: Aude, Gard, Hérault, Lozère and Pyrénées-Roussillon; also the four *départements* in the eastern half of the Midi-Pyrénées region: Ariège-Pyrénées, Aveyron, Haute-Garonne and Tarn.

The major cities featured are Albi, Carcassonne, Montpellier, Narbonne, Perpignan and Toulouse.

Though crowded along the coast in summer, the area is still predominantly rural. It offers the traveller the bonus of quiet roads and unspoilt landscapes – but be warned, hotels and restaurants are often few and far between in the countryside, and petrol stations scarce.

Until the 1960s, few people went to this part of southern France for holidays. In those days, too, its vineyards were better known for the quantity of their wines rather than the quality. The anonymous *vins de table* invariably hailed from the area.

Today Languedoc and its wines are up there with the best in the world – and the coastline is dotted with a string of well-planned resorts, the result of a far-sighted initiative by the French government. Furthermore, the building of marinas, apartments and villa complexes – some of the most imaginative in Europe – has been accompanied by careful conservation of the fragile dunes and shallow lagoons behind the long sandy beaches.

Driving inland you are very soon surrounded by vineyards. They cover the flat Languedoc plain and stretch up the sunny slopes of the Corbières hills and the Montagne Noire. The fact that an increasing number of the wines reach the *appellation d'origine contrôlée* standard is not only good news for everyone who enjoys them but is also helping to raise the area's profile.

Mountains frame both ends of the region, the Cévennes in the northeast and the Pyrenees in the south. Jagged ridges, deep river canyons and rocky limestone plateaux (with vast caves beneath) make it one of the most scenic too.

Not surprisingly, the mountains have become as popular as the coast, though without the crowds. Canoeists enjoy shooting the rapids, walkers and horse riders have miles of waymarked trails to explore and, when the snow arrives in winter, skiers flock to the Pyrenees.

Though so many of the buildings along the coast are modern, the area has plenty to show for over 2,000 years of history. Discoveries in a cave near the tiny village of Tautavel in the Corbières have revealed that people settled the area 700,000 years ago.

More recently – around the first century AD – the Romans left plenty of traces of their occupation, when Narbonne was capital of Gaul. A section of their Via Domitia highway, revealed during recent excavations and now the centrepiece of the city's main square, is just one of many relics from that remarkable era.

Touring the area today, you soon become aware of the havoc caused by religious and political conflicts over the centuries. The ruined castles which cling precariously to hilltops played a leading role in the struggles between Cathars and Catholics at the beginning of the 13th century. Others guarded the volatile border with Spain.

Whole communities were wiped out during the merciless campaigns to rid the area of the Cathar 'heretics' and later when Protestants fought for religious freedom. Many magnificent churches have survived, often fortress-like with a single nave designed to enable huge numbers to worship together and so be left in no doubt about the power of the clergy. Albi cathedral is the most outstanding of all.

Happier times and prosperity arrived when blue became the fashionable colour – woad, from which blue dye was produced, grew in profusion in the 'golden triangle' between Toulouse, Albi and Carcassonne. Local merchants were quick to capitalise on its availability and sold it around Europe. Their profits enabled them to build grand mansions which still grace the streets of Toulouse and other towns, some now converted into museums.

More than most areas of France, Languedoc changes with the seasons. In summer, the vineyards are a mass of vivid green leaves, yet come winter they are cut back to bare stumps that look more dead than alive. Each plant is neatly clipped by hand, a true labour of love. In autumn, those same vines transform the countryside once more when the leaves turn orange, maroon and purple.

The appearance of the mountains varies dramatically too. Autumn is the most beautiful time as the hillsides are patched with vivid yellows, reds and browns thanks to the beech and chestnut trees. In winter, snow covers the meadows and pine-covered slopes around the Cerdagne plateau in the Pyrenees, and also the highest parts of the Cévennes.

Despite having so much historical and scenic diversity to offer, the Languedoc has still to catch up with its neighbour, Provence, as an instantly recognisable tourist region. Holidaying on the coast in summer, it's pleasing to find more than enough room on the beach to spread out your towel. And there is certainly some way to go yet before the beaches begin to feel overcrowded. In high season, however, the coastal roads can become unpleasantly busy; but how delightful that so many places in the Languedoc and the Southwest are still off the beaten track. Visit and you will discover the best of the area and its diverse secrets.

# Travel facts

## Accommodation

The area's hotels range from basic to luxurious, though most are in the small and reasonably priced category. They tend to be in the cities and towns rather than in the countryside and many close out of season (usually November–March). Accommodation of all sorts can be booked on the Languedoc-Roussillon Holidays website: *www.sunfrance.com*

To help offset the summer heat, bedrooms are usually uncarpeted, and have shutters on the windows; they also help keep out the winter wind. If you don't like the look of the bolster on the bed, softer pillows (and extra blankets) can invariably be found in the wardrobe. Tea/coffee-making facilities are rarely provided.

Few hotels are part of international chains, except in the cities (particularly Toulouse and Montpellier). Chains represented include the modern four-star Holiday Inn Crowne Plaza, three-star Mercure and Novotel and two-star Campanile, Climat, Comfort Inn and Ibis.

Many of the smaller ones are members of the Logis de France association of privately owned hotels whose owners have signed a quality charter guaranteeing modern comforts and friendly service. These are marked by a distinctive yellow and green chimney sign outside. Their prices are always reasonable and the restaurants invariably feature home cooking with an emphasis on regional specialities. Many Logis hotels are in interesting old buildings and most are family-run, with the owners in residence to provide a homely welcome. The Logis directory, *3000 hôtels-restaurants de France*, is available free from the Atout (French Tourist Office) shop at *Lincoln House, 300 High Holborn, London WC1V 7JH (tel: 0906 824 4123 – premium rates apply)* or visit *www.logishotels.com*

## Gîtes

For self-catering, *Gîtes de France* are country properties, often part of a farm, whose owners have refurbished them for holiday accommodation (under a government grant scheme). Standards vary – from basic upwards. To book a gîte, go to **Gîtes de France:** *tel: 04 67 67 62 62; www.gites-de-france.com.* **Brittany Ferries** (*tel: 08705 360360*) also deals with enquiries about gîtes and other self-catering accommodation which are featured in its brochures; *tel: 08705 143 537; www.brittanyferries.co.uk*. A selection of country cottages, apartments and houses is also available through Interhome: *tel: 020 8780 6633; www.interhome.co.uk* or through local tourist offices and

### Hotel chains

**Accor** (includes Etap, Ibis, Mercure, Novotel, Pullman, Formule-1)
*Central reservation number:*
*UK tel: 0871 702 9469;*
*USA/Canada tel: 1 800 515 5679; www.accorhotels.com*

**Best Western**
*UK tel: 08457 73 73 73;*
*USA/Canada tel: 0800 393 130; www.bestwestern.com*

**Choice Hotels** (includes Comfort and Quality Inns)
*France tel: 0800 91 24 24;*
*UK tel: 0800 44 44 44;*
*USA/Canada tel: 1 877 424 6423; www.choicehotels.com*

**Holiday Inn & Crowne Plaza** *UK tel: 0800 40 50 60; USA/Canada tel: 1 800 465 4329;*
*www.holidayinn.com,*
*www.crowneplaza.com*

**Relais et Châteaux**
*UK tel: 0800 2000 00 02;
USA/Canada tel: 1 800 735
2478; email:
guide@relaischateaux.com;
www.relaischateaux.com*

**Fédération Nationale
des Logis de France**
*Reservation hotline: 01 45
84 83 84 (France);
email: info@logis-de-
france.fr; www.logis-de-
france.fr/uk*

agencies (*see page 29*). Another large selection, bookable direct with the owners, appears in the *Holiday France Direct* brochure: *tel: 0871 244 1408; www.holidayfrancedirect.co.uk*

## Bed & Breakfast

'Le B&B' is an internationally recognised term for accommodation in guest rooms in private homes, whether it's in a simple farmhouse, a town house or a grand château. The French also call it *chambres d'hôtes*. Thomas Cook Publishing, in cooperation with Bed & Breakfast (France), publish an annual directory – *Bed & Breakfast France* (price £14.99 plus p&p) – available from **Thomas Cook Publishing,** *PO Box 227, Peterborough PE3 8SB, UK; tel: 01733 416477; www. thomascookpublishing.com.* **Bed & Breakfast (France)** has a website at *www.bedbreak.com.* You can book your Bed & Breakfast on the website or by phone; *tel: 0871 781 0834 (UK); email: bab@bedbreak.com*

## Camping

Campsites are graded from one to four stars. Facilities and standards in the top category can be very impressive, including hot showers, supermarkets, takeaway restaurants and extensive sports amenities. Some have caravans (mobile homes) and chalets for hire; pre-erected tents and caravans can also be booked, including travel, through several UK tour operators (*see page 29*). The Camping France website at *www.campingfrance.com* handles online bookings for a range of owners covering more than one thousand campsites in southern France.

## Airports

Montpellier and Toulouse have international airports serving cities around Europe, including London and Paris. Low-cost flights from the UK go to them and also to Béziers, Carcassonne, Nîmes, Perpignan and Rodez. The only direct service to the area from North America is between Montreal and Toulouse; other transatlantic services go to Paris but there are frequent internal flights or you can continue your journey by train or car. All the major car rental companies have desks at Toulouse airport. Toulouse airport: *www.toulouse.aeroport.fr;* Montpellier-Méditerranée airport: *www.montpellier.aeroport.fr*

## Children

The sandy beaches along the Languedoc-Roussillon coast make its resorts very popular with families. The larger ones have children's beach clubs during the school holidays in summer (July and August). There are Aqualand water parks with slides in St-Cyprien-Plage (*see page 57*) and Le Cap d'Agde (*see page 271*), and a safari park, Réserve

## Customs regulations

Following the withdrawal of duty-free facilities within the European Union, Customs authorities in all member countries have introduced guidance levels for the import of tobacco, alcohol and other products bought by visitors for their own use, on which French duty and tax has been paid in shops and supermarkets. The levels for importing duty-paid cigarettes into the UK are currently higher than in the rest of the EU. For example, the current guidance limit for bringing duty-paid cigarettes into the UK from other EU countries is 3,200 but the limit within the rest of the EU is 800.

If you buy more dutiable goods than the amounts specified by HM Revenue & Customs, you must satisfy Customs Officers that the goods are for your personal use. For motorists returning to the UK on Eurotunnel trains, British Customs checks are made at the French station before you board the train.

Travellers from outside the European Union should check the duty-free allowances in their home countries.

Non-EU residents can claim the TVA (VAT) back on goods purchased in France when they spend a large sum in the same shop (though not all shops offer this facility).

Africaine de Sigean (*see page 120*), south of Narbonne. Inland, the area is short of man-made attractions but its many caves, hilltop castles and tortuous mountain roads can provide plenty of excitement for young visitors.

## Climate

The area enjoys some of the best weather in France with plenty of clear, dry days. During July and August, temperatures along the coast average around 28°C (82°F), dropping to 11°C (52°F) in February. Perpignan is one of the warmest places in France. However, the coast can also be windy due to the *Tramontane*, which frequently blows across the Corbières hills from the northwest, for three, six or nine days continuously. Another famous wind, the warm, gusty *Autan*, blows from the sea. 'It drives you mad,' they say in Toulouse and Albi. In the mountains the weather is always a little cooler. The higher areas in the Pyrenees have enough snow for skiing, and the Cévennes can also get a smattering of snow.

On doors and shutters of houses throughout the Causses you will often see a dried *chardon du causse* (thistle) hanging. When rain is imminent, the thistle closes up, but in good weather it stays open; thus it acts as a natural barometer.

## Currency

The unit of currency, the euro (€), is divided into 100 cents. When sums are written, a comma rather than a decimal point is used to separate euros from cents. Payments can be made in euro notes and coins from any of the countries in the eurozone. Airports and banks, as well as some shopping centres and tourist offices, have bureaux de change. Cash points (ATMs), known in France as *distributeurs*, are widespread. Payments can be made in euros by credit cards. Very few traders accept traveller's cheques as payment for goods and services and you will need to go to a major branch of a bank to change them for cash.

## Drinking

Languedoc-Roussillon is one of the most prolific wine-producing regions in France. In the vineyard areas on the plains just inland from the coast, there are frequent opportunities for a *dégustation* (sampling) at cooperative cellars and roadside stalls, as well as at the *domaines* (wine-producing estates) themselves. The red, white and rosé *vins de pays* (table wines) are inexpensive, though an increasing number of high-quality *appellation d'origine contrôlée* vintages are being produced.

If in doubt about what to drink with a meal, ask the waiter for advice. They are invariably knowledgeable and willing to help. The cheapest option is to have open wine, which comes in a *pichet* (litre

## Electricity

Plugs have either two or three round pins. As this is not a standard European design, you are likely to need an adaptor. The voltage is 220 (50 MHz).

## Regional specialities

A strong Arabic influence is noticeable in Catalan cakes, which ooze with honey and are flavoured with nuts and spices. *Crème Catalan* is a vanilla custard topped with crisp caramel, but lighter than crème brûlée.

The cherries which grow around Céret are the earliest variety in France and are followed by a succession of other fruits, particularly peaches, apricots, pears and apples. Seasonal fruit is used in flans for dessert.

Several towns have their own special cakes, including *petits pâtés* in Pézanas, *Glorias* and *Alleluias* in Castelnaudary and *jeannots* in Albi.

jug) or *demi-pichet*. If you ask for a beer – *une pression* or *une bière* – you automatically get a *demi* (½-litre) unless you specify more. Beer, pastis, kir (wine and cassis), Floc de Gascogne (sweet wine), whisky, fruit juice and mineral water are the accepted aperitifs – or sparkling wine. These are usually served with an *amuse-gueule* (cocktail snack) such as olives or small pastries. Note, however, that your food will not be served until the glasses are empty!

It is safe to drink tap water; indeed, restaurants invariably place a carafe on the table. It is 'not done' for men to drink only water with dinner in the evening, though driving or work are acceptable excuses for having soft drinks only. Mineral water can be more expensive than wine.

Café prices vary depending on whether you are served at the bar, at a table inside or at a table on the terrace, but price lists must be displayed both outside and inside. The staff are required to give bills for orders over €13; for lower amounts, they must give you one if you ask for it.

Selling or offering alcoholic drinks to children aged under 16 in bars (*cafés*), shops and other public places is banned, and you are not allowed to bring alcoholic drinks into establishments that provide fitness and sporting activities.

## Eating out

The larger towns offer an interestingly varied choice of restaurants, including many good ones in hotels. All are legally required to offer a set menu. Brasseries are less formal, stay open longer and offer snacks as well as two or three set menus. Sunday lunchtime is invariably busy everywhere (so it pays to make a reservation). Some restaurants are closed on Sunday evening and also on a weekday, often Monday. Many shut for a month or so in winter.

In the evening, restaurant menus (served from around 1900) are more expensive and elaborate than at lunchtime (1200–1400) when it is perfectly acceptable to order one dish and no alcohol. Bread is served automatically.

In restaurants, always wait to be shown to a table as it is 'not done' to choose one yourself. If you don't like it, you can then ask to be seated elsewhere. The bill (*l'addition*) will be brought to the table for payment.

Hotels and restaurants affiliated to the Logis de France association can be relied on to serve home cooking and regional specialities. In the countryside, you can also eat at *fermes-auberges* (farm restaurants) where the farmer's wife invariably provides a robust country meal using local seasonal ingredients. You usually need to book a day in advance and probably won't be offered a choice.

## Conversion tables

### Distances

| Metric | Imperial |
|--------|----------|
| 1m | 3ft 3in |
| 5m | 16ft 6in |
| 10m | 33ft |
| 50m | 164ft |
| 100m | 330ft |
| 1km | ²/₃ mile |
| 2km | 1¼ miles |
| 5km | 3 miles |
| 10km | 6¼ miles |
| 20km | 12½ miles |
| 50km | 31 miles |
| 100km | 62 miles |

### Weight

| Kg | Lb |
|----|-----|
| 1 | 2 |
| 2 | 4½ |
| 5 | 11 |
| 10 | 22 |
| 20 | 45 |
| 50 | 110 |
| 75 | 165 |
| 100 | 220 |

### Fluid measures

| Litres | Imperial gallons |
|--------|------------------|
| 5 | 1⅛ |
| 10 | 2¼ |
| 20 | 4½ |
| 50 | 11 |

### Area

1 hectare = 2.471 acres
1 acre = 0.4 hectares

## Entry formalities

Visas are not required by EU nationals or visitors from the USA, Canada and New Zealand staying not more than three months. Visitors from most other countries including Australia and South Africa need one, obtainable from their local French consulate.

## Festivals

Every town and village seems to have its own festival during the summer months, often with a bonfire and fireworks, processions, street entertainment and barbecues. No matter how small, they are an occasion not to miss and visitors are always welcome to join in. Bastille Day (14 July) is celebrated in great style.

Midsummer is also a time for street parties. Les Feux de la St-Jean takes place on 23 June, particularly around the Canigou mountain. Torches lit from bonfires on the mountain are carried down to more bonfires in the villages and towns below. When the embers begin to die down, everyone starts jumping over them. Many people join the grand procession into Perpignan.

Music festivals include sacred music in Perpignan (Holy Week), jazz in Albi (May and June), dance in Montpellier (June), riverside concerts in Toulouse (June); also a medieval festival in Narbonne (August).

## Food

Cassoulet, a sustaining meat stew with white beans, is one of the area's most famous dishes. Originally designed for hearty appetites, it features on menus in and around Toulouse and Carcassonne. Several kinds of fish stew are available on the coast, including *brandade de morue*, made from salt cod with milk and garlic. Bouziques oysters are cultivated in the Bassin de Thau; anchovies are a speciality in Collioure; and plump mussels are served stuffed with a herb and tomato sauce in Sète. Inland, you find mainly freshwater fish, particularly trout.

The area's most famous cheese is the creamy blue-veined Roquefort. Made from ewes' milk, it is matured for up to six months. Bleu des Causses is also a blue cheese, but made from cows' milk. Pélaradon des Cévennes is a small, round, mountain cheese made with goats' milk; it can be eaten fresh while soft, or left to mature and harden.

## Information

Most towns and some villages have a tourist office, though some are only open in high season. In smaller places, it is called the Syndicat d'Initiative (SI) and in larger ones the Office de Tourisme (OT). Many have an accommodation booking service, usually free. All have free local maps and accommodation lists.

## Postcodes

Postcodes (zip codes) in France are five-figure numbers inserted in an address in front of the city name. The first two digits indicate the *département* or county. Hérault postcodes, for example, begin with 34, Midi-Pyrénées 31, Pyrénées-Orientales (which includes Perpignan) 66 and Paris 75. The postcode is needed for letters sent in the mail, of course, but it is also very useful for locating an address on Internet map sites, in-car satellite navigation (satnav) and hand-held devices.

Unfortunately, many close at lunchtime, around 1200–1400, even at the height of summer. A solution is to seek out a café with a 'Bonjour' sign. This means it stocks local tourist information.

To get information on a particular area, bear in mind that France is divided into 22 regions. The regions in turn are split into *départements*. Do not expect an office to provide information about other *départements*.

The Languedoc-Roussillon Tourist Board – Comité Régional du Tourisme (CRT) – is based at *201 avenue de la Popignare, 34064 Montpellier; tel: 04 67 22 80 00; www.laregion.fr*

The Comités Départementaux du Tourisme (CDTs) in Languedoc-Roussillon are Aude: *11855 Carcassonne; tel: 04 68 11 66 00; www.audetourisme.com*; Gard: *3 place des Arènes, 30010 Nîmes; tel: 04 66 36 96 30; www.tourismegard.fr*; Hérault: *avenue des Moulins, 34034 Montpellier; tel: 04 67 67 71 71; www.herault-tourisme.com*; Lozère: *14 boulevard Henri Bourrillo, 48001 Mende; tel: 04 66 65 60 00; www.lozere-tourisme*; Pyrénées-Orientales: *16 avenue des Palmiers, 66005 Perpignan; tel: 04 68 51 52 53; www.cdt-66.com*

For Midi-Pyrénées the CRT is at *1 rue Rémusat, 31080 Toulouse; tel: 05 34 44 18 18; www.tourism-midi-pyrenees.co.uk*. The relevant CDTs in Midi-Pyrénées are Ariège-Pyrénées: *31 bis avenue du Général du Gaulle, 09004 Foix; tel: 05 61 02 30 70; www.ariegepyrenees.com*; Aveyron: *17 rue Aristide Briand, 12008 Rodez; tel: 05 65 75 55 75; www.tourisme-aveyron.com*; Haute-Garonne: *14 rue Bayard, 31015 Toulouse; tel: 05 61 99 44 00; www.tourisme-haute-garonne.com*; Tarn: *Moulin Albigeois, 41 rue Porta, 81006 Albi; tel: 05 63 77 32 10; www.tourisme-tarn.com*

Information about **walking tours** and **hiking** can be provided by the Parc National des Pyrénées: *tel: 05 62 92 52 56; www.parc-pyrenees.com*; or the Fédération Française de la Randonnée Pédestre: *64 rue du Dessous des Berges, 75013 Paris; tel: 01 44 89 93 93; www.ffrandonnee.fr*

For information about **campsites** in the region, contact Fédération de l'Hôtellerie de Plein Air Languedoc-Roussillon, *BP 21, 30220 Aigues-Mortes; tel: 04 66 35 99 99; email: camping@languedocroussillon.fr; www.campinglanguedocroussillon.com*

French tourist offices abroad are called Atout France: **Australia**: *Level 13, 25 Bligh Street, Sydney NSW 2000; tel: 29231 5244; email: info.au@franceguide.com*; **Canada**: *1800 avenue MacGill College, Suite 1010, Montreal H3A 3J6; tel: 514 288 20 26; email: canada@franceguide.com*; **Ireland**: *telephone or email access only; tel: 1560 235 235 (premium rates apply); email: info.ie@franceguide.com*; **South Africa**: *Village Walk Office Tower, Sandton, Johannesburg; tel: 11 523 8292; email: info.za@franceguide.com*; **United Kingdom**: *Lincoln House, 300 High Holborn, London WC1V 7JH; tel: 09068 244 123 (premium rates apply); email: info.uk@franceguide.com*; **United States**: *email access only; email: info.us@franceguide.com*

## Health

You should obtain a European Health Insurance Card (EHIC) before leaving the UK. The EHIC is available free of charge through most United Kingdom post offices, by telephoning: *0845 606 2030* or via their website *www.ehic.uk.com*. Their leaflet *Health Advice for Travellers* has more information and an application form.

The EHIC is not a substitute for medical and travel insurance, but entitles you to emergency medical treatment on the same terms as French nationals. The card does not cover you for medical repatriation, ongoing medical treatment or treatment of a non-urgent nature. Most UK insurance companies now give discounts or waive the 'excess' on travel health insurance policies if you use the EHIC.

There are no vaccinations specifically recommended for visitors to France, but rabies is prevalent in some areas and you are advised to avoid any contact with stray dogs.

## Maps

Michelin 1/200,000 (1cm:2km) Regional maps are a good scale for touring (including Nos 526 Languedoc-Roussillon and 525 Midi-Pyrénées). The larger-scale (1/150,000) Local maps for the area covered in this book are Nos 338, 339, 342, 343 and 344.

IGN (Institut Géographique National) publishes a regional 1/250,000 scale Carte-Routière series; No R16 covers Midi-Pyrénées and No R17 covers Languedoc-Roussillon. In its 1/100,000 Green series, the area is covered by Nos 58, 59, 64, 65 and 72. The 1/25,000 Blue series is designed for walkers. Available in the UK direct from Stanfords, *12–14 Long Acre, London WC2E 9LP; tel: 020 7836 1321; www.stanfords.co.uk*

Regional and departmental tourist boards issue free maps of their areas, marked with tourist attractions and listing useful addresses. Most newsagents and petrol stations sell local maps.

## Museums

National museums close all day on Tuesdays and municipal ones on Mondays; also some bank holidays. Privately run attractions normally open daily during high season; many close October–Easter. Opening hours vary but are usually from around 0900 or 1000 to 1700 or 1800 (often shorter hours at weekends); many close at lunchtime.

Most charge a small entrance fee with discounts for children. At national museums, under-18s are free and 18–25s and over-60s get a discount. At municipal museums, under-7s and over-60s are free; Sundays are free to everyone.

## National and regional parks

The mountainous and sparsely populated Cévennes National Park covers 1,000sq km and rises at Mont Lozère to 1,700m. It has large areas of open moorland, known for birds of prey such as eagles as well as butterflies and wild flowers. The park's information centre, Maison du Parc, is in the Château de Florac at Florac; *tel: 04 66 49 53 01; email: info@cevennes-parcnational.fr; www.cevennes-parcnational.fr*

Haut Languedoc Regional Park, a hilly forested region, is a good place to watch for eagles and other birds of prey, and is also excellent for walking. Information: *13 rue du Cloître, St-Pons-de-Thomières; tel: 04 67 97 38 22; email: pnr.haut-languedoc@wanadoo.fr; www.vivrehautlanguedoc.com/le_parc/index2.html*

## Opening times

Banks: open from 0800 or 0900 to 1200 and from 1300 or 1400 to 1600 or 1700, but close earlier before a bank holiday. They close Sunday and either Monday or Saturday.

**Opposite**
St-Guilhem-le-Désert

All hotels have a list of doctors and emergency medical services. Pharmacists are qualified to diagnose basic problems and suggest treatments, though you need a doctor's prescription to claim the cost back on insurance. As many people go mushrooming, pharmacists are also trained to identify which ones are poisonous! Pharmacies have a green cross sign outside. They are normally closed on Sundays but display a list of those on duty.

For the emergency medical service, SAMU, dial 15.

### Postal services

Postboxes are yellow. Post offices (la Poste) are generally *open Mon–Fri 0800–1900, often with a lunchtime break, and until 1200 on Sat.* There are eight price zones for mail, ranging from postcards and letters up to 20g within the EU to airmail to Australasia. Aerograms are the same for all countries. Stamps (*timbres-postes*) can also be bought at tobacconists (*tabacs*).

### Public holidays

1 Jan: New Year's Day
Mar/Apr: Good Friday
1 May: Labour Day
8 May: VE Day
May: Ascension Day
May/Jun: Pentecost
(Whit Monday)
14 Jul: National Day
15 Aug: Assumption
1 Nov: All Saints
11 Nov: Armistice Day
25 Dec: Christmas Day
When a national holiday falls on a Sunday, the next day is taken as a holiday instead.

Shops: normal hours are from 0900 or 1000 to 1830 or 1930; smaller ones close between 1300 and 1500 or 1600. Food shops open earlier and hypermarkets stay open later. *Boulangeries* (bakers) and *épiceries* (grocers) open Sunday morning, but other shops are closed, including hypermarkets. Many shops close on Monday, at least in the morning.

Churches: most are open 0800–1900, but usually close between 1145 and 1430. Entry is free. Visitors should not enter during services unless they intend to join the congregation.

## Packing

Swimwear and a sunhat are needed to enjoy the area's beaches (though many have nudist areas). Walking boots or shoes are essential for exploring the mountains on foot. In summer, a sweater and/or light jacket is advisable for evenings in case the wind gets up. Clothing requirements in winter depend on where you are going, from ski-wear in the Pyrenees to something lighter elsewhere, though the wind can be unexpectedly cold throughout the region.

## Reading

*The Cathars* by Malcolm Lambert, published by Blackwell.

*Travels with a Donkey in the Cévennes* by R L Stevenson.

### Safety and security

Emergency telephone numbers: *112* or Ambulance *15*, Police *17* and Fire *18*.

As in most places, it pays to keep to well-lit streets in towns after dark and to take care of handbags or wallets. When you park your car, hide luggage and valuables, especially cameras.

### Shopping

In the southwest of the region, colourful Catalan fabrics are on sale in specialist stores and craft shops, usually made up into household items, as well as skirts and dresses. To the east, potteries abound near the coast, often with attractive terracotta pots and glazed tableware stacked temptingly outside. You are unlikely to leave the region without investing in some wine as there are so many opportunities to buy it – hypermarkets, roadside stalls, *caves coopératives* and the vineyards themselves.

### Smoking

Throughout France smoking is prohibited inside public places such as bars, restaurants, museums, monuments, theatres and cinemas and on all public transport.

## Public transport

Frequent trains run between the main cities. Typical timings are: Toulouse–Albi 1 hour, Toulouse–Carcassonne 1 hour, Toulouse–Montpellier 2 hours 10 minutes, Montpellier–Narbonne 1 hour, Narbonne–Perpignan 40 minutes, Narbonne–Carcassonne 35 minutes. Information and bookings: *tel: 36 35.* Reservations are required on TGV (*train à grande vitesse*) services, which run between Montpellier and Perpignan. Bus services are very patchy. Toulouse has a one-line underground metro and Montpellier a tramway.

## Sport

Rugby, which arrived in the area a hundred years ago, is enthusiastically played and watched. ASB in Béziers is one of France's top teams. Around Carcassonne, rugby league is played too. Football is a particular passion in Toulouse. And in the shade of every dusty square, you are likely to see a game of pétanque (boules), played mostly by older men.

## Stores

Department stores are few and far between in the area except in Montpellier, Perpignan and Toulouse. Galeries Lafayette are smart fashion stores; Monoprix are middle-range stores selling food, inexpensive fashion, accessories and stationery.

Hypermarkets, which are situated on the outskirts of the largest towns, have a vast selection of food and kitchenware as well as cheap clothes, toys and electrical equipment. These include Auchan, Géant Casino and Leclerc.

## Telephones

The regional codes, 04 (Languedoc-Roussillon) and 05 (Midi-Pyrénées), are followed by eight digits; dial the whole number. Cheap rates (50 per cent extra time) are from 1900 (international calls from 2230) to 0800 weekdays and from 1400 on Saturdays and all day Sundays. At most telephone kiosks you will need a *télécarte* (phonecard) obtainable from post offices, *tabacs* and newsagents in 50 or 120 units. Kiosks marked with a blue bell can receive calls.

International calls can be made from most call boxes. To make an international call, lift the receiver, insert a *télécarte*, dial 00 to get an international line, then when the tone changes dial the country code followed by the number (omitting the first 0). International codes: UK 44; USA 1.

To dial France from abroad, the international access code is 00 33 followed by the number without the 0 of the local code. For directory enquiries, dial *12*. For the operator, dial *13*.

## Time

France is one hour ahead of GMT in winter (last Sunday in October to last Saturday in March) and two hours ahead of it during summer.

## Tipping

Service (15 per cent) is included on hotel and restaurant bills, but for particularly good service you may want to give an additional tip of 5–10 per cent; put it on the table as you leave.

It is usual to give taxi drivers, hairdressers and hotel porters a small tip.

## Toilets

Restaurants and cafés always have toilets for their customers. Public ones exist in most towns, often French-style (hole in the floor).

## Travellers with disabilities

The Hérault *département* has taken a leading role in promoting facilities for the disabled. It publishes a booklet listing adapted accommodation (hotels, campsites and gîtes) and special activity holidays and is available from Comité Départemental du Tourisme de l'Hérault, *avenue des Moulins, 34034 Montpellier; tel: 04 67 67 71 71; www.herault-tourisme.com*

Wheelchair access is not always available at hotels, though new ones are required to have at least one room adapted for disabled visitors.

*Guide Vacances*, a guide to accessible accommodation, is published by L'Association des Paralysés de France; *tel: 01 40 78 69 60; www.apf.asso.fr.* Available by post only from Direction de la Communication, *17 boulevard Auguste Blanqui, 75013 Paris; price €5.50.*

Tourism For All, a charity, provides information about tourism and travel for older and disabled people. Contact: *Tourism For All, Shap Road Industrial Estate, Kendal LA9 6NZ; tel: 0845 124 9971; email: info@tourismforall.org.uk; www.tourismforall.org.uk*

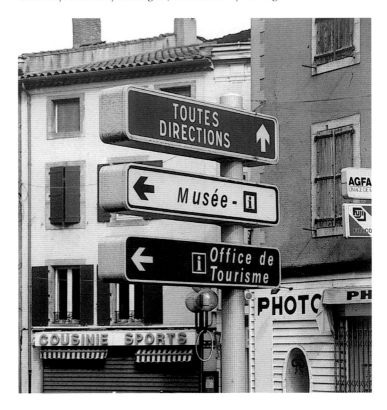

# Driver's guide

## Automobile clubs

Members of UK motoring organisations (AA or RAC) can extend their accident insurance and breakdown services to France. Both organisations offer a wide range of information and advice as well as suggesting itineraries and routes. *www.theaa.com* offers a free, turn-by-turn route map of your journey. See also *www.rac.co.uk* and *www.viamichelin.co.uk*

## Autoroutes

Most of the French autoroutes are toll roads. The commonest system of charging (*péage*) involves taking a ticket from a machine at the start of the toll section, which raises an automatic barrier. On leaving the system, or at an intermediate tollbooth, the ticket is presented and the amount to pay is displayed on an illuminated sign. Payment may be made in euros or by credit card. Signatures are not normally required. Traveller's cheques cannot usually be used for tolls. On autoroutes, speed is sometimes automatically computed from your time of entry and distance covered on arrival at the tollbooth. If a speeding offence is disclosed you may be prosecuted.

## Accidents

You must STOP after any accident. You can be in serious trouble if you don't. Call *15*, *17* or *18* to alert the Ambulance, Police or Fire Service as appropriate, or use the EU universal emergency number *112*. On an autoroute or main road, use one of the bright orange free SOS emergency roadside telephones located at frequent intervals.

Give whatever aid you are capable of to any person injured or in peril. It is an offence not to do this if it lies within your ability. This applies whether you are driver, passenger or witness. Safeguard against a secondary accident. Hazard lights or a warning triangle, which are compulsory in France, signal to other traffic. Exchange details of vehicles, driver's insurance, etc. (French cars display insurance details on a windscreen sticker.) Complete a 'European Accident Statement' form – ask your insurers for this before you leave; the French driver will almost certainly have one. This forms a factual record. It is not an admission of fault. Note as many details as you can. Photographs? Witnesses? If someone has been injured, you must inform the police. If you have damaged someone else's vehicle or property and you are unable to give the owner your details, you must inform the police. The police will not usually take details where an accident involves material damage only, unless there is evidence of an offence such as dangerous or drink driving. Inform your insurers as soon as possible.

## Breakdowns

If you are on an autoroute, stop your vehicle on the hard shoulder, getting it as far to the right as possible. On ordinary roads, consider using the verge but beware of roadside ditches. Put hazard lights on. Place a warning triangle at least 30m from the scene, visible from 100m away. (Remember, it can be very dangerous to walk on the hard shoulder of any motorway.) You and your passengers are probably safer out of the vehicle and well up the verge away from the traffic.

If you need assistance on an autoroute, you must use one of the free roadside telephones to connect you with the police. You cannot arrange recovery yourself, even if you are a member of a breakdown service. No garage will send a recovery vehicle on to an autoroute without police permission. There is a fixed scale of charges (€113 by day, €169.50 by night). You may not carry out a DIY tow on an autoroute and you may only do so on an ordinary road for 'a few metres' in an emergency.

## Documents

Members of EU countries and US citizens only need a valid national driving licence, but an international driving licence is essential for other nationals. Provisional licences are not valid and drivers must be over the age of 18. UK photo card licences are best. Paper licences are lawful but further proof of ID may be required. Registration papers (a logbook) and a letter of authorisation if the car is not registered in your name, insurance papers and Test Certificate (MoT) (originals – photocopies are not valid) and a nationality plate must be carried. The above documents must be produced at the time on request by the police. An immediate fine may be imposed if they are not to hand. For UK drivers a 'Green Card' is not required in France for car insurance. Your certificate of insurance issued in Britain conforms to French legal needs. However, this is minimum legal cover. You should ask your insurers to extend your normal, full cover for use abroad for the period of your stay. Should you visit the state of Andorra in the Pyrenees you will require a Green Card. Holders of US insurance must take out a European policy.

Continental breakdown insurance is strongly recommended and one phone call is all it takes to hand the whole problem over to multi-lingual operators, who are experts in sorting things out.

## Caravans and camper vans (Trailers and RVs)

France is probably the most 'camping and caravanning friendly' country in Europe and there are numerous attractive campsites from economical to de luxe in the area covered by this guide, especially in the most popular locations near the Mediterranean coast and in the Pyrenees. In the latter area, many are open all year to cater for winter sports enthusiasts. There is no need to book ahead, apart from the height of the winter/summer season. The Alan Rogers' campsite guides are very useful. *Camping sauvage* ('wild' camping) is completely banned. Camping in State Forests or any wooded area is virtually always prohibited because of the serious risk of fire. Overnight parking of motorhomes is frequently permitted (and often free) in the central square of smaller towns and villages where water and toilet facilities are available. There are no campsites in Monaco and while you may drive through the principality on the main roads, the parking of caravans or motorhomes is not allowed. There are no formalities about bringing a caravan into France if your stay is for less than six months.

Motorhomes and cars towing trailers have to pay a higher toll on autoroutes. Some caravanners use the facilities of the autoroute *aires de repos* (rest areas) for an overnight stop. This is quite lawful, as your autoroute ticket lasts for at least 24 hours. If you do this, you are advised to use common sense and stop in a well-lit spot, in view of passers-by. Thefts and break-ins are, unfortunately, not unknown.

Speed limits for cars towing trailers or caravans are the same as solo vehicles. Occasionally, there may be a reduced speed limit for caravans on long declines. This is to reduce the danger of instability when the caravan is being neither pulled nor braked but is 'floating' behind the towing vehicle.

If you intend driving in the Pyrenees or the Alps (and particularly if you are towing a trailer), you should remember that engine efficiency decreases with altitude, by about 10 per cent every 900m. This can mean that a heavily laden non-turbo car, just coping with the additional load at sea level, may not manage the incline as it climbs higher.

## Driving in Languedoc

There are three classes of road – motorway (*autoroute* – A); main road (*route nationale* – RN or N); and secondary road (*route départementale* – D). Many autoroutes and some N roads are part of the European international route network and have an E number assigned in addition to the A or N number, shown on road signs in green. The

## Drinking and driving

The French limit is 50mg of alcohol per 100ml of blood and penalties increase sharply if an 80mg limit is exceeded. There is a determined campaign to reduce incidents of drinking and driving, and penalties are severe, with heavy fines and imprisonment. Random breath tests are common and you should not underestimate the powers of the police or the consequences of failing a test. A large fine may be demanded on the spot and your vehicle may be impounded until it is paid. Any disqualification is immediate. If you are the sole driver, you will be stranded and any 'get-you-home' insurance will be invalidated by reason of your having committed an illegal act.

## Essentials

You *must* have a red warning triangle and hazard lights in case of accident, a headlight dip adjusted to the right, a first-aid kit, a high-visibility jacket and spare bulbs. You'll also need nationality (GB, IRL, etc) plates (or a sticker, usually supplied with Channel crossing tickets), a torch and a petrol container.

Petrol = *Essence*
Unleaded = *Sans plomb 95 and 98 octane*
Four-star = *Super*
Diesel = *Gazole, Gasoil or Diesel*
LPG = *GPL*

A75 north–south autoroute, for example, is also the E11. With the completion of the A75, including the new viaduct at Millau across the Tarn Valley, it is now possible to drive all the way from Calais to the south of France by motorway and without passing through Paris.

Some N roads are being transferred to *départements* for administration purposes and maintenance; the road numbers are being changed from N to D numbers progressively over the next few years in such cases, and road maps may not be up to date. At the same time, the main road link from the A75 autoroute into Montpellier has been renumbered A750, although the road is still in the process of being upgraded to autoroute standard in sections.

Drivers should also note that road numbers are sometimes not used on road signs in France, and direction-finding is usually by looking for signs to a town or city along the way. Only directions to autoroutes are indicated by their numbers on road signs.

Autoroutes are of excellent quality with frequent rest and service areas, offering the fastest means of covering long distances by car. The exit slip roads tend to have very tight curves and should be negotiated at much reduced speed, especially if towing a trailer or caravan.

*Routes nationales* and *départementales* in Languedoc and the Southwest are of a good standard but the closer one gets to the Pyrenees, the more twisting they become and hairpin bends are regular. Care must be taken, especially where black ice (*verglas*) is signed. In winter, snow chains or tyres are compulsory on some sections as indicated by signs and a lay-by is provided for them to be fitted. If skis are carried on a roof rack the points must face to the rear for safety. Any closure of a high-altitude pass is signed well in advance. These often sinuous roads may make for slow average speeds but drivers are rewarded by stunning views.

Coastal roads can become very congested in the peak season as the geography of the region funnels all north–south traffic on to them.

## Driving rules

Traffic drives on the right in France. A fundamental driving rule is that traffic from the right has priority at junctions, though not at roundabouts. In practice, priority from the right applies mostly in towns and on rural roads. Main roads are clearly signed as such by a yellow and white diamond sign which is repeated every 5km, or the conventional triangle showing a broad vertical black stripe with a narrow horizontal line crossing it (*see page 27*). Junctions marked with a simple X, or not marked at all, are governed by the 'Priority from the Right' rule. Any unmarked junction in a town or village must be treated as subject to this rule.

The rule applies to *junctions* and does not mean giving way to vehicles coming out of lay-bys, driveways, garages, parking spaces, etc. You should, however, give way to buses moving away from a bus stop.

## Fines

The police/gendarmes have wide powers to impose on-the-spot fines for a variety of motoring offences. Speed checks are frequent and merciless. Payment must be in cash and should you not be able to pay there and then, your vehicle and your passport may be impounded until you do. The fine is, in fact, a part payment (*amende forfaitaire*) and you may receive notification of a higher penalty later. Speed-trap detection devices are illegal.

## Information

You should take an up-to-date map with you. Changes in road numbers and motorway interchanges can booby-trap old editions. The Michelin 1/150,000 Yellow maps are ideal. Up-to-date information about traffic conditions throughout France can be seen on the Bison Futé website: *www.bison-fute. equipement.gouv.fr*

## 'Inforoute'

If your car radio is equipped with RDS, this will work in France, interrupting radio programmes with road news flashes (in French). You may also receive traffic news on 'Inforoute' on 107.7 MHz FM. These low-power transmitters cover the motorway routes and provide local up-to-date traffic reports, in French.

Traffic on roundabouts has priority and drivers entering the system must wait for a safe opportunity. Unfortunately, French drivers are very haphazard about signalling their intentions on roundabouts and care is needed.

Pedestrians have right of way when on marked crossings, but the practice of stopping for a pedestrian waiting to use a crossing is unknown. If you decide to display such courtesy, remember that following drivers may not anticipate your action.

## Fuel

Service stations are open all day but are normally closed on Sundays and public holidays. If a public holiday falls on, say, a Thursday, it is common practice to take the Friday off as well, rather than spoil a good weekend. This can mean that petrol stations are closed for four days, especially in the country. In rural areas, petrol stations can be few and far between, especially on *départementale* roads.

Fuel is cheapest at big supermarkets in out-of-town retail parks (*Centre Commercial*) and, not surprisingly, most expensive on motorways. Keeping the fuel tank well filled is good practice.

## Parking

Normally, parking is only a problem in large towns or cities. In the high season, however, especially in the coastal resorts, demand for parking spaces exceeds supply.

There is some free parking in Disc Parking zones, where the bays are marked out in blue. Purchase a disc (*Disque de stationnement*) at petrol stations or supermarkets. Setting your arrival time on the disc automatically displays the expiry time in a cut-out window. Meter or ticket parking follows the usual pattern. Very often parking is free 1200–1400. These times are displayed on the ticket machine.

If parking in the street, you *must* park facing the direction of travel, i.e. on the right in two-way streets. It is, in any case, bad practice to park on the left, as you may drive off forgetting to move to the correct side of the road.

It is illegal to leave a vehicle parked in the same place for more than seven days, and a lesser time in some cities. Obstructive or illegal parking, especially in cities, often results in the offending vehicle being uplifted and taken to a pound. Foreign number plates will not save you.

Some parking zones work on the basis of parking on the odd-numbered side of the street for the first fortnight of a month (1st–15th) and on the even-numbered side for the second. A special sign indicates the entry to the zone (*see page 27*). Changeover time is between 2030 and 2100 on the last day of each fortnight.

## Lights

All traffic must use headlights in rain or poor visibility. Right-hand-drive cars must have their headlight beam modified to prevent dazzle. This can take the form of masking off part of the headlamps (which unfortunately reduces the light output) or stick-on optical beam deflectors which cause the headlight to dip to the right. Some vehicles which have quartz-iodine headlamps cannot be modified in these ways and you should check with the car dealer. Driving with defective lights can result in a fine. The fine is less likely if you can remedy the defect right away. It is a legal requirement to carry a spare set of bulbs. Motorcycles must display headlights at all times.

### Mobile phones

The use of a hand-held phone when driving is specifically forbidden. The use of hands-free phones is strongly discouraged. The only safe and legal way for the driver to use a mobile is to stop and switch off the engine beforehand.

### Seat belts

Wearing of seat belts for front and rear passengers is compulsory when the vehicle engine is running. Children under ten must occupy the rear seats but an infant up to nine months may travel in the front seat if secured in an approved rear-facing seat, *but not if a passenger air bag is fitted.*

## Security

Sensible care should be taken, particularly where vehicles are left for long periods in vulnerable places such as tourist site car parks.

In the large cities, it is wise to keep car doors locked and windows up, if in slow-moving traffic or while stationary at traffic lights, as thieves on motorcycles occasionally reach inside to steal valuables.

Should you have the misfortune to become a victim of crime, your insurers will require you to report the circumstances to the police and obtain a record that you have done so. In the country go to the Gendarmerie and in larger towns the *Commissariat de Police.*

## Speed limits

Autoroutes – 130kph (110kph in rain). If windscreen wipers are needed it's 'raining'.
Dual carriageways – 110kph (100kph in rain)
Other roads – 90kph (80kph in rain)
All built-up areas – 50kph on roads between the entrance sign to a town and departure sign (place name crossed with diagonal bar)
There's a 50kph limit on any road when visibility is less than 50m.
Drivers with under two years' experience must not exceed the 'rain' speed limits even in fine weather.

## Road signs

All major routes are clearly signed; even most minor roads have their destinations marked. International European traffic signs are used throughout France.

*accôtement non-stabilisé* – soft verge
*aire de repos* – rest area
*cédez le passage* – give way
*chaussée déformée* – uneven surface
*défense de stationner* – no parking
*dépassement interdit* – no overtaking
*déviation* – diversion
*gravillons* – loose chippings
*passage protégé* – right of way
*péage* – toll
*poste d'essence* – petrol station
*priorité à droite* – priority to traffic from the right
*priorité aux piétons* – give way to pedestrians

*ralentir* – slow down
*rappel* – reminder of previous restriction
*renseignements* – information
*rives dangereuses* – dangerous roadsides
*route barrée* – road closed
*sens interdit* – no entry
*sens unique* – one way
*seulement riverains* – residents only
*sortie de camions* – HGV exit
*stationnement gratuit* – free parking
*stationnement interdit* – no parking
*stationnement payant* – paid parking
*toutes directions* – route for through traffic
*un train peut en cacher un autre* – one train may hide another
*virage* – bend
*vous n'avez pas la priorité* – you do not have priority

## FRENCH ROAD SIGNS

| (A) | (B) * | (C) * | | |
|---|---|---|---|---|
| You have Priority at *all* junctions on this road. | You have Priority at *next* junction. (Note: important difference with A.) | Be prepared to *Give Way* to traffic from right at next junction. | End of Priority road. | 'Give Way'. |

*Signs B and C may indicate a junction from either side, not necessarily a full crossroads.

You do not have Priority. *Give Way* at roundabout.

Signs attached to traffic lights are valid only if lights are OFF or yellow light is flashing.

Flashing yellow light = Proceed with caution. *Give Way* to traffic on right.

The red border on a town sign *means start of 50km/h limit*. If surmounted by 'Priority' sign (as here), you are on the Priority road through the town.

## PARKING

Disc Parking.

Parking on payment at meter.

Entry to zone where Parking is allowed first fortnight on odd-numbered side of street – second fortnight on even-numbered side.

## WARNINGS

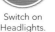

Risk of black ice.

Snow chains obligatory.

Switch on Headlights.

Minimum distance between vehicles.

**Itinéraire Bis**

**Déviation**

Alternative Route

Diversion

Frequently found at tunnels

# Getting to Languedoc and Southwest France

For up-to-date details of long-distance bus, ferry and rail services, consult the *Thomas Cook European Rail Timetable*, published monthly.

**Rail Europe**
*tel: 08448 484 064;*
*www.raileurope.co.uk* – bookings for Eurostar and TGV (high-speed) trains to destinations throughout France; also for Auto Trains within France.

**Eurotunnel** *tel: 08443 35 35 35; www.eurotunnel.com* – drive-on trains from Folkestone to Calais Coquelles through the Channel Tunnel (35 minutes), direct access to the French motorway system.

**Brittany Ferries** *tel: 0871 244 1400*, brochure line: *0871 244 1408; www.brittanyferries.co.uk* – Portsmouth to St-Malo (11 hours), Caen (6 hours, 3½ hours by high-speed ferry), Cherbourg (5 hours, 3 hours high-speed) and Santander in northern Spain (24 hours); Poole to Cherbourg (2¼ hours high speed); Plymouth to Roscoff (6 hours) and Santander (20 hours); Cork to Roscoff (13 hours), summer only.

**P&O Ferries** *tel: 08716 645 645; www.poferries.com* – Dover to Calais 1½ hours.

## By car

If you are taking your own car, the autoroute system (mostly toll roads) is an excellent means of getting to your destination. Using the A16 from Calais and the A10, A71, A20 to Toulouse and beyond, or the A10, A71, A75 to the Mediterranean offer virtually uninterrupted motorway driving with high average speeds. France is bigger than it looks and this 1,000km or so journey is best undertaken with an overnight break.

To reduce the driving distance in France, the longer sea crossings at the western end of the Channel, to St-Malo, Cherbourg, Caen or Le Havre, are an option. They also have the advantage of avoiding both the London and Paris areas. The Brittany Ferries overnight crossing from Portsmouth to St-Malo, arriving at 0800, for example, enables the drive to Toulouse of about 7 hours to be completed the same day, using motorways almost all the way.

SNCF, French Railways, ceased operating its car-carrying motorail services from Calais to southern France in 2010. Now the only alternative for those who want to avoid driving all the way is to go to Paris from where Auto-Train services carry cars overnight to several destinations including Avignon, Narbonne and Toulouse while the driver and passengers travel in a normal train of their choice; *www.voyages-sncf.com/services-train/auto-train*

While transporting your car in this way saves on fuel, tolls and hotels, as well as wear and tear on the vehicle, it does come at a price and is really based on your desire to use your own vehicle on holiday. It is worth calculating the total cost of vehicle transportation against 'ordinary' rail travel and car hire upon arrival.

Car hire is expensive in France. It is normally cheaper to make arrangements before you leave, or consider an inclusive deal or fly-drive. You must be over 21 and have held a licence for at least one year, perhaps two.

All the usual main car-hire firms have offices in France, and often at airports, main railway stations and ferry ports. It is wise to book ahead for peak holiday periods.

## By air

The main international airports are Montpellier for the eastern end of the Languedoc and Toulouse for the western part of the area.

British Airways (*tel: 0844 493 0787; www.ba.com*) flies to Toulouse from Gatwick. Ryanair (*tel: (UK) 0871 246 0000, (Rep. of Ireland) 0818*

**SeaFrance** *tel: 0871 423 7119; www.seafrance.com* – Dover to Calais 1½ hours.

**Transmanche** *tel: 0845 644 2737; www. transmancheferries.co.uk* – Newhaven to Dieppe (4 hours) and Ramsgate to Ostend (4 hours).

**LD Lines** *tel: 0870 420 1267; www.ldlines.co.uk* – Portsmouth to Le Havre (8 hours) and Dover to Boulogne (1¾ hours).

**Norfolk Line** *tel: 0844 499 0007 (France); www.norfolkline.com* – Dover to Dunkerque (2 hours).

**Condor Ferries** *tel: 01202 207 216; www.condorferries.co.uk.* Fast car ferry services from Portsmouth to Cherbourg (5½ hours), Poole to St-Malo (5 hours), Weymouth to St-Malo (5 hours).

**Irish Ferries** *tel: 00 353 0818 300 400 (GB), 0818 300 400 (Rep. of Ireland), www.irishferries.com* – Rosslare to Cherbourg (18 hours), Rosslare to Roscoff (17 hours) (summer only).

**Eurostar** *tel: 08432 186 186; www.eurostar.com* – London St Pancras International to Paris (2¼ hours), also Lille Europe for connecting high-speed TGV trains to Bordeaux and Toulouse.

*30 30 30; www.ryanair.com*) flies to Carcassonne from Stansted, East Midlands, Liverpool, Glasgow, Cork, Dublin and Shannon, to Montpellier from Leeds, to Perpignan from Stansted, to Nîmes from Luton and Liverpool, to Béziers from Bristol and Luton and to Rodez from Stansted. easyJet (*tel: 0871 244 2366; www.easyjet.com*) flies to Montpellier from Gatwick and Luton and to Toulouse from Gatwick and Bristol. Flybe (*tel: 0871 700 2000; www.flybe.com*) flies to Toulouse from Birmingham and to Perpignan from Birmingham and Southampton. bmibaby (*tel: 0905 828 2828; www.bmibaby.com*) flies to Perpignan and Toulouse from Manchester.

### By train

Eurostar trains take 1 hour 20 minutes through the Channel Tunnel from London St Pancras to Lille, linking with SNCF's high-speed TGV trains to Montpellier and Toulouse. Some stop at Ebbsfleet or Ashford in Kent. In July and August, Eurostar also runs a direct weekly service from London to Avignon (6 hours). Book through Rail Europe; *tel: 08448 484064; www.raileurope.co.uk*

From Paris, TGV services get you to the area in about 5 hours. TGV trains to Toulouse depart from the Gare Montparnasse and to Montpellier from the Gare de Lyon.

### Inclusive holidays from the UK

To hire a pre-erected tent or mobile home, contact Eurocamp, who feature a selection of sites along the Languedoc-Roussillon coast; *tel: 0844 406 0402; www.eurocamp.co.uk*

A comprehensive selection of self-catering accommodation and *Chambres d'hôte* is bookable through Brittany Ferries; *tel: 08705 360 360*. Operators featuring seaside villas, apartments and country houses include Interhome: *tel: 020 8780 6633; email: info@interhome.co.uk; www.interhome.co.uk*; Vacances en Campagne: *tel: 08700 771 771; www.holiday-home-pages.co.uk*. For walking or riding holidays and also short breaks at small hotels (many in the Logis de France chain), try Inntravel: *tel: 01653 617 009; www.inntravel.co.uk*

To get a full list of British tour operators to France, contact ABTOF (Association of British Tour Operators to France): *tel: 07813 344810; www.holidayfrance.org.uk*; or get the free *Traveller in France*, available from Atout France, *Lincoln House, 300 High Holborn, London WC1V 7JH; tel: 09068 244 123 (premium rates apply); email: info.uk@franceguide.com; www.franceguide.com*

# Setting the scene

## History

**The North–South Divide** Named after the ancient Langue d'Oc, the Languedoc was originally settled by people from various races who felt they had little in common with the French people who lived further north. This division came sharply into focus in the 12th century when the counts of Toulouse were powerful and independent. Later, Protestantism was warmly embraced in the Languedoc, another cause of bitter conflict with the Catholic north, which had subjugated it.

The Languedoc demonstrated a similar taste for independence during the French Revolution, but once again the forces of the north proved too strong.

**Above**
Festive decorations in Mirepoix

**Catharism** Having first emerged as a branch of Christianity during the 10th century, Catharism lasted for about 400 years. It first acquired a name in 1163 when Canon Eckbert of Cologne mockingly called its supporters by the Greek word *katharos* (pure). The Cathars sought absolute purity. Believing the world had been corrupted, they did not worship the cross, regarding it simply as the instrument of Christ's crucifixion. They also denied Catholic teaching by rejecting the Eucharist as they felt bread and wine could not possibly represent Christ's flesh. For them, the means to salvation was baptism, passed on by the laying on of hands from individual to individual in an unbroken line since Christ and the Apostles.

In many places, this 'heresy' never emerged from the shadows but in the Languedoc it thrived. The powerful counts of Toulouse were among many wealthy landowners who were sympathetic to its beliefs and willingly supported its followers, the *Parfaits*. But when it threatened to drive a wedge between political and religious power, both the king of France and the Catholic hierarchy got worried. At first, the bishops and priests were content to attack the 'heresy' from the pulpit, but this failed to check its advance and they became increasingly concerned.

Early in the 13th century, the counts of Toulouse and other *seigneurs* who owned parts of the Languedoc seemed likely to unite with Catalonia to form a powerful rival to France. King Philippe Auguste, already infuriated by their support for the Cathars, decided to act against them. Making the most of the wholehearted support he got from Pope Innocent III, who was anxious to see an end to Catharism, he embarked in 1209 on a ruthless campaign designed to get rid of the heretics. The Pope declared it to be as worthy as a pilgrimage to the Holy Land. Known as the Albigensian Crusade because Albi was the first place to offer refuge to Cathars, it led to the ravaging of many towns and villages. Hundreds of Cathars were martyred, mostly by being burnt. The Crusade dragged on for over 20 years until the Languedoc was firmly under northern rule – but Catharism still retained its hold.

In 1233, Pope Gregory IX took even more drastic action, setting up the Inquisition. As a result, everyone was forced to appear before tribunals made up of monks, usually Dominicans or Franciscans. Though run with ruthless efficiency and cruelty, their purge was severely handicapped by the fact that the Cathars had no fear of death as they believed hell was already on earth. Consequently, nearly a hundred years passed before the 'heresy' was finally eradicated.

The Cathars' doctrine and influence have remained of absorbing interest to theologians and historians ever since. The prime source of information is the Centre d'Etudes Cathares research centre in Carcassonne: *Maison des Mémoires, 53 rue de Verdun; tel: 04 68 47 24 66; www.cathares.org*

**Wars of Religion** The divisions between France's Catholics and Protestants reached a new peak during the Wars of Religion in the second half of the 16th century. Assassinations and massacres were widespread until the Edict of Nantes in 1598 when King Henri IV, who had renounced his own Protestant faith to become a Catholic, granted Protestants freedom of worship. Sadly, the edict was revoked in 1685 as part of the north's determination to control the south where there were large numbers of them. During the following years, many emigrated but others were tortured or killed by Catholics and their churches destroyed.

**Camisards** The peasants in the Cévennes mountains were among the most determined Protestants. They became known as the Camisards after *camiso*, the Languedoc word for 'shirt', because they sacked a shirt factory and wore the clothes they found in it. In July 1702, a group of them freed Protestant prisoners being held at Pont-de-Montvert and killed the abbot while doing so. All hell broke loose. Though the Camisards never numbered more than a few thousand, they were able to put up strong resistance against the 25,000 royal troops ranged against them because they had three enormous advantages (which later proved equally useful to the Resistance during World War II): the rough countryside was ideal for guerrilla warfare, they knew it intimately, and they had strong local support. However, in 1704, when the troops deliberately destroyed 466 small towns and villages, most of the remaining Camisards surrendered. In 1787, the Edict of Tolerance officially ended their persecution.

**Treaty of the Pyrenees** Centuries of Franco-Spanish conflict ended in 1659 when the Treaty of the Pyrenees laid down that the border between the two countries should run along the crests of the Pyrenees.

This meant that Roussillon became part of France after years of being pulled to and fro. A less satisfactory outcome was that the Catalan people found themselves split in two. Nevertheless, their language has survived and many place names and streets are signed in both French and Catalan.

One quirk left behind by the Treaty is a small Spanish enclave just inside the French border. About 3km across, it is based in the small town of Llívia, whose occupants refused to join with the neighbouring places in becoming French. Today their descendants are more likely to tell you they are Catalan than Spanish.

## Architecture

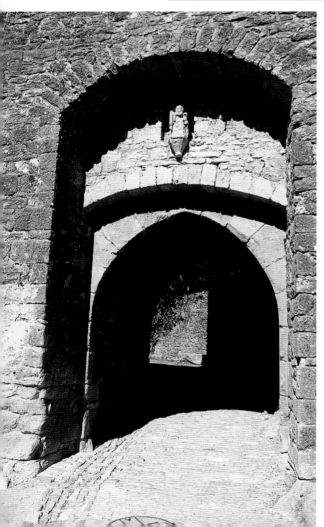

**Bastides** Many of the area's towns have developed from *bastides*, fortified medieval villages. The layout, still to be seen in places such as Carcassonne (Ville Basse), Mirepoix, Réalmont and Revel, was always similar – a grid of straight narrow streets and alleys with a square in the centre surrounded by covered arcades. Designed to enable the inhabitants to live safe from attack, they were surrounded by sturdy ramparts and gateways. Most date back to the height of the Franco-English wars in the 12th–14th centuries. At the time, parts of the area were governed by France, others by England, and both sides built *bastides* to strengthen their positions. The seeds of the conflict had been set in 1152 when a large part of France passed to English rule following the marriage of Eleanor of Aquitaine (who had divorced King Louis VII two months earlier) and the 19-year-old Henry Plantagenet. Two years later he became King Henry II of England.

**Southern Gothic** Churches built in the style known as Southern Gothic in the west of the area have more in common with the austere Romanesque architecture of the 11th and 12th centuries than with the more flamboyant design and decorative stonework of traditional Gothic ones. Due to the lack of local stone, many were built in brick, whose lightness, compared with stone, enabled them to have vaulted roofs supported by interior buttresses with chapels between them.

Stepping inside these churches, however, you are struck most by the lack of light due to small windows. They are also notable for the considerable width of their naves, which have no side aisles. After the Cathar movement had been stamped out, the Catholic clergy favoured this simple design, believing it helped unify their flocks and impressed on them who had the true and final word. The exterior of the churches is usually topped by a tower or wall of bells featuring tiers of arches.

**Coastal development** Until the 1960s, the 200km-long coast between the Camargue and the Spanish border was a desolate stretch of lagoons, bogs and sand, interspersed by occasional harbours and a few small and rather faded resorts. Anxious to ease pressure on the Riviera and concerned that increasing numbers of French holidaymakers were heading for Spain each summer, the government decided to capitalise on the area's major asset – its succession of long sandy beaches.

Billions of francs were spent on creating new resorts grouped around smart marinas at places such as Agde, Leucate and Port-Barcarès. The architects were told the buildings must look modern and attractive, have pleasant landscaped settings and be affordable to ordinary people. Top-class campsites with pools and sports facilities were encouraged too. At the same time, the hordes of mosquitoes that bred on the lagoons were eliminated, fast access roads constructed and sewage-treatment plants built to ensure that the beaches and sea remained unpolluted.

Just how successful the project has proved can be seen every summer when millions of holidaymakers descend on the area, not only from France but from all over the world.

## Landscape

The region has a number of distinctly different features.

**Mountains** The Cévennes on the northeastern edge of the area rise in rugged ridges above wooded valleys; their highest peaks are Mont Lozère (1,699m) and Mont Aigoual (1,567m). The Pyrenees which border the south of the area are significantly higher. The snowy peak of the Massif du Canigou (2,784m) is visible from high points across the whole region on clear days. The Pyrenees are also more extensive, stretching away into Spain and from the Mediterranean to the Atlantic.

The Montagne Noire and Corbières, which rise from the central Languedoc plain are hills rather than mountains. Nevertheless, much of their scenery is just as spectacular, thanks to their rugged cliffs, thickly wooded valleys and crags topped by castle ruins.

*Causses* Four massive limestone plateaux, the Grands Causses – Méjean, Noir, Larzac and Sauveterre – lie to the west of the Cévennes. Topped by poor, dry soil because water drains easily away through the rock, they are impressively bleak and barren, though grazed by sheep in summer. Their coarse tufty grass is dotted with hardy plants such as thistles, lavender and juniper which manage to survive the summer heat and winter frosts and snow when cold winds whistle relentlessly across them.

Rivers such as the Dourbie, Jonte and Tarn have cut their way between the Causses. They now flow in deep wooded ravines which twist below cliffs that often tower 500m above them. The roads cut into the cliffsides enable visitors to enjoy some of the most dramatic scenery in France.

*Etangs* The saltwater lagoons which border much of the coast behind sandbars are a comparatively recent arrival. Places such as Narbonne, Agde and Marseillan were ports in Roman times, though they required constant dredging to prevent their silting up. During the Middle Ages this became uneconomic. In any case, drifting sand was building up sandbars just offshore, creating a completely new coastline with seawater trapped in shallow lagoons behind it which were fed from the sea along *graus* (narrow channels).

Salt used to be extracted from the lagoons, but now they are put to much more profitable use as oyster and mussel beds. They are also home to many species of seabirds including hundreds of pink flamingos.

*Garrigue* This is the name of the natural scrubland that covers the limestone hills, mainly to the southwest of the Cévennes. Despite the unrelenting summer heat, clumps of holm oak, broom and sweet-smelling plants such as lavender, thyme and rosemary manage to grow abundantly among the white rocks.

**Caves** Under the area's many limestone plateaux, particularly in the Ariège and Aveyron, caves have formed over the centuries. It is largely thanks to Edouard-Alfred Martel (1859–1938), originally a Paris lawyer, that this underground world has been so extensively explored. Always an enthusiastic traveller, he set out in 1883 to penetrate and map the many caves and tunnels under the Causses. Until then, very little was known about what lay beyond the forbiddingly dark entrance holes, let alone how far the spaces stretched underground and whether any linked up. While exploring them, he also studied why the spaces had formed. By writing extensively about his discoveries, he inaugurated a new branch of science – speleology – based on the exploration and scientific study of caves. His work also had two other beneficial effects: it boosted both the area's water supplies and its tourist trade.

## Wine

Languedoc-Roussillon is the largest wine-producing region in France, accounting for around two-thirds of the country's production. The majority of those produced in the Languedoc area are inexpensive but highly drinkable red 'unclassified' *vins de table*. However, over the last 25 years an increasing number of *viticulteurs* (producers) have been planting different varieties of grape in order to produce wines of a higher quality. Fifteen from the Languedoc plain have now reached France's top *appellation d'origine contrôlée* (AOC) grading (the first was in 1985), while others have achieved *vin de pays* status, either *Pays d'Oc* or *Pays de L'Hérault*.

Some of the wines from the Languedoc plain are produced cooperatively by the Coteaux du Languedoc areas and some by individual châteaux and *domaines*. Predominantly red, they are best drunk young and chilled.

Wines from the Languedoc's two other large wine areas, the Corbières and Minervois, are mainly strong dark reds, as are those from the highly regarded neighbouring Fitou vineyards, which reach their peak when aged for a few years.

**Below**
A local favourite

In general, Roussillon produces better wines than Languedoc, having achieved its AOC status in 1977 for its Côtes du Roussillon, Côtes du Roussillon Villages (from 32 districts) and Collioure, which are mostly reds. In addition, there are five *vins de pays*.

Roussillon is also well known for its *vins doux naturels*, sweet wines made from muscat grapes and fortified with wine alcohol. Served chilled mainly as an aperitif, they include Banyuls, Maury and Rivesaltes. The town of Gaillac is in the centre of the smaller Côtes du Tarn area, which produces red, white and rosé wines. A Gaillac *appellation* denotes superior quality, yet prices are surprisingly low, even for Perlé, the top one.

The vineyards around Limoux have been producing sparkling white wine for 1,000 years – longer than any other vineyard in the world. Blanquette de Limoux, produced by the *méthode champenoise* (bubbles added chemically), is crisp and inexpensive compared with champagne. Around 3 per cent is produced by the *méthode ancestrale*, in which the bubbles occur naturally.

Armagnac, a brandy from the Gers *département* northwest of Toulouse, is thought to be the oldest distilled drink in France. It is made from white wine and matured in oak barrels.

## Food

The area's gastronomy is influenced by Languedoc and Catalan traditions. It owes its flavours to the fruits and vegetables, both wild and cultivated, which flourish in the hot Mediterranean sunshine. Herbs, berries and garlic are used extensively.

Languedoc dishes tend to be robust and straightforward, using plenty of young lamb, particularly on the Causses where sheep's cheese is made in many places. Catalan dishes are prepared with generous quantities of olive oil and use many wild ingredients, from partridges to snails as well as local tomatoes, olives, peppers and mushrooms. The chestnuts which grow in abundance in the hills inland are used in sauces and stuffings or served as a vegetable.

Throughout the region, there is a strong tradition of preserved meats, sausages and pâtés. Duck appears in many forms, especially confit where the meat has been conserved in fat to be used in stews such as cassoulet.

Several kinds of fish stew are available on the coast as well as grilled and barbecued fish, though seawater fish is surprisingly rare inland.

From spring to autumn, the wide variety of locally grown fruit and vegetables makes local markets a delight to visit. The triangle between Toulouse, Albi and Carcassonne, originally known as the 'land of milk and honey' because of the rich profits it made from growing woad, now produces all kinds of vegetables, particularly the white beans which are an indispensable component of both cassoulet and *fricassé de Limoux*.

**Below**
Collioure

## Language

In the Pyrénées-Roussillon *département*, once part of Catalonia, many people speak Catalan, though they also speak French (and probably Spanish too). Catalan vaguely resembles Spanish and both have a common origin in Latin.

Some of the most common Catalan words you are likely to meet are *puig* (mountain peak), *riu* (river), *pla* (plateau) and *aplech* (festival). You will also notice that place and street names often appear in both Catalan and French.

The sing-song French accent which you hear throughout the Midi – and indeed the word Languedoc – is a hangover from the Oc language, which was spoken locally in Roman times. Its name is derived from *hoc ille*, the Roman term for 'yes', which became 'oc' when spoken by the locals in the south. In northern France, people pronounced it 'oil' and the Langue d'Oil gradually developed into the French language.

However, the *langue d'oc* continued to thrive, a sign of the southern 'separatism' which troubadours helped to perpetuate between 1000 and 1200 by using this language to compose romantic poems. These were performed in stately homes around the Midi, as well as further afield.

Although an edict in 1539 made French the official language in the Midi, people continued to speak in the *langue d'oc* until the beginning of the 19th century when children were forbidden to do so in school. It then declined sharply and is now no more than a local dialect, though some streets still have two names. Montpellier University offers courses in Occitan, which is the 19th-century name for the *langue d'oc*.

## Some useful words

*Causse* – limestone plateau with dry rocky surface (a *can* is a small *causse*)

*Corniche* – escarpment (ledge)

*Département* – an administrative area; several make up a region such as Languedoc-Roussillon or Midi-Pyrénées

*Dos-d'âne* – hump in the road to slow down traffic (literally a 'donkey's back')

*Draille* – sheep track (often along a mountain ridge)

*Etang* – saltwater lagoon

*Garrigue* – poor terrain with scrub bushes, often rocky and hilly

*Grau* – narrow channel

*Hôtel particulier* – mansion

*Lauze* – flat slate or limestone slab used to cover roofs

*Lavogne* – man-made pond on the *causses* for sheep

*Mas* – prosperous 18th-century farm with lots of outbuildings

*Parfait* – Cathar

*Serre* – ridge

*Vieille ville/centre médiéval/ancien quartier* – oldest part of a town or village

*Vignoble* – vineyard

# Highlights

**Best art galleries**
- Hôtel d'Assézat, Toulouse (*see page 156*)
- Musée d'Art Moderne, Céret (*see page 62*)
- Musée Goya, Castres (*see page 182*)
- Musée Toulouse-Lautrec, Albi (*see page 175*)

**Best castles**
- Château de Brousse (*see page 182*)
- Château de Montségur (*see page 95*)
- Château de Peyrepertuse (*see page 100*)
- Palais des Rois de Majorque, Perpignan (*see page 44*)
- Château de Quéribus (*see page 102*)
- Château de Salses (*see page 121*)

**Best caves**
- Grotte de Lombrives (*see page 94*)
- Grotte de Niaux (*see page 94*)
- L'Aven Armand (*see page 250*)

**Best for children**
- Cité de l'Espace, Toulouse (*see page 155*)
- Four Solaire (*see page 86*)
- Réserve Africaine de Sigean (*see page 120*)

**Best churches**
- Basilique St-Nazaire, Carcassonne (stained glass) (*see page 128*)
- Basilique St-Sernin, Toulouse (*see page 154*)
- Cathédrale Ste-Cécile, Albi (*see page 174*)
- Église St-Pierre, Prades (altarpiece) (*see page 71*)
- Ste-Eulalie et Ste-Julie, Elne (cloister) (*see page 53*)
- St-Martin-du-Canigou (*see page 73*)

**Most unusual churches**
- Cathédrale Ste-Cécile, Albi (*see page 174*)
- Église Ste-Marie, Rieux-Minervois (*see page 195*)
- Maguelone cathedral (*see page 271*)

**Best events**
- La Foire de la Cocagne, St-Félix-Lauragais (*see page 168*)
- Les Feux de la St-Jean (*see page 16*)
- Procession de la Sanchí, Perpignan (*see page 45*)
- Carnaval de Limoux (*see page 139*)

**Best gorges**
- Gorges de Galamus (*see page 104*)
- Gorges de la Jonte (*see page 248*)
- Gorges du Tarn (*see page 250*)

**Best coastal towns**
- Le Cap d'Agde (*see page 271*)
- Collioure (*see page 51*)
- Sète (*see page 275*)

**Best medieval towns/villages**
- Carcassonne (Cité) (*see page 128*)
- La Couvertoirade (*see page 239*)
- St-Guilhem-le-Désert (*see page 224*)
- St-Jean-d'Alcas (*see page 243*)
- Villefranche-de-Conflent (*see page 74*)

**Most interesting towns/villages**
- Cantobre (*see page 238*)
- Minerve (*see page 194*)
- Mirepoix (*see page 165*)
- Mont-Louis (*see page 88*)
- Rennes-le-Château (*see page 104*)
- Villeneuvette (*see page 224*)

**Best museums**
- Amphoralis (Musée des Potiers Gallo-Romains), Sallèles d'Aude (*see page 195*)
- L'Horreum, Narbonne (*see page 111*)
- Musée de Tautavel (*see page 121*)
- Oppidum d'Ensérune (*see page 195*)
- Parc Pyrénéen de l'Art Préhistorique, Tarascon-sur-Ariège (*see page 96*)

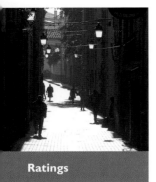

# Perpignan

### Ratings

| | |
|---|---|
| Food and drink | ●●●●● |
| Architecture | ●●●● |
| Shopping | ●●●● |
| Entertainment | ●●● |
| History | ●●● |
| Museums | ●●● |
| Art | ●● |
| Children | ● |

**B**asking almost continuously in Mediterranean sunshine, Perpignan has an attractive Franco-Spanish ambience – it used to be capital of French Catalonia – and always seems to buzz with activity. Its shops and pavement cafés are patronised as enthusiastically by its well-heeled citizens as by visitors taking time off from the beach. The Mediterranean is only 10km away at Canet-Plage. In the old town area, which is traffic-free and paved with glistening red marble, the narrow streets are crammed with shops and stalls. An aroma of spices wafts from the Arab quarter. By contrast, the avenues around the area are wide and lined with plane trees and palms, particularly beside the small River Basse, which runs into the broader and less appealing Têt nearby. On high days and holidays, dancers take to the streets in traditional costumes to perform the *sardana*.

## Getting there and getting around

**ⓘ Tourist Information** *Palais des Congrès, place Armand Lanoux; tel: 04 68 66 30 30; email: contact-office@perpignan.fr; www.perpignantourisme.com.* Guided walking tours.

Branch office in the Espace Palmarium, *place Arago. Open daily all year.*

**By air: Aéroport Perpignan-Rivesaltes** (*avenue Maurice Bellonte; tel: 04 68 52 60 70*) is 7km northeast of the town centre. Facilities include car hire, restaurant and shop. A shuttle bus to the SNCF station (*avenue Général de Gaulle*) connects with flights.

**By car:** Leave A9 (La Catalane) autoroute at exit Perpignan Nord/Airport. This leads across Pont Arago over the River Têt and to a convenient car park just beyond place de Catalogne.

**By train:** High-speed TGV trains run from Paris Gare de Lyon to Perpignan. A direct TGV service from Brussels calls at Lille Europe where it connects with Eurostar services from London at around noon each day.

Perpignan

0        100 metres
0        100 yards

PLACE DE LA RESISTANCE
BOULEVARD WILSON
BLVD JEAN BOURRAT
RUE PIERRE RONSARD
Le Castillet–Musée Catalan des Arts et Traditions Populaires
Cathédrale St-Jean
Chapelle St-Dominique
Musée des Monnaies et Médailles J. Puig
PLACE DE VERDUN
RUE REMPART VILLENEUVE
RUE L. BLANC
PLACE GAMBETTA
Couvent des Minimes
Préfecture
RUE FABRIQUES NABOT
Loge de Mer
RUE ST-JEAN
Campo Santo
PLACE DE LA RÉVOLUTION FRANÇAISE
RUE ST FRANÇOIS DE PAULE
QUAI VAUBAN
Hôtel de Ville, Palais de la Députation
Conseil Général
RUE DE LA LOGE
RUE DE LA BARRE
RUE DE L'ARGENTERIE
QUAI SADI CARNOT
PLACE BARDOU JOB
PLACE JAURÈS
RUE JEAN DENIS
Eglise St-Jacques
PLACE ST-JACQUES
N
RUE DE LA MAIN DE FER
RUE DE LA MANCHE
RUE DU RUISSEAU
Gare SNCF
PLACE PÉRI
RUE DE LA CLOCHE D'OR
Théâtre Municipal
Bibliothèque Municipale
PLACE ARAGO
RUE DU THÉÂTRE
QUAI LATTRE DE TASSIGNY
RUE DE L'ANGE
RUE VOLTAIRE
PLACE RIGAUD
RUE EMILE ZOLA
CCI Tribunal
Musée des Beaux Arts Hyacinthe Rigaud
RUE DE LA FUSTERIE
PLACE DES POILUS
Archives Communales, Ancienne Université, Hôtel Pams
RUE DES AUGUSTINS
Palais des Rois de Majorque
RUE GRANDE LA REAL

○ ........ Attraction
▬ ........ Important Building
........ Park
—— ........ Main Road
—— ........ Other Road
ℹ ........ Information

ℹ **Comité Départemental du Tourisme** *16 avenue des Palmiers; tel: 04 68 51 52 53; email: tourisme.roussillon.france@ wanadoo.fr; www.cdt-66.com*

**Gare SNCF** *place de la Gare. Train information: tel: 36 35.*

**Getting around:** The main sights and main shopping area are easily manageable on foot. At night the streets in the St-Jacques quarter are best avoided. The free P'tit Bus operates on a circle route around the town; *Mon–Fri 0800–1200, 1345–1815, Sat from 0900.* Bus No 1 runs every 30 minutes between place Péri and Canet-Plage, 30 minutes away *(until 2300 in summer).* CTP bus information at the kiosk on place Péri; *tel: 04 68 61 01 13. Open Mon–Sat.* **Taxis:** *tel: 04 68 35 15 15; www.accueilperpignantaxi.fr*

**Parking:** Large parts of the old town area are pedestrian-only and others one-way only, so park on the streets around it which are pay-and-display, or head straight for an underground car park. Handiest for the town centre are those in place du Pont d'En Vestit and place de la République. You can also park free near the Palais des Rois de Majorque and on Promenade des Platanes.

# Sights

🏛 **Campo Santo** *rue Amiral Ribeil. Open Wed–Mon.*

## Campo Santo
This former cemetery next to the cathedral is completely surrounded by cloisters. One of only two of this kind in Europe (the other is in Pisa), it is now used for exhibitions and concerts.

**Musée Catalan des Arts et Traditions Populaires** € *Le Castillet, place de Verdun; tel: 04 68 35 42 05. Open May–Sept Wed–Mon 1000–1830; Oct–Apr Wed–Mon 1100–1730. Closed Tue & some holidays. Admission free on first Sun of the month.*

**Cathédrale St-Jean**
*place de Gambetta.*

## Le Castillet

This 15th-century red-brick gatehouse with two towers, crenellations, windows with wrought-iron grilles and a pink dome is the only surviving part of the town's fortified walls. At one time used as a prison, it is now called Casa Païral and houses the **Musée Catalan des Arts et Traditions Populaires**, which is devoted to local crafts, agriculture and festivals. One of the most striking exhibits is a life-size reconstruction of a typical home in the foothills of the Pyrenees. Climb the 142 spiral steps to the top for a splendid panorama stretching over the town's rooftops to the sea in one direction and the snowy Canigou mountain in the other.

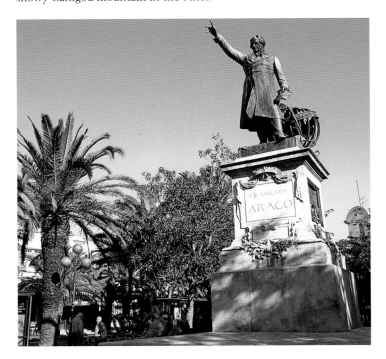

## Cathédrale St-Jean

The cathedral is a grand Gothic building, topped by a bell encased in an intricate wrought-iron cage. The attractive façade is made of river pebbles – frequently used in Roussillon because of the scarcity of stone – and thin red bricks. Inside, its most outstanding features, on either side of the large single nave which is typical of the Southern Gothic style, are sumptuously gilded Baroque altarpieces dating from the 16th and 17th centuries. Whether they are to your taste or not, you cannot but marvel at the craftsmanship that went into sculpting the wood and then painting it, a process which occupied two artists for three

**Above**
Local hero: memorial to François Arago

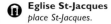

**Eglise St-Jacques** *place St-Jacques.*

**Hôtel de Ville** *rue de la Loge.*

**Loge de Mer** *rue de la Loge.*

**Musée Rigaud** € *16 rue de l'Ange; tel: 04 68 35 43 40. Open Wed–Mon all year.*

**Musée Puig** € *42 avenue de Grande-Bretagne; tel: 04 68 62 37 64; email: Musee-puig@mairie-perpignan.com. Open Wed & Sat all year.*

years. There is also a splendid organ whose unusual painted shutters are now displayed on the wall opposite. Outside, a doorway in the south transept leads to a chapel built specially to house the Dévôt Christ, a rather harrowing crucifix in gilded wood, thought to date from the early 14th century.

### Eglise St-Jacques
This 14th-century sanctuary is in the St-Jacques quarter, which is now somewhat sleazy. Its large chapel was added in the 18th century for the Confrérie de la Sanch, the Brotherhood of the Holy Blood, formed in 1416 to comfort those condemned to death. The members are famous for the Procession de la Sanch on Good Friday when, hooded and dressed in macabre red or black robes with pointed hats, they parade a crucifix and huge *misteris* (scenes from the Stations of the Cross) through the streets to the cathedral.

### Gare SNCF
The town's railway station was immortalised as the 'Centre of the World' by Salvador Dalí. Arriving there in 1965, he claimed he suddenly felt free of the constraints of living in his native Spain.

### Hôtel de Ville
The town hall is typical of the local Roussillon architecture, having wide wrought-iron gates and a façade of river pebbles. You have to be attending a wedding to visit its splendid Salle des Mariages but anyone can peep through the gates and see Maillol's famous bronze nude, *La Méditerranée*, on the patio.

### Loge de Mer
Built in 1397 as the headquarters of the town's maritime trade, the Loge de Mer is an impressive Gothic building with a decorative Renaissance extension added 200 years later. A wrought-iron weather vane on one side shaped like a galleon is a reminder of its connections with the sea, though the building has served many purposes and now, somewhat incongruously, a restaurant occupies the ground floor.

### Musée des Beaux Arts Hyacinthe Rigaud
Paintings by Hyacinthe Rigaud are displayed in this imposing 17th-century mansion. Born in the town in 1659, she became court painter to Louis XIV and Louis XV. The museum also has works by Picasso, Dufy and Maillol, a native of nearby Banyuls-sur-Mer (*see page 49*).

### Musée des Monnaies et Médailles J. Puig
This museum in Les Tilleuls, a turn-of-the-century villa, is devoted to a collection of coins donated by a local collector, Joseph-Puig, though less than half – about 1,500 – are on show. Attractively displayed, they are mainly old Catalan and Mediterranean coins.

🛈 **Palais des Rois de Majorque** €€ *4 rue des Archers; tel: 04 68 34 96 26. Open Jun–Sept daily 1000–1800; Oct–May daily 0900–1700.*

### Palais des Rois de Majorque

The palace of the kings of Majorca was built in 1276 when the town, part of the kingdom of Majorca, became the mainland capital but lacked a residence deemed fit for a king. More a fortress than a residence, it stands boldly on a hill, Puig del Rey, a few quiet streets away from the old quarter, reached by flights of steps which zigzag up to the ramparts and gardens surrounding it. The kings of Aragon once kept lions in the moat, while the mighty beasts' food – goats – grazed on the lawns. From the roof of the entrance tower, **Tour de l'Hommage**, there are splendid views over the town to the Massif du Canigou, ancient symbol of Catalan unity. Two stairways on either side of the palace courtyard lead to various grand rooms, including a reception hall and three chapels. The large courtyard in the centre is often used for concerts.

## Shopping

The narrow streets in the old quarter are crowded with specialist shops. Look out particularly for traditional Catalan fabrics, and jewellery in the local red stone, *grenat*, at shops such as **Gilles et Jean**, rue Blanc. For gifts such as high-quality pottery, glass and household items, head for **Maison Quinta** (*3 rue Grande des Fabriques*), or **du Côté de l'Orangerie** (*2 rue de la Révolution Française*). Shops around Marché de la République specialise in dried fruits and spices. Rue de l'Ange is good for clothes. The main department store, **Galeries Lafayette**, is just across the River Basse in boulevard Clémenceau, with Monoprix store opposite. Two arcades of small shops, **Galerie Rive Gauche** and **Galerie Centre Ville**, lead off quai Vauban. The citizens love their

**Above**
Perpignan's popular daily produce market

🍴 Eating outdoors on balmy evenings along the palm-lined avenues and narrow streets in the old quarter is one of the town's great pleasures, heightened by the wide choice of French and Catalan specialities. The most popular spot of all is square Arago, a square with brasseries and cafés under magnolia trees. Small restaurants can also be found up what look like impossibly narrow alleys. Rue Fabriques-Nadal, for instance, is given over almost completely to small restaurants.

**Casa Sansa** € *2 rue Fabriques-Nadal; tel: 04 68 34 21 84. Open daily all year.* Has gypsy musicians who serenade diners late into the night.

**Al Très** €€ *3 rue de la Poissonnerie; tel: 04 68 34 88 39. Open Tue–Sat all year.* A small restaurant with ochre walls, which specialises in Catalan-style seafood.

**L'Arago** €€ *l place Arago; tel: 04 68 51 81 96. Open daily all year.* Is one of the lively brasseries with a shaded terrace around the relaxed place Arago.

**La Galinette** €€ *23 rue Jean-Payra; tel: 04 68 35 00 90. Open Tue–Sat all year.* Serving regional dishes, some using chocolate as an ingredient.

markets, particularly the daily fruit and vegetable one on place de la République. A flea market is held every Sunday morning outside the Palais des Expositions and a bric-a-brac market on the second Saturday of each month at Promenade des Platanes.

# Entertainment

Discos, piano and jazz bars, American theme bars, brasseries and pubs are scattered throughout the old quarter. Thursday is party night for the locals when you are bound to find live music in the old town at bars such as **Le Barabul** (*26 boulevard Cassanyes; tel: 04 68 80 70 60. Open Tue–Sun all year*) and **Républic Café** (*2 place de la République; tel: 04 68 51 11 64. Open daily all year*).

# Events

Easter: **Festival of sacred music** during Holy Week and Spanish-style **Procession de la Sanchí** on Good Friday when sacred relics and a crucifix are carried to the cathedral by the Brotherhood of the Holy Blood.
June: **Midsummer Festival of St-Jean** is celebrated in grand style with folk music, fireworks and dancing the *sardana*. Fires are lit on the 2,784m Canigou mountain (40km inland) and torches from the surrounding villages are paraded into the town.
September: **International Festival of Photojournalism** and **Medieval Market**.

# Accommodation and food

Perpignan has a good choice of hotels of all prices, from modern to traditional. Avenue Général de Gaulle, leading to the railway station, is well endowed with one- and two-star hotels, though parking is a problem in the centre as only the larger hotels can offer garage facilities.

**Hôtel de la Loge** € *1 rue Fabriques-Nabot; tel: 04 68 34 41 02; email: hoteldelaloge@wanadoo.fr; www.hoteldelaloge.fr. Open all year.* Small and smart, occupying a 15th-century mansion in the old town centre. Twenty-two rooms. No garage.

**Park Hotel** €€ *18 boulevard Jean Bourrat; tel: 04 68 35 14 14; email: contact@parkhotel-fr.com; www.parkhotel-fr.com. Open all year.* Overlooks a leafy boulevard only steps from the old town. Sixty-nine rooms.

**La Villa Duflot** €€€ *Rond-Point Albert Donnezan; tel: 04 68 56 67 67; email: contact@villa-duflot.com; www.villa-duflot.com. Open all year.* The top hotel, situated in large grounds on the southwest outskirts of town. Twenty-four rooms.

# Suggested walk

**Length:** 3km.

**Duration:** 1½ hours, allowing time to go up to the Palais des Rois de Majorque (though not inside).

The town is best explored on foot by wandering along the narrow streets and alleyways of the old quarter to admire its 14th- and 15th-century buildings and shady squares. Peep through the sturdy doorways of the old *hôtels particuliers* (mansions) whenever you get the chance as many have pretty courtyards, often featuring a well and balconies with carved stonework and wrought-iron balustrades. Even their drainpipes can be interesting as some of the old ones are made of glazed ceramic shaped with 'Dauphin' faces at the bottom. And note how the street names often appear in both Catalan and French.

Begin at **LE CASTILLET** ❶ where narrow streets lead straight to the **LOGE DE MER** ❷. Take rue St-Jean to the **CATHEDRALE ST-JEAN** ❸. On its left is St-Jean-le-Vieux, Perpignan's first church, consecrated in 1025. A century ago it was taken over by a M Bartissol to use as a store when he was in charge of installing electricity in the town. Though it is now being restored, it seems unlikely to reopen for some time yet. Nearby a wall plaque commemorates the visit of Frédéric Chopin and George Sand on their way to set sail from Port Vendres to Majorca in 1838.

Past the **CAMPO SANTO** ❹ you arrive at the small **place de la Révolution Française** where **rue du Ruisseau** slopes up to the old St-Jacques quarter, now largely populated by Arab families and the scene of a lively market every morning on **place Cassanyes**. The **PALAIS DES ROIS DE MAJORQUE** ❺ dominates this part of the town.

For a short cut, walk through place Rigaud and place des Poilus, window-shopping along the way, to **Maison Julia**, a 14th-century mansion in rue Fabriques-Nabot. With an attractive courtyard surrounded by two storeys of pillared galleries, it is one of the best preserved of Perpignan's *hôtels particuliers*. This is the old *parayres* area where drapers used to live.

The terrace brasseries and cafés around **place Arago** are ideal for lingering in the sunshine before strolling along the gardens bordering the **River Basse** back to **Le Castillet**. For a quieter retreat, the broad **Promenade des Platanes** is shaded by plane trees, palms and mimosas.

## Also worth exploring

**Jardin Sant-Vicens**
*rue de Sant Vicens.*
*Open daily.*

In the attractive Mediterranean-style **Jardin Sant-Vicens**, on the southeast side of the town centre, an arts centre has been created in

100-year-old wine cellars. Named **Centre d'Artisanat et d'Art Sant-Vicens**, it displays striking ceramic pieces, tapestries and paintings by contemporary artists, including Jean Lurçat (1892–1966). Works by local artists are on sale.

## The *sardana*

This traditional Catalan dance dates from the 16th century. Dressed in red and white, the dancers, young and old, move rhythmically and precisely in concentric circles, arms raised high, as they nimbly perform the intricate steps to the accompaniment of Catalan music. This is played on ancient woodwind instruments by bands called *cobles*. The *sardana* is performed frequently on summer evenings in Perpignan on place de la Loge and in front of Le Castillet. You can also see it at summer festivals in other Catalan towns and villages throughout Roussillon.

# The coast south from Perpignan

## Ratings

| | |
|---|---|
| Art | ●●●●● |
| Beaches | ●●●●● |
| Coastal villages/ towns | ●●●●● |
| Wine | ●●●●○ |
| Children | ●●●○○ |
| History | ●●●○○ |
| Scenery | ●●●○○ |
| Walking | ●○○○○ |

The Languedoc's flat coast is totally transformed when it reaches Les Albères, the foothills of the Pyrenees, shortly before the Spanish border. The long sandy beaches and sea-water lagoons suddenly give way to the rocky coves and steep hillsides of the Côte Vermeille, named after the silver-red glint of its rocky schist stone.

At the beginning of the 20th century, the painter Matisse discovered Collioure. Soon other Impressionist painters followed him. It's easy to see why, as the harbour is one of the prettiest on the Mediterranean.

Like the railway line which first brought tourism to the area, the coast road south of Argelès is highly scenic, twisting around cliffsides and dipping through the small resorts. Sunset on the beach at Argelès (which boasts more campsites than anywhere else in France) is always a dreamy time as the Pyrenees become silhouetted above the sea.

## ARGELÈS-PLAGE

**ⓘ Argelès Tourist Information**
*I place de l'Europe; tel: 04 68 81 15 85; email: infos@argeles-sur-mer.com; www.argeles-sur-mer.com. Open daily Jun–Sept.*

**Ⓗ Musée Casa de les Albères € 4 place** *des Castellans-Argelès village; tel: 04 68 81 42 74; email: accueil-musée-argeles@ wanadoo.fr. Open daily Jun– Sept; Wed–Mon Oct–May.*

**◉** *There's a market on Wed and Sat.*

Argelès has the reputation of being the campsite capital of Europe! Over 60 sites are set in a 5km stretch of dunes and woods near the sea. Most have sophisticated facilities such as large swimming pools, tennis courts and restaurants. In summer, many organise children's clubs and sports activities. Well-equipped pre-erected tents and mobile homes can be booked through tour operators in the UK (*see page 29*).

A promenade shaded by pines runs between the long sandy beach and a row of small hotels, holiday apartments, villas and shops. The beach offers children's clubs and watersports, as well as umbrellas for those who want to do nothing more strenuous than laze in the sun. However, the sand shelves quickly and is rather coarse for digging, so small children are best taken to the shallow lagoon beside a stream at the northern end.

**Argelès-sur-Mer**, slightly inland, is the oldest part of the town with narrow streets and alleys. In the centre, **Musée Casa de les Albères** is a

Catalan museum showing traditional art and craft including wooden toys, rope sandals and corks for bottles.

# BANYULS-SUR-MER

With its pale pink and white buildings and shady squares, Banyuls feels distinctly Catalan. It spreads around two sheltered bays bordered by eucalyptus, palms and pavement cafés, with vineyards stretching over the hillsides around it.

**ℹ Banyuls-sur-Mer Tourist Information** *avenue de la République; tel: 04 68 88 31 58; email: ot.banyuls@banyuls-sur-mer.com; www.banyuls-sur-mer.com. Open daily Jun–Sept; Mon–Sat Oct–May.*

**🏰 Cellier des Templiers** *Le Mas Reig, rue du Balcon de Madeloc; tel: 04 68 98 36 92. Open daily May–Sept. Guided visits (free) include sampling.*

**Musée Maillol €€** *Vallée de la Roume; tel: 04 68 88 57 11; email: contact@musee-maillol.com; www.musee-maillol.com. Open daily all year.*

**☾ Les Elmes €€** *Plage des Elmes; tel: 04 68 88 03 12; email: info@hotel-des-elmes.com; www.hotel-des-elmes.com.* Modern family-run hotel with 31 smart air-conditioned rooms and terraces beside the beach.

The sweet, dark brown aperitif, Banyuls, was first made here by the Knights Templar in the 13th century and there are plenty of opportunities for a free *dégustation* (tasting). On the edge of the town, you can see it being made at the **Cellier des Templiers**, the 600-year-old vaulted cellars of Le Mas Reig, the castle where it was first produced. There is also a free exhibition and film about Banyuls in the **Grande Cave** (*open daily*) opposite.

The **Aquarium €€** (*tel: 04 68 88 73 39. Open daily*) on the headland near the harbour is a centre for marine research as the sea on the Côte Vermeille is exceptionally clear, deep and well stocked with fish.

The sculptor Aristide Maillol (1861–1944) was born in Banyuls. One of his famous bronzes, *La Jeune Fille Alongée* (*Girl Lying Down*), stands on the seafront in Allée Maillol. He also sculpted the war memorial on the Ile Grosse, a small island at the southern end of the bay. Although he lived mostly in Paris, he returned every autumn to his aunt's country house, now the **Musée Maillol**, where he had a studio and is buried. His sculpture, *La Pensée* (*Thought*), can be found on his tomb (*see page 58*).

A lively festival, Fête Catalan, takes over the town every year from 3 to 11 July.

**Right**
Banyuls-sur-Mer

# CANET-PLAGE

**Canet Tourist Information** *Espace Méditerranée; tel: 04 68 86 72 00; email: infos@ot-canet.fr; www.ot-canet.fr*

**L'Aquarium €€** Beside the harbour; *tel: 04 68 80 49 64. Open daily Jul–Aug; Tue–Sat Sept–Jun 0900–1800.*

Unlike many of its neighbours, Canet is a long-established seaside resort – with a casino – though it got a facelift in the late 1960s when the coast was redeveloped. More recently, it has transformed its long seafront, lined with bars, restaurants, shops and apartments, by restricting traffic and creating a large central piazza. At the north end, there is a busy harbour and boatyards.

The **Aquarium** attracts visitors of all ages as it contains over 350 species of fish from all over the world; it is also an important research centre.

## Accommodation and food in Canet-Plage

**Hôtel le Galion €€** *20 avenue du Grand Large; tel: 04 68 80 28 23; email: contact@hotel-le-galion.com; www.hotel-le-galion.com.* Comfortable 28-room hotel with restaurant, a mile from the sea.

# CERBERE

**Cerbère Tourist Information** *avenue du Général de Gaulle; tel: 04 68 88 41 85; email: mairie@cerbere-village.com; www.cerbere-village.com. Open daily in summer; Mon–Tue & Fri in winter.*

The coast road winds south to the French–Spanish border at Cap Cerbère, a magnificent viewpoint on both sides over sea and mountains. The little town itself huddles around a small pebbly bay surrounded by steep vineyards. Trains on the Paris–Barcelona line stop at its 'international' station. On the seafront, a striking bronze statue of a woman holding a basket of oranges commemorates the workers who from 1878 to 1970 transferred freight, particularly oranges, between the French trains and the wider-gauge Spanish ones.

# COLLIOURE

**Collioure Tourist Information** *place du 18 Juin; tel: 04 68 82 15 47; email: contact@collioure.com; www.collioure.com. Open daily Apr–Sept; Mon–Sat Oct–Mar.*

Nestling by the Mediterranean at the foot of the first hills after miles of flat coastline to the north, Collioure is the gem of the Roussillon coast. A charming little port, it has been a magnet for artists since Matisse settled there in 1905. His disciples, dubbed the 'Fauves' (wild beasts), noted for their wild use of colour, soon followed. Narrow cobbled streets, now crowded with galleries and souvenir shops, lead back from its much-painted harbour and the small Eglise Notre-Dame-des-Anges, whose tower, which has a small pink dome, was once a lighthouse. Inside the church, remarkable Baroque wooden altarpieces, ornately carved and gilded, include a high altar by the Catalan artist Joseph Sunyer, sculpted in 1698.

Along the quay, colourful fishing boats tie up to deposit their catch, mainly the anchovies for which the town is renowned.

**Château Royal €€**
*tel: 04 68 82 06 43.*
*Open daily.*

A succession of traditional fêtes *from May to Sept* includes **Fêtes de La St-Vincent** *in mid-Aug,* when you can rely on seeing the *sardana* danced. Don't forget to sample the local anchovies.

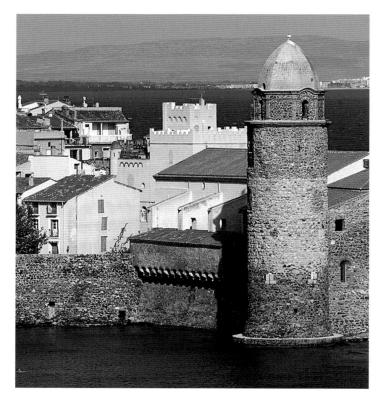

The **Château Royal**, which juts out into the centre of the harbour, was built by the Knights Templar in the 13th century and reinforced by the military architect Vauban in 1679, after Catalonia became part of France.

The town's four beaches are sandy but small so are usually crowded in summer. There are also diving and windsurfing schools.

## Accommodation and food in Collioure

**Hôtel Madeloc €** *24 rue Romain Rolland; tel: 04 68 82 07 56; email: hotel@madeloc.com; www.madeloc.com. Open Apr–mid-Nov.* Small modern hotel with a pool in a quiet position on a hill behind the harbour (10-minute walk). No restaurant.

**Les Templiers €** *12 quai de l'Amirauté; tel: 04 68 98 31 10; www.hotel-templiers.com. Open Feb–Dec.* Restaurant overlooking the harbour and Château Royal, famous for its paintings which almost cover its walls. Many are by artist friends of the family who run it. Also notable for its fish.

**Above**
The harbour at Collioure

**Opposite**
Elne: cloister carving

# ELNE

**ⓘ Elne Tourist Information** *place St Jordi; tel: 04 68 22 05 07; email: contact@ot-elne.fr; www.ot-elne.fr. Open daily all year.* Follow the signs to the free parking place at the top of the town to join marked walking routes of different lengths around the old streets.

**ⓗ Ste-Eulalie et Ste-Julie (cloister €€)** *tel: 04 68 22 70 90. Open daily all year.* Admission includes entrance to the cathedral and archaeological and history exhibits in the cloister and **Musée Terrus** (paintings) opposite; *tel: 04 68 22 88 88.*

**ⓒ Hotel Week-end** *€€ 29 avenue Paul Reig; tel: 04 68 22 06 68; www.hotel.weekend.chez-alice.fr.* Small eight-room hotel handily placed at end of main street with restaurant. Garden. Bicycles for hire. Private secure car park.

Surrounded by apricot and peach orchards, Elne became the capital of the Roussillon area in Roman times so was superior to its now much bigger neighbour Perpignan. The Romans named it after Helena, mother of Emperor Constantine. Narrow streets wind up to the majestic Gothic cathedral, **Ste-Eulalie et Ste-Julie**. Its two towers, the original in stone and a 19th-century brick addition, are a landmark for miles around. Built between the 11th and 15th centuries (apart from the second tower), it has six chapels on its south side, all with fine vaulting showing how the Gothic style developed over the centuries. There is also a beautiful cloister, almost completely intact, with arches supported by superbly carved twin pillars telling the story of Adam and Eve. The view from the cathedral terrace high above the town stretches from the sea to the Pyrenees.

## Hannibal

In 218 BC, Hannibal arrived from Spain with 34 elephants on his way to attack the Roman Empire. Learning of his intentions, the Romans tried to persuade the local people to stop him, but they had no wish to get involved in battles to protect another country. Instead, they signed a treaty with Hannibal at Elne, then one of the area's most important towns, and invited him to set up his headquarters there. Unusually, one clause stated that any dispute between his soldiers and the local men should be judged by a tribunal of Elne women.

# PORT-VENDRES

ℹ **Port-Vendres Tourist Information** 1 quai François Joly; tel: 04 68 82 07 54; email: infos@portvendres.com; www.port-vendres.com. Open daily in summer; Mon–Fri in winter.

🐚 Daily fish auction at around 1600 at 1 Anse-Jerbal Tue–Sun.

Port-Vendres – meaning the 'port of Venus' – has played many different maritime roles. Built around a deep cove which offered shelter for the Roman sailing galleys, it later developed into an important naval port when the military architect Vauban began strengthening the coast's defences in the late 17th century. Following bomb damage during World War II, it was largely rebuilt. When Algeria was part of France, passenger ferries operated regularly to Algiers. Today the port is home to many fishing boats and has a well-equipped marina.

# SOREDE

ℹ **Sorède Tourist Information** Off rue de la Caserne; tel: 04 68 89 31 17; email: ot-sorede@club-internet.fr; www.ot-sorede.com. Open daily Jul–Aug; Mon–Fri Sept–Jun.

🏭 **Les Micocouliers** rue des Fabriques; tel: 04 68 89 04 50; email: esat.micocouliers@orange.fr. Exhibition and shop open Mon–Fri Sept–Jul.

In the days of horse transport, this small town used to make the whips and crops for which Perpignan was famous. Now production is confined to one factory, **Les Micocouliers**, a rehabilitation centre which is the only place where whips are still made by hand.

# TOUR MADELOC

This 14th-century signal tower, situated at a height of 652m, is ideally placed for keeping watch out to sea in this once sensitive border area. Very exposed, it is built in the local schist slate and topped with battlements. The road up to it off the D86 is narrow, steep and twisting and is often subject to strong winds, but offers superb views. From here, you can see down across vineyards to Banyuls, Port-Vendres and Collioure, each tucked into its rocky cove, and to the flat sandy coast stretching away north.

**Above**
Sorède door detail

**Opposite**
Elne cathedral cloister

Children's beach clubs operate on the long sandy beach at Cerbère *in Jul–Aug*. Watersports are available at several points and there is an Olympic-sized open-air heated pool.

**Below**
Elne cathedral

# Suggested tour

**Total distance:** 125km. The detour to the Tour Madeloc adds 3km and the detour to Lavall adds 8km.

**Time:** 4 hours' driving. Allow 2 days to explore the little towns and enjoy the scenery and seaside. Those with limited time should concentrate on the coastal stretch from Collioure to Cerbère.

**Link to another tour:** From Sorède, the D2 and D618 lead west to Le Boulou (*see page 63*), 13km away.

Leave Perpignan on the straight D617, which runs through vineyards to the popular seaside resort of **CANET-PLAGE** ❶. The D81 enables you to skirt round it, but to see the sea – and get a better flavour of the

**Restaurant de la Plage** € *avenue du Général de Gaulle, Cerbère; tel: 04 68 88 40 03. Open daily Jul–Aug; Thur–Tue Sept–Jun. Large blue and white seafront restaurant with terrace in the centre of the bay at Cerbère, specialising in Catalan fare, especially fish.*

coast – continue to the beachside road before turning right. Be warned, however, that this tends to be very busy at the height of summer.

On the way south to **St-Cyprien-Plage**, you have water on both sides – the sea on the left and the **Etang de Canet et de St-Nazaire** on the right. Continuing on the D81, you come next to **ARGELES-PLAGE** ❷, the last of the beach resorts at the southern end of the French Mediterranean. Campsites can be found in the pine woods bordering the long straight road into the busy little town.

Afterwards the road begins to climb into the **Albères Hills** but drops down again into **COLLIOURE** ❸ and then up and down over the headland to **PORT-VENDRES** ❹. Joining the D914, you hug the hillsides, now covered by terraces of vineyards, on the scenic run down into **BANYULS-SUR-MER** ❺. Continue winding midway between sea and hilltop to **CERBERE** ❻ where the Spanish border lies at the top of the high pass, 4km on the far side, though its Customs' post is now invariably deserted.

Returning to Banyuls, follow the **TOUR MADELOC** ❼ sign (just after the river bridge) by turning left to climb inland on the narrow D86. Several *tables d'orientation* beside the road identify the landmarks and explain the history of the vineyards.

**Detour:** The turn to the Tour Madeloc off the D86 takes you up a steep 1.5km climb around narrow hairpin bends.

The D86 continues along the appropriately named **Balcon de Madeloc** hillside past **Notre-Dame de la Consolation** chapel to rejoin the D914. Leave this at Junction 12, turn left through the centre of **Argelès-sur-Mer** ❽ town and take the D2 to **SOREDE** ❾.

**Detour:** About 2km before Sorède, a left turn along a narrow road leads for 4km beside the River Massane into the **Gorges de Lavall** and the village of **Lavall**, with its tiny 12th-century chapel, **St-Martin**.

**Above**
*La Pensée* by Aristide Maillol

From Sorède, the D11 takes you to **ELNE** ❿ and along the straight Roman road, now the D914, back into Perpignan.

**La Paella €** *Les Arcades Centre, avenue de St-Cyprien, Latour bas, Elne; tel: 04 68 22 23 72. Open daily Jul–Aug except Sun evening; otherwise lunchtime only. Small roadside restaurant where you eat inexpensively and well.*

## Getting out of the car

The best reason to get out of the car along this route is to sit on the beach, but if you want to be a lot more energetic, try tackling the steep walk from the top of the village in Lavall to the **Tour de la Massane**, which takes you through a forest of ancient oaks and beeches. The tower at the top, 793m up and only 2km from the Spanish border, is a breathtaking viewpoint. Allow 2–3 hours. Alternatively, there's a gentler and shorter route up, starting from the Château de Valmy just outside Argelès, beside junction 12 on the D914.

# Into the foothills of the Pyrenees

## Ratings

| | |
|---|---|
| Mountains | ●●●●● |
| Scenery | ●●●●● |
| Food | ●●●●○ |
| History | ●●●●○ |
| Castles | ●●●○○ |
| Architecture | ●●○○○ |
| Art | ●●○○○ |
| Spas | ●●○○○ |

This is a route of contrasts, starting in flat countryside covered in vineyards, orchards and cork woods which edges up to Les Albères, the foothills of the Pyrenees. The further you go towards the Spanish border, the more alpine the scenery and architecture become. Prats de Mollo is very much a mountain town and in winter a cross-country skiing centre.

The area is also Catalan country. Many of the place names are distinctly un-French; you can often see the *sardana* danced and restaurants offer specialities such as spicy sausages and *anchoïade* (garlic and anchovy paste). The area did not become part of France until the border was finally settled in 1659 by the Treaty of the Pyrenees.

Though basically circular, the route has spurs up valley roads which lead to mountain passes on the border with Spain.

## AMELIE-LES-BAINS-PALALDA

The particularly mild winters enjoyed by this spa town which spreads along the winding River Tech have given it an abundance of subtropical plants such as palms, oleanders and mimosa. It also has two spa centres, dating from 1902, using sulphurous springs, first discovered by the Romans, which are highly regarded for the treatment of rheumatism. General de Castellane, whose construction of a military hospital in the 1850s put the town's medicinal qualities on the map, was also responsible for the network of footpaths in the hilly woods all around. A short walk from the town centre in the direction of the Modony Gorge leads to the remains of Roman baths, the best preserved in France.

Across the Tech from the town centre, **Palalda** is a medieval hillside village of steep narrow streets whose 400-year-old Chapelle du Rosaire has a fine carved wood altarpiece. The **Musée de la Poste en Roussillon** is devoted to the local postal service, including the invention of stamps by

**Tourist Information**
*22 avenue du Vallespir;
tel: 04 68 39 01 98; email:
ot.amelie@wanadoo.fr;
www.amelie-les-bains.com.
Open Mon–Sat all year.*

**Musée de la Poste
en Roussillon €**
*Carrer de la Placette, Palalda;
tel: 04 68 39 34 90; email:
musée.poste.amelie.66
@wanadoo.fr. Open Tue–Fri,
Mon, Sat & public holidays
afternoon only. Shuttle bus
services to Palalda from
Amélie or 2km on foot.*

a local man, Etienne Arago, and the code of smoke signals which could be sent from the nearby tower to alert the area in case of invasion from Spain.

## Accommodation in Amélie-les-Bains-Palalda

**Hôtel de Paris €€** *37 avenue du Vallespir; tel: 04 68 39 00 86; email: hotel2paris@orange.fr. Open mid-Feb–Nov.* Handily located in the town centre, this 24-room hotel has a large terrace and garden.

**Hôtel Lion d'Or €€** *3 carrer del Pardal; tel: 04 68 39 13 04; email: le-lion-dor-amelie@wanadoo.fr. Open all year.* Twenty-room hotel with a swimming pool in a pleasant garden.

# ARLES-SUR-TECH

**ℹ Tourist Information**
rue Jean-Baptiste
Barjou; tel: 04 68 39 11 99;
email: arles.tourisme@
neuf.fr; www.tourisme-haut-
vallespir.com. Open daily
Jul–Aug; Mon–Fri Sept–Jun.

**Tissages Catalans**
rue des Usines; tel: 04
68 39 10 07. Open Mon–Fri
May–Oct. Shop and
museum.

The tall 14th-century bell tower of the Eglise St-Sauveur welcomes you to this little town which grew up in the 10th century around a Benedictine abbey. The church has a soaring vaulted nave and peaceful 13th-century cloister. Don't miss the Sainte Tombe by the doorway, as water, said to be holy, seeps into it for no explicable reason.

The small **Tissages Catalans** factory, which has produced traditional Catalan fabrics for over a hundred years, has a **museum** beside it and a shop crammed full of colourful items from table napkins to dresses.

# CERET

**ℹ Tourist Information**
avenue Georges
Clemenceau; tel: 04 68 87
00 53; email: contact@ot-
ceret.fr; www.ceret.fr. Open
Mon–Sat all year. Guided
visits in English available.

**Musée d'Art
Moderne €€** 8
boulevard Maréchal Joffre;
tel: 04 68 87 27 76; email:
contact@musee-ceret.com;
www.musee-ceret.com. Open
daily May–Sept; Wed–Mon
Oct–Apr.

**Maison de
l'Archéologie €** porte
d'Espagne, place Picasso;
tel: 04 68 87 31 59. Open
Mon–Fri all year.

Saturday morning is a
good opportunity to
buy tielles, the local tartlets
of cuttlefish and tomato, in
the market.

**Sardana festival**
Mid-Jul.

This lively little town is known throughout France for the delicious plump red cherries which grow in the local orchards, providing a mass of beautiful white blossom in spring. On sale in markets and shops from April, they are one of France's earliest varieties.

Being strong in Catalan traditions, Céret is a good place to watch the *sardana* being danced and, if to your taste, attend a bullfight. Avenues of plane trees, plenty of smart shops and the remains of ancient fortifications around its web of narrow streets and small squares make it a pleasant place to stroll round. Picasso was a frequent visitor and many of his ceramics are on show in the small but excellent **Musée d'Art Moderne**, together with works by contemporary artists, particularly from the local area. A small Picasso memorial based on one of his drawings stands opposite the Arènes bullring. The **Maison de l'Archéologie**, an archaeological museum, occupies one of the town's old towers.

## Accommodation and food in Céret

**Les Arcades €** *1 place Picasso; tel: 04 68 87 12 30; email: info@hotel-arcades-ceret.com; www.hotel-arcades-ceret.com.* Has 30 rooms with cheerful Catalan-style furnishings and pictures by Ecole de Céret artists. B&B only but some rooms have a kitchenette.

**Hôtel La Terrasse au Soleil €€€** *route Fontfrède; tel: 04 68 87 01 94; email: terrasse-au-soleil.hotel@wanadoo.fr; www.terrasse-au-soleil.com/en. Open mid-Feb–mid-Dec.* You pay for the hillside setting of this comfortable, 36-room hotel on the edge of the town with beautiful views to the Canigou mountain and the Roussillon plain. Outdoor pool. Congenial surroundings.

# GORGES DE LA FOU

**Gorges de la Fou**
€€ *Off the D115, 2km west of Arles-sur-Tech; tel: 04 68 39 16 21; email: arles.tourisme@neuf.fr. Open Apr–Nov 1000–1800, except in bad weather. Visits last 1½ hours, including a 15-minute walk from the car park.*

Reputed to be the narrowest canyon in the world, this 250m-deep slit has been cut through rock by a stream (*fou* in Catalan means 'precipice'). The canyon is 2km long and often less than a metre wide; you walk between its often slimy sides on a metal 'bridge'. Though so much smaller than America's mighty Grand Canyon, it is no less impressive.

# LE BOULOU

**Tourist Information**
*1 rue du Château; tel: 04 68 87 50 95; email: contact@ot-leboulou.fr; www.ot-leboulou.fr. Open Mon–Sat all year.*

**Espace des Arts**
*2 rue des Ecloes; tel: 04 68 83 36 32; email: contact@mairie-leboulou.fr*

**Les Thermes** €€ *On the road to Le Perthus; tel: 04 68 87 52 00; email: leboulou@ chainethermale.fr. Open daily Mar–Nov. Casino tel: 04 68 83 01 20.*

Situated beside the River Tech on the edge of cork woods which stretch up the Albères hillsides, Le Boulou is a relaxed little spa town which benefits from its proximity to both sea and mountains. In the oldest quarter, the tiny 15th-century Chapelle de St-Antoine is a gem, particularly its gilded wooden altarpiece. Next door, the works of the local sculptor François Pous and other modern Catalan artists are on show in the **Espace des Arts**. The Eglise Ste-Marie, in the town centre, is remarkable for its splendidly carved 12th-century stone porch and a flamboyant Baroque altarpiece in red and white Céret marble.

Le Boulou's most glorious moment in French history was in 1794 when it was the site of a battle which resulted in the French army pushing the Spanish back over the Pyrenees. The soldiers' success is commemorated by an imposing round monument and on the Arc de Triomphe in Paris.

Today the town's main industry is cork, which is stripped from the woods around to make corks for the local Roussillon wine producers. Its spa, **Les Thermes**, with a casino beside it, still offers treatments based on the thermal springs and gas.

## Accommodation and food in Le Boulou

**Le Grillon d'Or** €€ *40 rue de la République; tel: 04 68 83 03 60; email: le-grillon@wanadoo.fr; www.grillon-dor.com.* Family-run hotel on the edge of town with hillside views, and 38 good-sized rooms, outdoor pool and garage. The restaurant (€) offers a wide choice of menus in congenial surroundings.

**Above**
Playing pétanque

## Maureillas-las-Illas

**ⓘ Tourist Information**
*At the Musée du Liège;*
*avenue Maréchal-Joffre;*
*tel: 04 68 83 48 00.*

**ⓜ Musée du Liège €**
*avenue Maréchal-Joffre;*
*tel: 04 68 83 15 41. Open*
*Wed–Mon afternoons all*
*year.*

The main reason for pausing in this large village is its cork museum, the **Musée du Liège**, which shows the full process of cork-making from tree to wine bottle. Cork sculptures by local artists are also on show alongside a collection of oak casks.

The ancient church, Chapelle St-Martin-de-Fenollar (*open Wed–Mon all year*), has frescoes dating back to the 12th century which provided inspiration for Picasso and Braque.

## Le Perthus

**ⓜ Fort de Bellegarde**
**€** *tel: 04 68 83 60 15.*
*Open daily Jun–Sept.*

This little town has an almost South American feel as its long main street, avenue de la France, is crowded with shops and stores catering for day-trippers from Spain. Earlier travellers were more likely to have been nomads, armies and refugees as it was a major border crossing point until 1976 when the A9 autoroute (La Catalane) opened, sweeping most of the traffic straight past it.

**Fort de Bellegarde**, an impressive fortress, stands guard over the town on a rock (420m). You reach it over a drawbridge beyond a smaller fort. Originally Spanish, it was strengthened by the military architect Vauban in the 1680s and most of his improvements are still intact. There is a large central courtyard and terrace with extensive views. Permanent exhibitions are devoted to its history and the Romans' Via Domitia highway.

### Vauban

Sébastien le Prestre de Vauban (1633–1707), Louis XIV's military engineer, was the principal exponent of the new design of fortress required to meet the challenge presented by the introduction of the cannon. Until then, attacks involved digging tunnels to undermine fortresses, weakening the walls with battering rams or building towers so the marauders could climb over the top. The only alternative was to wait until the defenders ran out of food or water which, if they had livestock and a well, might not happen for months.

The cannon changed the situation completely, necessitating a major re-think in military architecture. Huge curtain walls, sometimes 6m thick, became essential and towers lost their importance.

Although Vauban built or strengthened a large number of the area's fortresses and castles, he claimed to be much more proud of his work on the Canal du Midi, where he oversaw the construction of 49 aqueducts.

**Opposite**
Le Perthus: the Fort de
Bellegarde

# PRATS-DE-MOLLO-LA-PRESTE

**ℹ Prats-de-Mollo-la-Preste Tourist Information** *place du Foiral; tel: 04 68 39 70 83; email: info@ pratsdemollolapreste.com; www.pratsdemollolapreste.com. Open daily Jul–Aug; Mon–Fri Sept–Jun.*

**🏰 Fort Lagarde €€** *tel: 04 68 39 70 83. Open daily Apr–Oct; live shows Sun–Fri,* including cavalry displays, fencing, shooting and actors re-enacting life there in the 18th century.

**🌙 Hôtel le Bellevue €€** *place El Firal; tel: 04 68 39 72 48; email: info@hotel-le-bellevue; www.hotel-le-bellevue.fr. Open mid-Feb–Nov.* Small hotel with 17 en-suite rooms situated just outside the old quarter. Some rooms have balconies overlooking the lively town square.

**Above**
Prats-de-Mollo-la-Preste

This lively mountain town is overlooked by **Fort Lagarde**, a formidable citadel which Vauban constructed in 1692 around the remains of an older castle. Below it beside the River Tech, the original medieval part of the town, Ville d'Amoun, has straight narrow streets and thick ramparts. Among its interesting old buildings are the **Maison des Rois d'Aragon**, once the hunting lodge of the kings of Aragon, and the **Eglise Ste-Juste et Ruffine**, which has several splendid altarpieces. The town's large square, outside the old walls, is the scene of festivities throughout the year which often include *sardana* dancing; it is also popular for the game of pétanque (boules). In winter, cross-country ski routes lead around the base of the Costabonne peak (2,465m) from the little spa of La Preste (1,130m), 8km up the valley.

# ST-LAURENT-DE-CERDANS

**ℹ St-Laurent-de-Cerdans Tourist Information** *7 rue Joseph Nivet; tel: 04 68 39 55 75; email: contact@ville-saint-laurent-de-cerdans.fr; www.ville-saint-laurent-de-cerdans.fr. Open daily Jul–Aug; Mon–Fri Sept–Jun.*

Traditional Catalan fabrics and espadrilles are made in this unexpectedly busy little town surrounded by mountains. The **Musée d'Arts et Traditions Populaires €** (*rue Joseph Nivet. Open daily Jul–Aug; Mon–Fri Sept–Jun*), housed in a redundant textile factory, shows traditional crafts including the production of shoes.

# THUIR

**Left**
Prats-de-Mollo-la-Preste church

The Cusenier wine cellars have made a name for this otherwise unremarkable town. On a visit to the **Caves-Byrrh**, you can see its 800

**① Caves-Byrrh €**
*6 boulevard Violet; tel:
04 68 53 05 42; email:
contact@byrrh.com;
www.byrrh.com. Guided tours
daily Jul–Sept; Mon–Fri Oct
& Apr–Jun; Mon–Tue &
Thur Nov–Mar.*

vats, including the world's largest oak one which holds more than a million litres, and can watch aperitifs such as Byrrh, Cinzano and Dubonnet being made.

# Suggested tour

**Total distance:** 150km. The detour to Le Perthus adds 18km, the detour to St-Laurent-de-Cerdans adds 20km, the detour to La Preste adds 16km and the detour to Batère adds 26km.

**Time:** 4 hours' driving. Allow a day for the main route, but more with detours. Those with limited time should concentrate on the stretch from Céret to Prats-de-Mollo.

**Link to another tour:** From Le Boulou, the D618 and D2 lead east to Sorède (*see page 54*), 13km away.

From Perpignan (*see page 40*), take the D900 south to **LE BOULOU ①** – a quieter and more peaceful road than the A9 autoroute, which runs parallel with it.

**Detour:** To visit **LE PERTHUS ②** on the Spanish border, leave Le Boulou on the N9, once a busy cross-border road but now superseded by the autoroute which soars over lofty viaducts beside it. At the start of the detour (9km each way), the tiny **Chapelle St-Martin-de-Fenollar** on the left is noteworthy for its 12th-century murals in bold ochres, reds and greens; they provided inspiration for both Picasso and Braque.

From Le Boulou, take the D618 through **MAUREILLAS-LAS-ILLAS ③** and **CERET ④** to join the D115. Follow it beside the Tech through **AMELIE-LES-BAINS-PALALDA ⑤** and **ARLES-SUR-TECH ⑥**. Just after Arles-sur-Tech, the **GORGES DE LA FOU ⑦** are prominently signed on the right.

**Detour:** Shortly after the Gorges de la Fou sign, turn left off the D115 on to the D3 to **ST-LAURENT-DE-CERDANS ⑧** (10km each way).

Continuing on the D115 through a wide wooded gorge, you come to **PRATS-DE-MOLLO ⑨**.

**Below**
Céret

**Detour:** About 8km beyond Prats-de-Mollo on the D115a, **La Preste** is a small spa town offering thermal treatments.

From Prats-de-Mollo, you can return towards Arles-sur-Tech along an even more scenic route by turning left off the D115 at **Le Tech** on to the narrow D44. This goes through the village of **Montferrer** where you can pause to admire the mountain views from the terrace of its tiny museum.

**Detour:** Just before **Corsavy** on the D44, take the D43 for a detour (13km each way) on the lonely road up to the abandoned mine workings and remote inn at **Batère**.

From Corsavy, return to the D115 at Arles-sur-Tech and head back towards Céret but skirt it by turning left on to the D615 to go through **Llauro** to **THUIR ⑩**. As the road climbs through cork woods, it passes the **Ermitage de St-Ferréol** with views over the coast and to the snowy Canigou mountain inland. The hills give way to flat countryside covered in the neat vineyards which produce the famous aperitifs of Thuir.

Return to Perpignan on the D612, going through **Toulouges**, which was put on the map in 1027 when the Synod held there tried to promote peace throughout Western Europe by proclaiming the Truce of God, which restricted warfare to certain days of the year.

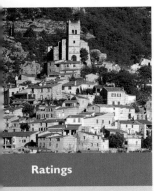

# In the shadow of the Canigou

## Ratings

| | |
|---|---|
| Architecture | ●●●●● |
| Mountains | ●●●●● |
| Scenery | ●●●●● |
| Churches | ●●●●○ |
| Outdoor activities | ●●●●○ |
| Walking | ●●●●○ |
| Villages | ●●●○○ |
| Spas | ●●○○○ |

You can't escape the spell of the Pic du Canigou, the dramatic snow-topped mountain, when you are in the Perpignan area. Rarely out of sight, it has been loved and revered for centuries by the local Catalans. They light the first midsummer bonfire on it and enjoy walking, riding, cycling and climbing on the wooded slopes that stretch for miles below it. For those who prefer less energetic pursuits, the castles, monasteries and picturesque little towns ranged around offer plenty to explore.

An opportunity not to be missed in summer is to look in the village churches, which are usually closed out of season, to see the surprising wealth of treasures inside. Many have beautiful carved and gilded wooden altarpieces inspired by the work of the 17th-century Catalan sculptor Joseph Sunyer. His own most famous pieces are to be seen in Perpignan and Prades.

## ABBAYE DE ST-MICHEL-DE-CUXA

**ⓘ Abbaye de St-Michel-de-Cuxa €**
*Codalet; tel: 04 68 96 15 35; email: contact@cuxa.org; www.cuxa.org. Open daily except Sun morning.*

After being abandoned during the French Revolution, this ancient monastery at Codalet, where Benedictine monks first settled in 878, was eventually restored, becoming a monastery again in 1919. Parts of the building are original, dating back to the 10th to 12th centuries, including the attractive four-tier square bell tower and delicately sculpted cloisters.

## ILLE-SUR-TET

**ⓘ Ille-sur-Têt Tourist Information** *place de la Poste; tel: 04 68 84 02 62; email: office-tourisme.ille@libertysurf.fr; www.ille-sur-tet.com. Open daily all year.*

This little town nestles between two rivers, the Têt and Boules. Its main tourist attraction is the **Centre d'Art Sacré** (*tel: 04 68 84 83 96. Open daily Jul–Aug; Wed–Mon Sept–Nov & Feb–Jun*), housed in Hospici d'Illa, a 16th-century pilgrims' hospice which highlights the treasures of the area's churches by staging different exhibitions each summer as well as having permanent displays.

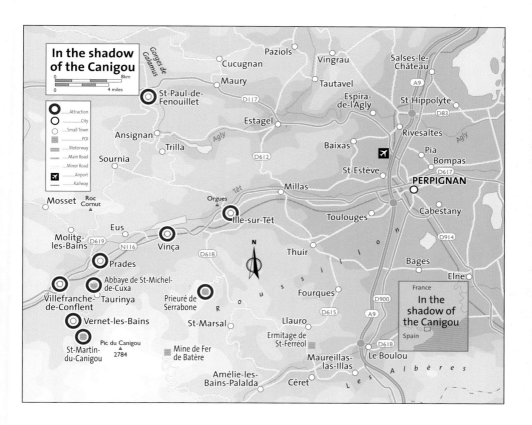

## In the shadow of the Canigou

0 ___ 8km

0 ___ 4 miles

- ◎ Attraction
- ○ City
- ○ Small Town
- ▬ POI
- ▬▬ Motorway
- ▬▬ Main Road
- ▬▬ Minor Road
- ✈ Airport
- ▬▬ Railway

Gorges de Galamus

Paziols
Cucugnan
Vingrau
Salses-le-Château
Maury
St-Paul-de-Fenouillet
D117
Tautavel
Espira-de-l'Agly
St-Hippolyte
D83
Estagel
Ansignan
Trilla
Agly
Baixas
Rivesaltes
Agly
Pia
Bompas
Sournia
D612
St-Estève
D617
**PERPIGNAN**
Mosset
Roc Cornut ▲
Orgues
Tét
Millas
Ille-sur-Tét
Toulouges
Cabestany
Eus
Molitg-les-Bains
D619
N116
Vinça
D618
Thuir
D914
Prades
Bages
Abbaye de St-Michel-de-Cuxa
Fourques
Elne
France
Villefranche-de-Conflent
Taurinya
Prieuré de Serrabone
D900
**In the shadow of the Canigou**
Vernet-les-Bains
St-Marsal
Llauro
D615
A9
Spain
St-Martin-du-Canigou
Pic du Canigou ▲ 2784
Mine de Fer de Batère
Ermitage de St-Ferréol
Maureillas-las-Illas
D618
Le Boulou
A l b è r e s
Amélie-les-Bains-Palalda
Céret
L e s

# PRADES

**ℹ️ Prades Tourist Information** *4 rue des Marchands; tel: 04 68 05 41 02; email: infos@prades-tourisme.fr; www.prades-tourisme.fr. Open daily Jul–Aug; Mon–Fri Sept–Jun.*

Surrounded by peach orchards, Prades nestles below the Canigou mountain. The town, which has many street names in Catalan, is strung out along narrow straight streets, some with kerbstones and doorsteps made of the local pink marble quarried at Villefranche-de-Conflent (*see page 74*). Dominating the central square, the 17th-century **Eglise St-Pierre** has a tall, square bell tower, 500 years older, with three tiers of open paired arches, typical of the area's Lombardy style. Inside, the church has a single nave lined with side chapels. Its rather austere design sets off the lavish altarpiece, which takes up the entire wall behind the high altar. Elaborately carved, painted and gilded, the altar is the largest in France and depicts scenes from the life of St Peter. The artist was Joseph Sunyer, the famous Catalan sculptor who came to Prades with his brother around 1690 and worked in churches throughout the area.

**P** Pay-and-display parking on market square; free on streets further away.

**Eglise St-Pierre** tel: 04 68 05 41 02. Open Mon–Fri Jul–Sept. Church silver on show in the Treasury €.

**Villa Lafabrègue €€** 15 avenue Louis Prat; tel: 04 68 96 29 90; www.villafrench.com. Five en-suite B&B rooms and two self-contained apartments (gîtes) near the centre of Prades. Built in 1873.

**Market** Tue.

**Music Festival** Late Jul–early Aug. Tickets bookable by credit card through the tourist office; booking opens May.

The distinguished Spanish cellist Pablo Casals made Prades his home in 1939 when he could no longer stomach life in Spain under Franco. An exhibition about his life and work can be seen in the **Mediathèque** (33 rue de l'Hospice; tel: 04 68 96 52 37. Admission free. Open Tue–Sat all year). In 1950, he inaugurated a Bach Festival which, with several other musical events, continues today, staged mainly in the Abbaye de St-Michel-de-Cuxa (see page 70.) in the countryside 3km south of the town.

## Accommodation and food in Prades

**Les Glycines €€** 129 avenue du Général de Gaulle; tel: 04 68 96 51 65; email: les-glycines2@wanadoo.fr. Simple but comfortable town-centre hotel noted for its floral displays. Nineteen attractively furnished rooms. Bright, cheerful restaurant.

**L'Hôtel Hexagone €€** La Plaine St-Martin; tel: 04 68 05 31 31; www.hotel-hexagone-prades.federal-hotel.com. Plain but comfortable modern hotel (definitely the town's best) with garden and sun terrace on the edge of the town, handy for the N116. No restaurant. Thirty rooms.

# PRIEURE DE SERRABONE

**Prieuré de Serrabone €** Boule d'Armont; tel: 04 68 84 09 30. Open daily all year.

This 12th-century priory is regarded as one of the area's best examples of the Romanesque style. Although the outside is rather austere, the interior is richly decorated, including flowers and animals on the capitals and an elaborate pink marble tribune (bishop's throne) with carving so delicate it looks like embroidery. Take a stroll, too, in its small botanic garden.

# ST-MARTIN-DU-CANIGOU

**St-Martin-du-Canigou €** tel: 04 68 05 50 03. Open daily Jun–Sept; Tue–Sun Oct–May. Walk up to it from the village of Casteil (45 minutes) or book to go by 4WD vehicle with a guide from Vernet-les-Bains or Villefranche-de-Conflent.

Perched on a rocky outcrop (1,055m), 3km south of Vernet-les-Bains, this monastery's red rooftops and square bell tower provide a landmark for miles around. When founded in the 11th century, its church was one of the first to have a vaulted nave and aisles supported by massive pillars. Since then it has had a chequered history. It was severely damaged by an earthquake in 1428 and the monks had to abandon it during the French Revolution. In 1902, the ruins were bought by the bishop of Perpignan and gradually restored until the monks were finally able to move back in 1972.

**Left**
Prades church

# St-Paul-de-Fenouillet

**ℹ St-Paul-de-Fenouillet Tourist Information** 26 boulevard de l'Agly; tel: 04 68 59 07 57; email: contact@st-paul66.com; www.st-paul66.com. Open Mon–Sat Jul–Aug; Tue–Sat Sept–Jun.

**🏛 Le Chapitre de St-Paul-de-Fenouillet** € Next to tourist office. Open Mon–Sat Jul–Aug; Tue–Sat Sept–Jun.

Situated between the Fenouillèdes and Corbières hills, this little town promotes itself as a base for a wide variety of outdoor activities, from mountain biking to canyoning. You can see layers of its long history in what remains of its ancient church, which was part of a chapter house, **Chapitre de St-Paul-de-Fenouillet**.

## Accommodation in St-Paul-de-Fenouillet

**Le Chatelet €€** *route de Caudiès; tel: 04 68 59 01 20; email: chatelet.rauss@orange.fr; www.hotel-lechatelet.com. Open mid-Mar–mid-Oct.* Small, pink, countryside hotel on the D117 towards Quillan. Fifteen rooms, swimming pool May–September.

# Vernet-les-Bains

**ℹ Vernet-les-Bains Tourist Information** 2 rue de la Chapelle; tel: 04 68 05 55 35; email: tourisme.vernet-les-bains@wanadoo.fr; www.vernet-les-bains.fr. Open daily Jul–Aug; Mon–Fri Sept–Jun.

**🚴 Championnat du Canigou** is a 30km race, on footpaths on the Canigou mountain. To take part, just turn up on the day (first Sun in Aug).

**⛰ Fête de la Belle Epoque** takes place on Ascension weekend in May when everyone dresses up and old vehicles parade through the streets.

Vernet-les-Bains is a relaxed hillside town with lush gardens, thermal springs and shaded boulevards. In its heyday as a fashionable spa around the turn of the 20th century, it attracted many British visitors, including Rudyard Kipling. Today some people still come to drink its waters (reputed to help the treatment of rheumatism and ear, nose and throat diseases) but most visitors are more interested in walking, riding or mountain biking in its glorious mountain surroundings. The square bell tower of the Eglise St-Saturnin beside the restored castle crowns the old quarter at the top of narrow streets whose old houses are bedecked with flowers. The castle's terraces have good views of the wooded mountains.

## Accommodation and food in Vernet-les-Bains

**Le Mas Fleuri €€** *25 boulevard Clémenceau; tel: 04 68 05 51 94; email: hotel.masfleuri@wanadoo.fr; www.hotellemasfleuri.fr. Open daily Apr–Oct.* Comfortable family-run hotel in sunny position with large pool and gardens. Thirty rooms.

# Villefranche-de-Conflent

**ℹ Tourist Information** place de l'Eglise; tel: 04 68 96 22 96; email: infotourisme@villefranche66.fr; www.villefranchedeconflent.fr. Open daily Feb–Dec.

Walking round the **ramparts** of this strongly fortified medieval town, you can easily feel transported back in time. Twenty-two of the buildings within its thick two-storey-high walls are classed as historic monuments. Often built in pink marble from the nearby quarry, they date from the 13th and 14th centuries. Though most are now occupied by souvenir shops or restaurants, Villefranche is definitely a

**Ramparts €** *tel: 04 68 96 22 96. Open daily, Feb–Dec.*

**Fort-Libéria €€** *tel: 04 68 96 34 01; www.fort-liberia.com. Open daily. Shuttle bus (navette) from Le Canigou café, place du Génie.*

place to linger and absorb the unique atmosphere. It is also the starting point of Le Petit Train Jaune (Little Yellow Train), one of Europe's most scenic railway lines (*see page 79*). **Fort-Libéria**, which stands guard on a hillside above the town, was built by the military architect Vauban in 1679 as a deterrent to any snipers who might have been tempted to take potshots down into the town. It has three tiers and high stone walls topped by bricks and wrought-iron rails. **L'Escalier de Mille Marches** ('staircase of 1,000 steps', though there are actually 734) leads up to it from the town across **Pont St-Pierre**, an attractive fortified bridge. The climb is rewarded by a magnificent panorama over the valley and the Canigou mountain.

**Grotte des Grandes Canalettes** €€ *2 rue Saint-Jacques; tel: 04 68 05 20 20; www.grotte-grandes-canalettes.com. Open daily Apr–Oct; Sun afternoon Nov–Mar.*

**Grotte des Grandes Canalettes,** one of several large caves in the area, is in the hills on the southwest edge of the town. It is part of a collection of caves, which are part of an underground river. Visitors can follow man-made pathways to explore the rich earth history and beauty of the chambers. There is an auditorium which holds son-et-lumière musical entertainments every evening at 1830 during July and August. Group bookings can be made for this.

# VINÇA

**Tourist Information** *9 place Bernard Alart; tel: 04 68 05 84 47; email: otvinca@orange.fr; www.ville-vinca.fr. Open Mon–Sat Jul–Aug. Visits to the local church in the mornings during summer.*

Big old houses with decorative stone doorways are gathered along a network of narrow streets and tiny squares, all clustered around the village's fine Southern Gothic church, Eglise St-Julien, which has several beautiful altarpieces and an organ built by the famous Cavaillé-Colls family (*see page 164*). There are organ recitals in July and August.

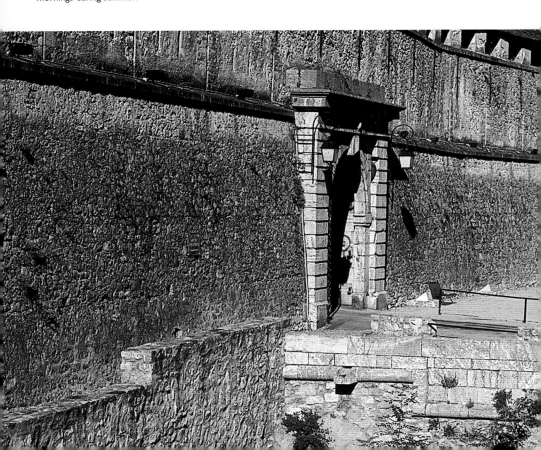

## Suggested tour

**Total distance:** 140km, plus 25km each way between Perpignan and Ille-sur-Têt. The detour to Prieuré de Serrabone adds 24km, the detour to St-Martin-du-Canigou adds 6km and the detour to Eus adds 8km.

**Time:** 5 hours' driving. Allow at least a day for the main route, more with detours. Those with limited time should concentrate on the circuit from Prades through Vernet-les-Bains and Villefranche-de-Conflent. A trip on the Little Yellow Train can take almost a full day.

**Links to other tours:** From St-Paul-de-Fenouillet, the D117 leads east to Maury (*see page 106*), 8km away, and the D10 leads north to Cubières-sur-Cinoble (*see page 106*), 10km away. From Villefranche-de-Conflent, the N116 leads west to Mont-Louis (*see page 88*), 30km away.

**Below**
Ramparts, Villefranche-de-Conflent

Take the N116 west out of Perpignan to **ILLE-SUR-TET** ❶ where the route proper begins, then continue on it as it climbs from the

**Le Petit Train Jaune** runs between Villefranche-de-Conflent and Latour-de-Carol, a distance of 63km, and makes stops at 20 stations, including Bolquère-Eyne, the highest station in France; *tel: 04 68 96 63 63*. Information and a timetable can be downloaded from the French Railways website at *www.trainstouristiques-ter.com*

Roussillon plain along the valley into the mountains, getting nearer to the snow-capped Canigou (on the left) all the way. In early spring, the peach orchards which thrive in the shelter of the valley are a mass of pink blossom.

**Detour:** To visit the **PRIEURE DE SERRABONE ❷**, turn left off the N116 3km beyond Ille-sur-Têt on to the D618 and then follow the River Boulés on the D84 (12 km).

As the N116 bypasses **VINÇA ❸** and **PRADES ❹**, leave it each time and follow their *centre ville* signs to visit them.

On the edge of Prades, turn south on the D27 (signed Codalet). This leads up through cherry orchards to the **ABBAYE DE ST-MICHEL-DE-CUXA ❺** and has a glorious view of the Canigou ahead. Continuing to climb through open countryside, you pass the village of **Taurinya** and its attractive 11th-century bell tower, enjoying superb views back

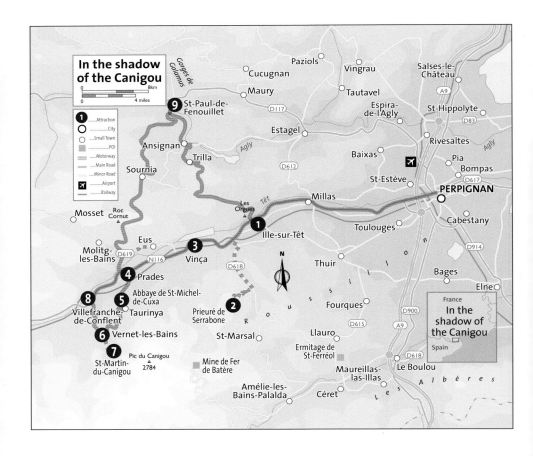

A leaflet about walks and places to visit from various stations is available from stations and tourist information offices. The train can be hired as a whole for a private party.

down over Prades and ahead of **VERNET-LES-BAINS** ➏ spreading down from its ancient church.

**Detour:** To visit **ST-MARTIN-DU-CANIGOU** ➐, follow the D116 south from Vernet-les-Bains for 3km.

## Le Petit Train Jaune

Constructed between 1910 and 1927 to connect the remote villages in the foothills of the Pyrenees, the line is now mainly used by tourists. Its bright yellow metre-gauge electric trains (with open-top carriages in summer) climb to the 1,200m-high Cerdagne plateau near the Spanish border on their way to Latour-de-Carol where they connect with the Toulouse–Barcelona line on the main SNCF network. On the 63km journey, they rattle around hillsides, through deep gorges, over lofty viaducts, in and out of 19 tunnels and past terraced vineyards and tiny red-tiled villages that cling to the hillsides. Several run each day and the full journey takes 2½–3 hours.

After following the wooded Têt Valley in the shadow of the Canigou, the line crosses wide mountain pastures below Font-Romeu and passes the huge solar oven at Odeillo. The scenery becomes positively alpine at the highest point (1,593m) where it crosses the Col de la Perche at Bolquère-Eyne, the highest SNCF station in France.

**Below**
Le Petit Train Jaune

From Vernet-les-Bains, the D116 leads north down a wide gorge to **VILLEFRANCHE-DE-CONFLENT** ❽, with Fort-Libéria brooding over it on the hillside beyond. A ride on **Le Petit Train Jaune**, which starts from Villefranche-de-Conflent, is a memorable experience. The 63km line to Latour-de-Carol is one of the most scenic in Europe.

From Villefranche-de-Conflent, take the N116 towards Prades, turning left on to the D619 to **Sournia**.

**Detour:** A short detour (4km each way) off the D619 on the D24 leads to **Eus**, a picturesque hillside hamlet whose old houses cluster around a fortified church in typical Catalan style. It spreads down the sunny side of the valley among boulders of granite and patches of broom.

Then as the D619 twists and climbs towards Sournia in the Fenouillèdes hills, you get splendid views south across the valley not only to the Canigou but also the mountains across the border in Spain. Trees give way to scrubby bushes as the road winds up and up through wild rocky moorland past huge boulders and strangely shaped rocks, such as the **Roc Cornut**. You'll certainly want to stop and get

**Below**
Les Orgues, at Ille-sur-Têt

your binoculars out at the highest point, the Col de Roque-Jalère (976m), where the white ridge of the Corbières hills comes into view to the north and the Mediterranean to the west. The Compoussey plateau beyond it is a very quiet stretch of countryside with just a few red-roofed villages clustered around their square bell towers. The final descent into **ST-PAUL-DE-FENOUILLET** ❾ is dramatic as the road drops down to go through the Clue de la Fou, a narrow gap between two cliffs gouged out by the River Agly. From St-Paul-de-Fenouillet, the D619 and D77 return you south via **Ansignan** where the road passes close to an aqueduct built by the Romans. Bear right on the D9b via **Trilla** for the scenic run down to the Têt Valley and the N116 back to Perpignan. Just before Ille-sur-Têt the road passes **Les Orgues**, curious pillars of rock which look remarkably like organ pipes. There are two groups of these *cheminées de fées* ('fairies' chimneys'). The one on the eastern side, in the middle of an 'amphitheatre' of craggy white walls, is easily accessible. Enjoy this spectacular site while you can as geologists reckon it will disappear within about 50 years due to erosion by wind and rain.

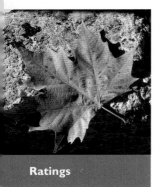

# Up into the Pyrenees

## Ratings

| | |
|---|---|
| Mountains | ●●●●● |
| Outdoor activities | ●●●●● |
| Scenery | ●●●●● |
| Spas | ●●●●○ |
| Architecture | ●●●○○ |
| Food | ●●●○○ |
| History | ●●○○○ |
| Wildlife | ●●○○○ |

This route takes you south through the Pyrenees to the wide Cerdagne plateau on the border with Spain. Although the tops of the mountains do not match the height of the Alps, this part of Catalan-speaking Roussillon – fought over with Spain for centuries – is all high. Its meadows, where sheep, cattle and horses graze, blaze with wild flowers in summer when wild crocuses, gentians and lupins mingle with the buttercups and daisies. And a huge variety of mushrooms sprout up in the woods.

Criss-crossed by footpaths, the area rewards those who get out of their car to enjoy the fresh mountain air and scenery on foot – or, in winter, on skis. Indeed, snow makes many of the minor roads impassable until spring and the narrow mountain road which twists between Ax-les-Thermes and Mijanès often remains blocked until even later.

## Ax-les-Thermes

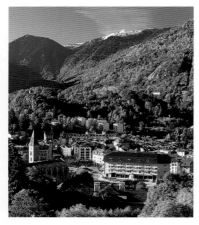

This elegant town is typical of the 19th-century spas which became fashionable with the arrival of the railway. Today most summer visitors prefer to go walking and winter ones to go skiing, but it still has two pump rooms – the Teich and Grand Tétras – and 80 thermal springs. These range in temperature from 18 to 78°C (64–172°F) and are used to treat rheumatism, skin problems and breathing disorders. Anyone can use the Bassin des Ladres (lepers), the public pool on place du Breilh which was built in 1260 for soldiers suffering from leprosy. You could take a very public dip in it but most people are content simply to soak their feet; wonderful after a long walk or day's skiing! The town also has a large selection of hotels. The **Eglise St-Vincent**, built in 1811 on the site of an earlier church, is remarkable for its 4-tonne granite altar and modern stained glass.

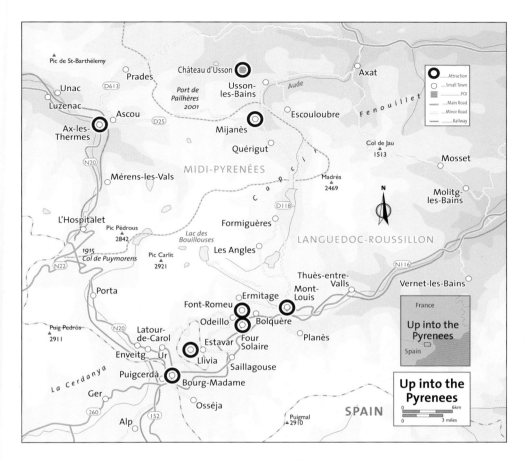

**ⓘ Ax-les-Thermes Tourist Information** 6 avenue Delcassé; tel: 05 61 64 60 60; www.vallees-ax.com. Open daily all year.

**Thermal information** 6 avenue Delcassé; tel: 05 61 65 86 60; www.thermes-ax.com

**Opposite**
The stunning backdrop to Ax-les-Thermes

## Accommodation and food in Ax-les-Thermes

**Auberge l'Orry le Saquet €** *route de l'Espagne; tel: 05 61 64 31 30.* Fifteen-room hotel with pretty garden on southern edge of town. Parking.

**Hôtel l'Auzeraie €€** *1 avenue Delcassé; tel: 05 61 64 20 70; email: auzeraie@auzeraie.com; www.auzeraie.com. Open mid-Dec–mid-Nov.* Noted for its regional cuisine. Fitness room, garden and car park. Thirty-three rooms.

**Hôtel le Chalet €€** *4 avenue Turrel; tel: 05 61 64 24 31; email: contact@le-chalet.fr; www.le-chalet.fr. Open Jan–Nov.* Smart modern hotel beside the River Oriège with extensive views.

# Bourg-Madame

**ⓘ Bourg-Madame Tourist Information** *place de la Catalogne; tel: 04 68 04 55 35; email: tourisme.bourg-madame@wanadoo.fr; www.bourg-madame.fr. Open Mon–Sat Jul–Aug; Mon–Fri Sept–Jun.*

**ⓗ Eglise St-Martin** Guided visits to Hix.

**◔ Two-week Hix festival** *in Aug.*

As befits a border village, Bourg-Madame once thrived on smuggling. It was originally called Guingettes d'Hix because people from Hix, a hamlet 1km away, liked to go to its *guingettes* (cafés with dancing) for a night out; the first opened in 1693. Its present name was given after the Duc d'Angoulême and his wife, known as Madame Royale, passed through on their return from exile in Spain after the downfall of Napoleon. He gave permission for it to be renamed in honour of the event.

Hard as it is to believe, Hix was the capital of the region until the 12th century, mainly because of the country fairs which were held there. Today it consists only of a few stone buildings beside a small Romanesque church, **Eglise St-Martin**.

# Chateau d'Usson

**ⓗ Château d'Usson €** *Tel: 04 68 20 43 92; email: ot@donezan.com; www.languedoc-france.info. Open daily Jul–Sept; Sat–Sun May–Jun. Other days by appointment through Mijanès tourist office; tel: 04 68 20 41 37.*

This ruined castle stands on a rocky outcrop above the village of Usson-les-Bains. Originally constructed in wood in the 10th century, it was a Cathar refuge when the 'heretics' were in retreat. Later it became redundant and fell into ruin during the French Revolution when much of its stone was removed for other buildings. The village below has also seen better days as its former spa buildings beside the River Bruyère are fast falling into disrepair.

# Font-Romeu

**ⓘ Font-Romeu Tourist Information** *82 avenue E Brousse; tel: 04 68 30 68 30; email: office@font-romeu.fr; www.font-romeu.fr. Open daily all year.*

**ⓗ Chapel** *300m before the Col du Calvaire de Fort-Romeu on the D618, 1km east of Font-Romeu. At the Col itself, on the other side of the D618, a footpath leads past Stations of the Cross to a panoramic view over the Cerdagne and surrounding mountains.*

**Left**
A rural community

This large year-round holiday resort, the highest town in France (1,800m), was purpose-built in the 1920s on the edge of pine forests. Occupying a sheltered sunny position on a south-facing hillside, it enjoys a panoramic view aross the Cerdagne plateau to the ridges of the Pyrenees.

In winter, it is a busy ski resort, equipped with 460 snow cannons to ensure the season remains in full swing until April. Throughout the year leading sportsmen and women arrive from all over the world for altitude training, as well as holidaymakers who go walking or climbing. The Grand Hotel, which occupies a commanding position on the skyline, was built as a prestigous railway hotel but is now divided into holiday apartments.

The town got its name from the nearby pilgrims' spring (*foun roumeu* in Catalan) which has been the site of pilgrimages since – the story goes – the *Vierge de l'Invention*, a statue of the Virgin Mary, was discovered in a crack in the rock by a bull as it scraped earth from the spring. The small 17th-century **chapel** beside it has a lavish altarpiece by the Catalan sculptor Joseph Sunyer. The statue spends each summer in the chapel until 8 September when it is carried downhill

**Hôtel Carlit €€**
*8 avenue d'Espagne;
tel: 04 68 30 80 30; email:
contact@carlit-hotel.com;
www.carlit-hotel.com.*
Modern family-run
58-room hotel in town
centre enjoying good
views over the plain.
Swimming pool.

with much pomp and ceremony to the church in Odeillo. It is brought back with similar ceremony on Trinity Sunday. The large hermitage building beside the chapel is now used as university accommodation.

# FOUR SOLAIRE

**Four Solaire €€**
*Odeillo; tel: 04 68 30
77 86; email:
soleil@promes.cnrs.fr;
www.foursolaire-fontroneu.fr.
Open daily all year.*
Exhibition with video on
how the solar oven works.

The Four Solaire, a vast 40m-high curving screen of tiny mirrors near the village of Odeillo, dominates the countryside. Built in 1969, it is the world's largest solar oven and is used to research the effects of very high temperatures on materials. The sun's rays are reflected on to the screen from 63 large mirrors set up on the hillside facing it and then reflected again into a single spot where the temperature can reach over 3,000°C (5,400°F).

# LLIVIA

**Llívia Tourist
Information** *Musée
Municipal de Llívia, Spain;
tel: (Spain) (+34) 972 89 63
13; email:
patronat@llivia.com;
www.llivia.org. Open
Mon–Sat all year.*

You are now entering Spain. This small enclave, only 3km across, remained Spanish when everywhere around it became part of France following the Treaty of the Pyrenees in 1659. On the road which crosses it you slip over the 'border' without realising until you stop and find everyone speaking Catalan (though they also understand Spanish). A large number of holiday villas enjoying views over the Cerdagne are springing up around the road, but if you turn off it into the old part of Llívia you are immediately plunged into narrow streets

## Spain's Llívia

Llívia has remained 'temporarily' part of Spain since 1659 when the Treaty of the Pyrenees ceded 33 villages on the northern slopes of the Cerdagne to France. At the time, the exact course of the border was not precisely specified but was basically understood to be the North–South watershed where rivers flowed into either France or Spain.

The population of Llívia strongly objected to being moved into France, arguing that it could not possibly be classed as a 'village' as it had been capital of the Cerdagne since the 10th century. They also pointed out that the River Sègre, which passes it flows into Spain even though its source is a spring on the northern side of the Pic de Sègre.

No one has yet got round to settling the matter, but meanwhile Llívia determinedly retains Spanish signs and Spanish menus and – until the euro – used Spanish currency. The tiny village of Eyne, 7km east of Llívia, has tried to become a second Spanish enclave, but so far the French government has loftily ignored its petitions.

**l'Esquirol** € *Avinguda Catalunya, 17527 Llívia; tel: (Spain) (+34) 972 89 63 03.* For a taste of genuine Catalan food, including specialities such as duck with peas and *crème Catalan*.

**A music festival** takes place in the church at *weekends in Aug*. For information, *tel: (Spain) (+34) 972 89 60 49; www.llivia.com/festival/ index.htm*

**Right**
The solar oven (Four Solaire) on Mont-Louis

clustered beneath an imposing 15th-century church with a spired bell tower. The stone buildings house a handful of shops and restaurants. The old pharmacy is now a small museum.

### Accommodation and food in Llívia

**Hostal Ruso €€** *2 Pujada de l'Esglesia; tel: (+34) 972 14 62 64; email: hostalruso@jmail.com. Open all year.* Atmospheric nine-room hotel in an attractively restored old mansion in the town centre. Popular with skiers in winter.

# MONT-LOUIS

**Tourist Information**
*3 rue Lieutenant Pruneta; tel: 04 68 04 21 97; email: otmontlouis@wanadoo.fr; www.mont-louis.net. Open daily Jul–Aug; Mon–Sat Sept–Jun.*

**Puits des Forçats**
*€ In the military fort. Guided visits Jul–Aug. Tickets available at the Office de Tourisme.*

**Four Solaire €€**
*Résidence Vauban; tel: 04 68 04 14 89; email: contact@four-solaire.fr; www.four-solaire.fr. Open daily all year.*

Still completely surrounded by ramparts which have never had to withstand an attack, Mont-Louis is a perfect example of an old fortified town. Its watchtowers and bastions have remained intact since Louis XIV instructed his military architect, Vauban, to build it in 1679 to guard the border between France and Spain following the Treaty of the Pyrenees when Roussillon was ceded to France. Today the citadel is used as a commando training centre – so don't be surprised to see soldiers out and about. Inside it the original well, the **Puits des Forçats**, built in case of siege, still has its wooden winding gear in working order.

**Four Solaire**, the world's first solar oven, an amazing combination of mirrors and panels, was installed in the Résidence Vauban in a corner of the ramparts in 1949, predating the Four Solaire at Odeillo (*see page 86*). Guided tours show how solar energy is produced, reaching temperatures of over 3,000°C (5,400°F). Pottery baked in the oven is on display.

# MIJANES

**Mijanès Tourist Information** *At Le Pla (2km south on the D16); tel: 04 68 20 41 37; email: ot@donezan.com; www. donezan.com. Open daily Jul–Aug; Mon–Fri Sept–Jun.*

This quaint little terraced village, whose stone houses spread along narrow cobbled streets down a sunny hillside, has been occupied since prehistoric times. Once home to Gauls and Romans, it was at its busiest during the 18th century when iron was mined in the area. Now in winter it turns into a mini ski resort for slopes about a 10-minute drive away.

# Suggested tour

**Total distance:** 135km. The detour to Lac des Bouillouses adds 28km and the detour to Château d'Usson adds 6km.

**Above**
Magnificent autumn colours in
the Pyrenees

**Time:** 4 hours' driving. Allow at least a day for the main route, two with detours. Those with limited time should concentrate on the Cerdagne area, particularly Font-Romeu and Mont-Louis.

**Links to other tours:** At Ax-les-Thermes, the route meets the 'Castles and caves from Foix' route (*see page 96*). From Mont-Louis, the N116 leads east to Villefranche-de-Conflent (*see page 74*), 30km away.

Leave **AX-LES-THERMES** ❶ along the N20, which climbs beside the railway up the River Ariège Valley in a wide wooded gorge. It's easy to sweep through **Mérens-les-Vals** without noticing its ruined chapel, one of the oldest in the region. Thought to date back to the 10th century, it has a three-tier bell tower in typical Catalan style.

Further south, you can shorten the journey over the **Col de Puymorens** (1,915m) by paying the toll to go through the 6km-long tunnel under it from **L'Hospitalet**, but the ride over the top on the twisting road through the mountains is much more scenic. Dropping down along the wide valley of the River Carol, still beside the railway, you pass the twin towers of a ruined castle, Tours Carol, and reach the villages of **Latour-de-Carol** and **Enveitg**, where trains on the Toulouse–Barcelona line meet up with Le Petit Train Jaune (*see page 79*).

Continuing south, the N20 goes through **Ur** on the way to **BOURG-MADAME** ❷ and its tiny suburb **Hix**, framed by a ridge of the Pyrenees across the border in Spain. Take the N116 east (towards the charcuterie-producing town of **Saillagouse**), but turn left after 4km on to the D30 and then right on to the N154. This whisks you imperceptibly into the Spanish enclave and its small town of **LLIVIA** ❸. Leaving Llívia is trickier as you need to spot the sign to **Estavar** in the town centre. Beyond Estavar the D33e runs scenically up to **FONT-ROMEU** ❹ past **Odeillo** and its extraordinary-looking solar oven, **FOUR SOLAIRE** ❺. Leaving Font-Romeu on the D618, you soon come to the hermitage on the left with the chapel behind it and then go over the Col du Calvaire de Font-Romeu (1,836m) on the way to **MONT-LOUIS** ❻.

**Detour:** The D60 (left off the D198 just north of Mont-Louis) leads up a wooded road through the Fôret de Barrés to the **Lac des Bouillouses**, 14km north. This big mountain reservoir, over 2,000m high, feeds irrigation channels and hydroelectric plants in the Têt Valley. Altogether there are over 20 lakes on the bleak Bouillouses plateau between the Carlit, Péric and Aude peaks.

From Mont-Louis, the D118 runs north past **Formiguères**, a village notable for its distinctly alpine feel and 14th-century church, Ste-Marie. Six kilometres beyond it, turn left on to the D32 and then the D16 for Quérigut and **MIJANES** ❼. In Napoleonic times, this was an important stretch of highway. Named the Chemin des Canons, it was built in 1659 following the Treaty of the Pyrenees so munitions could be transported to the Mont-Louis fort. Indeed the village of **Quérigut**, watched over by the ruins of a castle abandoned after the Treaty, boasted a population of 600 inhabitants at the end of the 19th century.

**Detour:** From Mijanès the D16 leads to **CHATEAU D'USSON** ❽ (3km).

From the car park in Mijanès, a 25-minute woodland walk leads to one of the few remaining Catalan forges, a relic from the 18th-century iron industry. Oxen were used to operate the presses which enabled a team of eight men to do work which previously required a hundred – clearly a significant step towards industrialisation.

Along the D25, which takes this route back to Ax-les-Thermes from Mijanès, the mountain tops are crowned by cairns, thought to have been placed there by Napoleon's officers to mark the summits. It is one of the remotest mountain roads in the area, often steep and narrow with hairpin bends over the Col de Pailhères (2,001m). It is invariably blocked by snow in winter and can remain closed until May; the alternative route back to Ax-les-Thermes is via Usson-les-Bains, Aunat, Espezel and Belacaire, but this adds 20km to the journey.

Various trips are possible on Le Petit Train Jaune as it makes frequent stops on its scenic 63km journey between Villefranche-de-Conflent and Latour-de-Carol. Timetable and information: *tel: 04 68 96 63 63* (*see page 79*).

# Castles and caves from Foix

## Ratings

| | |
|---|---|
| Castles | ●●●●● |
| Caves | ●●●●● |
| Historical sights | ●●●●○ |
| Children | ●●●○○ |
| Mountains | ●●●○○ |
| Outdoor activities | ●●●○○ |
| Scenery | ●●●○○ |
| Museums | ●●○○○ |

Two of the region's most characteristic features are included in this route – castles and caves. Foix Castle was a major political stronghold in the 13th century and Monségur, one of the most historic sites in France, was the scene of the terrible slaughter that ended the Albigensian Crusade.

In the limestone hills crossed by the River Ariège and its tributaries, hundreds of caves have formed. The prehistoric paintings in the Grotte de Niaux are among the finest in Europe – and are being carefully cherished. The Grotte de Lombrives is the largest cave open to the public in Western Europe.

Although several towns along the route have an industrial side, this scarcely impinges on their attraction. The busy main roads which link them take you through peaceful countryside and hills where it is easy to head off along less beaten tracks and find places to explore on foot.

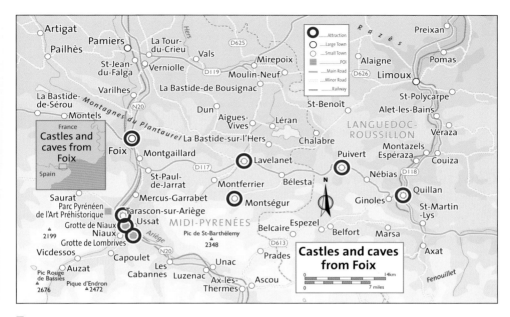

**Castles and caves from Foix**

# FOIX

**Foix Tourist Information** 29 rue Delcassé; tel: 05 61 65 12 12; email: foix.tourisme@wanadoo.fr; www.ot-foix.fr. Open daily Jul–Aug; Mon–Sat Sept–Jun.

**Château des Comtes de Foix** and **Musée de l'Ariège** €€ tel: 05 61 65 56 05. Open daily, weekends Jan.

**Large regional market** Fri.

**Son-et-Lumière** Tue & Thur–Fri Jul–Aug.

The most important town between Toulouse and Carcassonne benefits from its commanding position on the edge of the Plantaurel hills where two rivers meet, the Arget and Ariège. Though comparatively small, its castle, **Château des Comtes de Foix**, occupies an impressive position on a rock in the centre, with its three towers silhouetted against the mountains. One of the lower rooms houses the **Musée Départemental de l'Ariège**, a collection of weapons and prehistoric finds from over 60 caves around the Ariège area (250 more caves have been identified but not yet explored). The castle's finest hour was early in the 13th century when the count of Foix was a force to be reckoned with. Indeed, Simon de Montfort never dared attack it during the Albigensian Crusade though the town was a Cathar stronghold (*see page 30*). There are good views from the top of the 15th-century round tower (the two 13th-century ones are square) and the terrace.

The town has two distinct areas. In the old part, narrow streets and alleys with half-timbered buildings radiate from small squares including place de Labistour, which has a charming bronze fountain in the shape of a swan. The newer area has broad boulevards and two 19th-century covered markets. Traditional Catalan fabrics are made in the town but nobody now pans for gold in the river. Iron was mined nearby until 1931. The composer Gabriel Fauré (1845–1924) grew up in the town, attending school at the Ecole Normale d'Instituteurs in Montgauzy, just above the castle on the north side of town, which has

**Left**
Foix château

**P** Pay-and-display parking.

a good view over the town. The Chapelle Notre-Dame, next to the Ecole, was formerly part of a convent.

## Accommodation in Foix

**Hôtel Pyrène €€** *rue Serge Denis; tel: 05 61 65 48 66; email: hotel.pyrene@wanadoo.fr; www.hotelpyrene.com. Open mid-Feb–mid-Nov.* Well placed at southern entrance to the town with good view of the castle. Garden and pool. No restaurant. Twenty rooms.

# GROTTE DE LOMBRIVES

**Grotte de Lombrives €€€**
*Ussat, beside the N20, 4km southeast of Tarascon-sur-Ariège; tel: 05 61 05 98 40; email: grotte.lombrives@laposte.net; www.grotte-lombrives.fr. Open daily Apr–Oct for 90-minute tours of the caves on a little train.*

This extensive network of caves near Tarascon-sur-Ariège has featured in the *Guinness Book of Records* as the biggest open to the public in Western Europe. The galleries extend for over 3km and the main cathedral-like chamber (100m high) has an almost vaulted roof. Stories abound about activities in the caves over the centuries. Hercules is said to have buried Pyrène, his beautiful young mistress, there. Religious and political refugees sought refuge in them. And did the Cathars hide their treasure somewhere inside?

# GROTTE DE NIAUX

**Grotte de Niaux €€€** *Above Niaux village, 5km south of Tarascon-sur-Ariège, off the D8; tel: 05 61 05 88 37; email: info@sesta.fr; www.niaux.net, www.showcaves.com. Open daily but reservations essential as only 20 people allowed in at a time for the 90-minute guided tours.*

Extensive galleries have been excavated in this network of caves halfway up a steep rocky hillside south of Tarascon-sur-Ariège. The remarkably well-preserved prehistoric paintings in them are the best of all those discovered so far in 23 caves in the area. Dating from Palaeolithic times around 12,000 BC, they depict mainly animals – bison, ibex, deer and horses – all neatly outlined in black and red. The colours were created by using animal fat and charcoal made from burnt twigs. Visitors are restricted to 200 a day to prevent the sort of deterioration that has necessitated closing the caves at Lascaux in the Dordogne.

# LAVELANET

**Lavelanet Tourist Information** *place Henri du Nant; tel: 05 61 01 22 20; email: tourisme@paysdolmes.org. Open daily Jul–Aug; Mon–Sat Sept–Jun.*

This is a busy industrial town with several fabric factories, plenty of shops and a museum, the **Musée du Textil et du Peigne en Come €€** (*65 rue Jaurès; tel: 05 61 03 01 34. Open Mon–Sat afternoons Jul–Aug*), devoted to local cloth-making, with looms from the 18th century to the 1980s and a reconstruction of a typical mountain mill. During the summer, the town holds festivals with fireworks.

# MONTSEGUR

**ℹ Montségur Tourist Information**
*tel: 05 61 03 03 03; email: tourisme.montsegur@ alsatis.net; www. montsegur.org. Open daily Jul–Aug; Tue–Sat Sept– Nov & Apr–Jun.*

**⛫ Château de Montségur €€**
*Access from the car park above the village on the D9. Guided tours tel: 05 61 01 06 94; www.languedoc-france.info. Open daily all year.*

**Village museum €**
*tel: 05 61 01 10 27; www.montsegur.org. Open daily Feb–Dec.*

The small village of Montségur, with its craft studios and souvenir shops, nestles at the bottom of a 300m-high crag where a ruined castle, the **Château de Montségur**, the third to occupy the site, perches (1,216m), silhouetted above a white cliff. The second castle once provided refuge for over 200 Cathars in 1244 during the Albigensian Crusade until they were martyred on a burning pyre after they left it. The crusade was over but the Inquisition continued for 80 more years. Speculation has continued ever since about whether Cathar treasure is hidden on the site, though excavations, on show in the village's small **archaeological museum**, have not revealed it – yet!

## Accommodation and food in Montségur

**Hôtel Costes €** *tel: 05 61 01 10 24*. Small 13-room hotel with modern comforts in well-converted stone farm buildings in the centre of the village. Lots of atmosphere, sun terrace and good selection of books and souvenirs. Tasty home-cooked meals.

# PUIVERT

**⛫ Château de Puivert €€** *tel: 04 68 20 81 52; www.chateau-de-puivert.com. Open daily mid-Dec–mid-Nov.*

**Musée du Quercorb €€**
*16 rue Barry du Lion; tel: 04 68 20 80 98; email: musee. quercorb@wanadoo.fr; www.quercorb.com/musee. Open daily Apr–Oct.*

**Right**
Puivert

All that remains of **Château de Puivert**, this sleepy village's medieval castle, once a Cathar stronghold, is its 32m-high keep, now a dominant landmark as you approach. The **Musée du Quercorb** in the village has a model showing how the castle would have looked in its heyday in the 14th century. The most interesting section of the museum (which covers local history) is devoted to medieval musical instruments displayed in a reconstruction of the castle's music room – a reminder of the time when troubadours were frequent visitors.

# QUILLAN

Set in a bowl of wooded hills beside the River Aude, the town (once a famous shoe-making centre) offers visitors a variety of activities from

**Quillan Tourist Information**
*boulevard Charles de Gaulle; tel: 04 68 20 07 78; email: tourisme.quillan@wanadoo.fr; www.ville-quillan.fr. Open daily Jul–Aug; Mon–Sat Sept–Jun.*

**Folklore Festival**
*During Jul–Aug.*

## The Pyrenees

The mountain range that stretches for 430km from the Atlantic to the Mediterranean, separating France from Spain, is said to be named after Pyrène, a beautiful young girl who fell in love with Hercules, the Roman hero famed for his strength. She was the daughter of King Berbryx, who lived in the huge Lombrives cave and ruled the mountain folk, the Bekrydes.

When Hercules was called away to continue his labours she found she was expecting his child. Too frightened to tell her father, she fled into the mountains but was mauled by a bear. Hearing her agonised cries echoing around the peaks, Hercules rushed to her aid, leaping over mountains and raging rivers. But he arrived too late to save her. As he buried her in the Lombrives cave, he said, 'Gentle Pyrène, so that your name will always be remembered by those who people this land, these mountains where you now sleep for eternity will henceforth be named the Pyrenees.'

potholing to horse riding and is a good base for exploring both the foothills of the Pyrenees and the Corbières hills. Its ruined 12th-century castle, high above the river, is shaped in a perfect square.

### Accommodation and food in Quillan

**Hôtel Cartier €€** *31 boulevard Charles de Gaulle; tel: 04 68 20 05 14; email: contact@hotelcartier.com; www.hotelcartier.com. Open mid-Mar–mid-Dec.* Comfortable 28-room hotel facing the station with renowned restaurant, Les 3 Quilles.

**Opposite**
Tarascon-sur-Ariège

# TARASCON-SUR-ARIEGE

**Tarascon-sur-Ariège Tourist Office** *Espace François Mitterrand; tel: 05 61 05 94 94; email: otauzattarascon@wanadoo.fr; www.paysdetarascon.com. Open daily Jul–Aug; Mon–Sat Sept–Jun.*

**Parc Pyrénéen de l'Art Préhistorique**
*€€€ route du col de Port; tel: 05 61 05 10 10; www.sesta.fr. Open daily Apr–Oct.*

The round 14th-century St-Michel clock tower watches over this small town from a hilltop near the remains of its medieval quarter. The large square, place Garrigou, has several 16th-century buildings around it including L'Eglise de la Duarade. The area's many caves have made the town an important base for speleologists. At the **Parc Pyrénéen de l'Art Préhistorique** (just off the N20 1km north of the town), full-size replicas of paintings from the nearby Grotte de Niaux are on show.

# Suggested tour

**Total distance:** 190km. The detour to Grotte de Niaux adds 10km.

**Time:** 4 hours' driving. Allow at least a day for the main route. Those with limited time should concentrate on Montségur and the Grotte de Niaux.

**Links to other tours:** At Ax-les-Thermes, the route meets the 'Up into the Pyrenees' route (*see page 88*). From Foix, the N20 leads north to Pamiers (*see page 166*), 20km away. From Quillan, the D118 leads northeast to Couiza (*see page 103*), 12km away.

From **FOIX** ❶ (87km south of Toulouse on the N20), follow the scenic N20 south beside the River Ariège to **TARASCON-SUR-ARIEGE** ❷.

**Boulangerie Saint Roch Francerie**
*3 avenue St-Roch (on the N20 just south of Tarascon-sur-Ariège).* Very handy for picnic items, cakes and ice cream.

**Hôtel Bayle €**
*38 avenue d'Ax-les-Thermes, Belcaire; tel: 04 68 20 31 05; email: hotel-bayle@ataraxie.fr.* Open mid-Nov–Oct. Twelve-room hotel with garden and exhilarating mountain views. Restaurant.

## Caves

The reason why the area has so many caves is that the limestone ground readily absorbs rainwater. This causes a chemical reaction which can slowly dissolve some of the limestone, creating shafts or tunnels inside it. When these widen out they can become underground rivers and caves, often linked in a complex network. Rushing water and roof falls help enlarge the spaces, sometimes creating enormous cathedral-like caverns.

Just north of the town, the Parc Pyrénéen de l'Art Préhistorique is signposted 1km off the N20.

**Detour: GROTTE DE NIAUX ❸** is 5km south of Tarascon-sur-Ariège. To visit it, turn right on to the D8 off the N20.

Leaving Tarascon-sur-Ariège, stay beside the Ariège on the N20, which passes **GROTTE DE LOMBRIVES ❹**. Go through **Les Cabannes** and **Unac** to **AX-LES-THERMES ❺** (*see page 82*) and then take the long climb out of it on the D613 up to the Col de Chioula (1,431m), a popular base for cross-country skiing in winter. After passing wooded hillsides and terraces and crossing plains, you come to **Belcaire** and the wide flat Plateau de Sault. Four kilometres beyond Belcaire, turn right on to the D29 to **Espezel** and drop sharply down to the D107. This goes along a valley to **Belfort**, the Défilé de Joucou Gorge and Marsa (whose church has a distinctive flat bell tower), before dropping gently to **Axat**, a pretty village beside the River Aude, with a medieval quarter clustering around the church, where the D117 leads beside the River Aude through **St-Martin-Lys** to **QUILLAN ❻**. The 8km stretch between St-Martin-Lys and Quillan is named the Défilé du Pierre-Lys. In 1814, Félix Armand, the priest of St-Martin-Lys, got his parishioners to build it by hacking through solid rock; he is commemorated by a small monument in front of Quillan's railway station. From Quillan take the D117, which climbs west on to a plateau of farmland towards **PUIVERT ❼**, whose castle is silhouetted on the skyline as you approach, and then **Bélesta**. Turn left there on to the D5 and head for **MONTSEGUR ❽**, past the roadside cave where water often gushes from the Fontaine des Fontestorbes spring.

From Montségur, take the D107, through the cloth-making town of **Montferrier** with its distinctive bell tower, to **LAVELANET ❾**. From there, the quiet D10 (signed Raissac) is a much more pleasant way to return to Foix than the faster D117 as it crosses hillsides and farmland.

### Getting out of the car

From the car park beside the D9 above Montségur village, a short track leads to the foot of the steep path which leads up through trees and bushes to the ruins of its bleak fortress. Part steps, part rocks, it takes

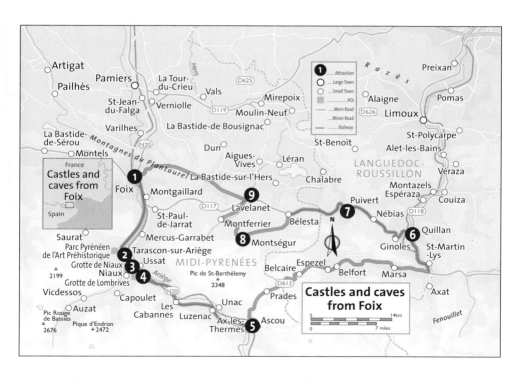

**Grotte du Mas d'Azil** €€ *tel: 05 61 69 97 71. Open for guided tours (1 hour) of caves and museum daily Jul–Aug; Tue–Sun Sept & Apr–Jun; Sun Oct–Nov & Mar.* More information about the caves is shown in a small museum in the village, **Musée du Mas d'Azil**; *tel: 05 61 67 69 05.*

**Tourist Information** *17 avenue de la Gare; tel: 05 61 69 99 90; email: tourisme.arize.leze@ wanadoo.fr; www.tourisme-drize-leze.com*

about 20 minutes to climb. Sensible shoes are essential. Seeing the small area at the top, it's hard to believe that over 1,000 Cathars once lived there under siege. The last 205 were surrounded by an army of 10,000 Catholics. When they eventually descended on 16 March 1244, refusing to recant, they were burnt alive. A memorial stone at the bottom in the 'Prat dels crematz' (field of the burnt) commemorates them – 'Martyred in the name of pure Christian love'. How ironic that the name Montségur means 'safe mountain'.

## Also worth exploring

To visit the **Grotte du Mas d'Azil**, take the D117 west from Foix, turning right just beyond La Bastide-de-Sérou on to the D49 (34km). This cave is of great importance to archaeologists because in 1887, Edouard Piette found evidence of human habitation there between 30,000 and 9500 BC. The cave, 420m long and about 50m wide, has winding galleries beside a river. Painted stones were found there but no one has yet come up with an explanation for what they depict.

# A taste of Cathar country

**Ratings**

| | |
|---|---|
| Castles | ●●●●● |
| Scenery | ●●●●● |
| History | ●●●●○ |
| Children | ●●●○○ |
| Nature | ●●●○○ |
| Villages | ●●●○○ |
| Architecture | ●●○○○ |
| Walking | ●●○○○ |

History was made in the Corbières hills during the Middle Ages. If you let your imagination roam, this route will take you back to the noble, ferocious and mysterious events which took place there in the days of the Cathars, the troubadours and the Knights Templar.

Although the Corbières themselves are hills rather than mountains, the scenery is often dramatic with rocky limestone ridges and crags peeping above the *garrigue* and small vineyards. The roads can twist and turn but are never difficult.

Two famous castles, Peyrepertuse and Quéribus, which both played a crucial part in the Cathar movement, stand on rocky pinnacles that look startlingly inaccessible even today. It would be a pity not to allow time to walk up to at least one of them. The reward is not only superb views but a better understanding of former lifetimes and struggles.

## ARQUES

🛈 **Château d'Arques**
€€ *tel: 04 68 69 82 87; www.chateau-arques.fr.* Combined admission with La Maison Déodat Roché; *tel: 04 68 69 82 87. Open daily Apr–Oct.*

Only the sturdy four-storey orange sandstone keep survives from **Château d'Arques**. Built in 1284, it was severely damaged during the Wars of Religion. It overlooks the flat countryside around the village which was the birthplace of Déodat Roché, a leading historian on the Cathars. After he died in 1978, his home, **La Maison Déodat Roché €€** (*tel: 04 68 69 82 87. Open daily all year*), became a small museum devoted to Catharism.

## CHATEAU DE PEYREPERTUSE

Seen at its best from the village of Rouffiac-des-Corbières, this medieval fortress is the least ruined of the area's castles. Built on top of a rocky crest, a site first used by the Romans, it is one of the marvels of the Corbières. As you discover when you climb up, the ruins of two castles are spread along a 300m-long ridge. The upper one (796m) has

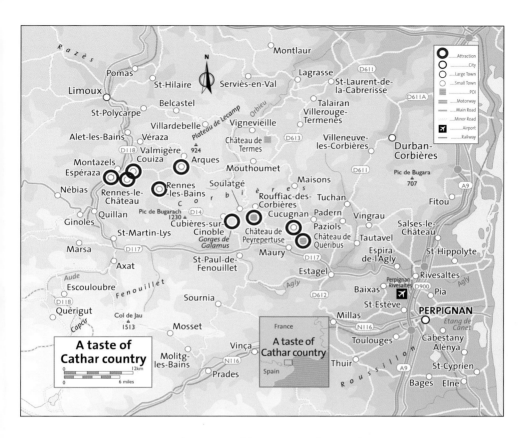

**A taste of Cathar country**

**Legend:**
- ◎ Attraction
- ○ City
- ○ Large Town
- ○ Small Town
- ○ POI
- ━ Motorway
- ━ Main Road
- ━ Minor Road
- ✈ Airport
- ━ Railway

*(Map labels, reading across the map:)*

Razès · Montlaur · Pomas · St-Hilaire · Serviès-en-Val · Lagrasse · D611 · St-Laurent-de-la-Cabrerisse · D611A · Limoux · St-Polycarpe · Belcastel · Vignevieille · Plateau de Lecamp · Orbieu · Talairan · Villerouge-Termenès · Villardebelle · Alet-les-Bains · Véraza · Château de Termes · D613 · Villeneuve-les-Corbières · Durban-Corbières · D118 · Valmigère · Couiza · Arques · 924 · Montazels · Espéraza · Mouthoumet · D611 · Pic de Bugara 707 · A9 · Nébias · Rennes-le-Château · Rennes-les-Bains · Soulatgé · Corbières · Maisons · Rouffiac-des-Corbières · Tuchan · Fitou · Quillan · Pic de Bugarach 1230 · D14 · Cubières-sur-Cinoble · Cucugnan · Padern · Vingrau · Salses-le-Château · Ginoles · St-Martin-Lys · Gorges de Galamus · Château de Peyrepertuse · Paziols · Château de Quéribus · Tautavel · Marsa · D117 · Maury · Espira-de-l'Agly · St-Hippolyte · Axat · St-Paul-de-Fenouillet · D117 · Estagel · Rivesaltes · Aude · Escouloubre · Fenouillet · Agly · Baixas · Perpignan-Rivesaltes · D900 · Pia · D118 · Quérigut · Sournia · D612 · St-Estève · PERPIGNAN · Capcir · Col de Jau 1513 · Mosset · Millas · N116 · Étang de Canet · France · A taste of Cathar country · Vinça · Toulouges · Cabestany · Alénya · Molitg-les-Bains · N116 · Thuir · Roussillon · St-Cyprien · Prades · Spain · A9 · Bages · Elne

*(Map scale:)* 0 — 12km / 0 — 6 miles

---

🅷 **Château de Peyrepertuse €€**
*Duilhac-sous-Peyrepertuse; tel: 06 71 58 63 36; email: chateau.peyrepertuse@wanadoo.fr; www.chateau-peyrepertuse.com. Open daily Feb–Dec.*
Access to the winding 3.5km road up to the car park is from Duilhac, just below it at the foot of the ridge; then allow at least 15 minutes to walk up – and wear walking shoes. On a windy day the experience can be particularly exhilarating!

never been accessible except on foot, as the steps cut in the rock to it are too steep even for mules. As you wander round the remains of the courtyards, towers and arches, the most amazing thing to reflect on – apart from the view – is the feat of building them with the simple tools of the 12th century.

## Accommodation and food near Château de Peyrepertuse

**La Giraudasse €** *2 place de la Fontaine, Soulatgé; tel: 04 68 45 00 16; email: info@giraudasse.com; www.giraudasse.com. Open Mar–Nov (Dec–Feb for groups only).* Five miles west of the château on the D14, this 17th-century hotel has five rooms, mountain views and a south-facing terrace and garden.

**Hostellerie du Vieux Moulin €** *24 rue de la Fontaine, 11350 Duilhac-sous-Peyrepertuse; tel: 04 68 45 02 00. Open Feb–mid-Mar.* Old mill converted into a 14-room inn.

# CHATEAU DE QUERIBUS

**Château de Québirus €**
Cucugnan; tel: 04 68 45 03
69; email: queribus
cucugnan@orange.fr;
www.queribus.fr. Open daily
Feb–Dec. Combined ticket
with Théâtre Achille Mir
(see opposite). Access from
the D123 south of
Cucugnan, signposted
left up a steep narrow
road to the car park
and ticket office.

The ruined Château de Québirus is one of the Languedoc's most dramatic sights, perched perilously on the Grau de Maury, a narrow rocky crag 728m high above the village of Cucugnan. From a distance, it's hard to believe there is any way up, but a steep rocky path leads to this 'eagle's nest' from the car park. The walk up, always exhilarating, is distinctly perilous in wind so it's definitely not suitable for anyone without a good head for heights.

The ruin itself is a maze of passages, staircases and doorways with a high vaulted wall supported by a sturdy pillar in the centre. First recorded in 1020, it was a Cathar stronghold in the 13th century and was the last refuge, sheltering the bishop of Razès until 1254. Subsequently, it was a royal fortress guarding the Spanish border until Roussillon became part of France in 1659. Arrow slits provide hair-raising views down, though you get a 360-degree panorama from the terrace – across the Roussillon plain to the Mediterranean in the east and south to the Canigou mountain with the Pyrenees beyond.

**Right**
Château de Peyrepertuse

# COUIZA

**Tourist Information**
*18 bis route des
Pyrénées; tel: 04 68 74 02
51; email:
pays.couiza@orange.fr;
www.paysdecouiza.fr. Open
Mon–Fri all year.*

On the River Aude, Couiza's fortunes grew from the hat-making industry but declined when uncovered heads became fashionable. It boasts a totally restored 16th-century castle, the Château des Ducs de Joyeuse, whose four round towers, typical of the Languedoc, are a landmark on the edge of the town. Used as a military hospital and then as a prison, it is now a hotel.

## Accommodation and food in Couiza

**Château des Ducs de Joyeuse €€** *tel: 04 68 74 23 50; email: direction@chateau-des-ducs.com; www.chateau-des-ducs.com. Open Apr–mid-Nov.* A 35-room hotel in the 16th-century castle. Top-class restaurant, swimming pool and four-poster beds in ten of the rooms. For a real treat, book the Gothic suite.

# CUCUGNAN

**Théâtre Achille Mir**
*€€ tel: 04 68 45 03
69. Open daily Feb–Dec.
Combined ticket with the
Château de Quéribus (see
opposite).*

This smart little village was surrounded by olive groves until 1956 when they were destroyed by frost. Few people have heard of Cucugnan unless they are fans of the French writer Alphonse Daudet. An audiovisual version of *Le Sermon du Curé de Cucugnan*, his short story based on verses by Achille Mir, a local teacher who died in 1901, is presented in the **Théâtre Achille Mir**, the village's 49-seat theatre.

## Accommodation and food in Cucugnan

**Auberge du Vigneron €€** *2 rue Achille-Mir; tel: 04 68 45 03 00; email: contact@auberge-vigneron.com; www.auberge-vigneron.com. Open Mar–mid-Nov.* Small six-room hotel with terrace looking down on vineyards and up to Château de Quéribus.

# ESPERAZA

**Musée de la
Chapellerie €€**
*avenue Gare; tel: 04 68 74
00 75; www.
museedelachapellerie.fr.
Open daily Feb–Dec.*

**Musée des Dinosaures**
*€€ avenue Gare; tel: 04 68
74 26 88;
www.dinosauria.org.
Open daily Feb–Dec.*

The **Musée de la Chapellerie** occupies an old warehouse in this small town. Laid out like a factory, it shows the different stages in the making of hats. Over 150 wigs, ancient and modern, are also on display, and hats are for sale. Next to it, **Musée des Dinosaures** displays the enormous skeleton of a dinosaur which was found locally, together with fossils and a life-size tableau of an archaeological dig. **Campagne-sur-Aude €** *(open daily Jul–Aug)*, 2km south of Espéraza, has an archaeological trail where some of Europe's most important dinosaur remains have been excavated.

# GORGES DE GALAMUS

**Ermitage St-Antoine-de-Galamus** € is a 15-minute walk from the car park on the D7; www.st-paul66.com

The drive along this rugged 3km-long gorge high above the River Agly is one of the most dramatic in the region. The road, built in 1892, twists tightly along a shelf carved out of the white rock which frequently overhangs it as the gorge becomes narrower and narrower. At the southern end, from a car park/viewing platform you look down on the small **Ermitage St-Antoine-de-Galamus**, now a café, clinging to the hillside halfway down the gorge. Its tiny chapel is behind it in a cave.

# RENNES-LE-CHATEAU

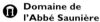
**Domaine de l'Abbé Saunière** €€ Villa Bethania; tel: 04 68 74 72 68; email: rlctourisme@wanadoo.fr; www.renneslechateau.com. Open daily all year.

The village bookshop (tel: 04 68 74 26 71; email: librairie@atelier-empreinte.fr) has a good selection of books about l'Abbé Saunière, Catharism and the local area.

From its hilltop position above the Aude Valley, this intriguing little village has a good view of the red rooftops of Espéraza and Campagne-sur-Aude nestling in the valley below. How could the parish priest, Béranger Saunière (1852–1917), afford to build himself the grand Villa Bethania and the curious neo-Gothic Tour Magdala on the cliff edge as his library? And where did the money come from in 1891 to restore the almost derelict village church, Ste-Marie-Madeleine?

A visit to the **Domaine de l'Abbé Saunière**, the priest's former home and now a museum, sheds a little light on the mystery of his unexplained wealth. Maybe he discovered the treasure of the Knights Templar who, in the 12th century, had one of their headquarters nearby. He had been arrested for digging up graves at night, and he refused to allow the use of his water tower when the villagers were fighting a fire – so was it really full of water?

# RENNES-LES-BAINS

**Rennes-les-Bains Tourist Information** grande rue des Thermes; tel: 04 68 69 88 04. Open daily Jul–Aug; Mon–Fri Sept–Jun.

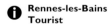
**Thermes de Rennes-les-Bains** grande rue des Thermes; tel: 04 68 74 71 00; email: regie.thermale@renneslesbains.org; www.renneslesbains.org

You can do your body a favour by bathing in mineral and thermal water in this village nestling beside the crystal-clear River Sals. Its spa, **Thermes de Rennes-les-Bains**, offers various medicinal programmes and also has a large outdoor pool overlooking a pretty riverside walk.

## Accommodation and food in Rennes-les-Bains

**Hostellerie de Rennes-les-Bains** €€ 17 rue des Bains Forts; tel: 04 68 69 88 49; email: hotel-rlb@orange.fr; www.hotel-renneslesbains.com. Open Mar–Dec. Riverside hotel with seven rooms, pool and sun terrace.

**Opposite**
Château de Quéribus

## Blanquette de Limoux

Vines have been cultivated in the Limoux region since ancient times but in 1531 the Benedictine monks at St-Hilaire abbey made a historic discovery. They found that wine produced in glass flasks with a cork top – rare at the time – acquired a natural fizz. This was the origination of Blanquette de Limoux, the world's first sparkling wine, now enjoyed all over the world. The production process begins with crushing grapes in whole bunches as soon as they are picked and then involves a careful timetable of fermentation and ageing lasting almost a year or, for special vintages, up to three years. Most is produced by the *méthode champenoise* where the bubbles are added chemically, but about 3 per cent is the sweeter organic *méthode ancestrale* version, which has no additions and is always bottled on the third day after a full moon.

**Above**
Arques

**Le Presbytère €**
*Bugarach; tel: 04 68 69
82 12; email:
info@presbyterebugarach.fr;
www.presbyterebugarach.fr.
Open Feb–Oct & Dec.*
Wonderfully
atmospheric little
guesthouse owned by a
Dutch couple in a 17th-
century former
presbytery beside the
village church (the bells
only ring for funerals).
Four en-suite rooms
and a garden apartment.
Meals served in its
secluded garden in
summer.

# Suggested tour

**Total distance:** 185km. The detour through the Gorges de Galamus
adds 8km, the detour to Espéraza and Campagne-sur-Aude adds 12km
and the detour to Rennes-le-Château adds 10km.

**Time:** 5 hours' driving. Allow at least a day for the main route or two
to include walking up to the Château de Peyrepertuse and Château de
Quéribus. Those with limited time should concentrate on the stretch
between the Château de Quéribus and Rennes-le-Château.

**Links to other tours:** From Maury, the D117 leads west to St-Paul-de-
Fenouillet (*see page 74*), 8km away. From Cubières-sur-Cinoble, the D10
leads south to St-Paul-de-Fenouillet, 10km away. From Couiza, the
D118 leads southwest to Quillan (*see page 95*), 12km away, or north to
Limoux (*see page 136*), 15km away. From Mouthoumet, the D613 leads
northeast to Villerouge-Termenès (*see page 139*), 13km away. From
Padern, the D14 leads east to Tuchan (*see page 123*), 8km away.

From Perpignan, take the D117 past the airport beside the River Agly
to **Estagel** and then **Maury**. Turn right here into the Corbières hills on
the steeply climbing D19, which takes you over the Grau de Maury, a
432m-high pass, remarkable for both its views and its vegetation. The
Maury Valley below, made up of fossils having originally been covered
by the sea, is famed for its scented bushes such as thyme as well as
boasting several varieties of wild orchids. Just beyond the pass, the
CHATEAU DE QUERIBUS ❶ is on the right; then 2km beyond it,
turn left at CUCUGNAN ❷ on to the D14. This takes you over the
Col du Tribi (344m), through **Duilhac-sous-Peyrepertuse** (below the
CHATEAU DE PEYREPERTUSE) ❸, and over the Col de Grès (406m)
to the quaint little village of **Rouffiac-des-Corbières** from where the
Château de Peyrepertuse looks like a piece of the rocky ridge.
Continue through **Soulatgé** to **Cubières-sur-Cinoble**.

**Detour:** At Cubières-sur-Cinoble, turn left off the D14 to drive
through the narrow GORGES DE GALAMUS ❹; the distance to the
viewpoint at the end is 4km.

After Cubières-sur-Cinoble, the D14 goes through **Bugarach**, a thriving
hat-making centre in the 19th century, which is overlooked by a rugged
massif. It then continues through wooded valleys to join, 3km beyond
RENNES-LES-BAINS ❺, the D613. Turn left on to it to COUIZA ❻.

**Detour:** From Couiza, the detour (4km) to ESPERAZA ❼ crosses over
the River Aude to **Montazels** and then south along the D12. The
Campagne-sur-Aude trail is 2km further beyond Espéraza. While in
Montazels, watch for the signs to Domaine St-Jacques, 1km north of
the town, as it is one of the few vineyards which produce sparkling
white wine, Blanquette de Limoux, by the *méthode ancestrale*. This
means the bubbles form naturally rather than by chemical injection.

**Detour:** Also from Couiza, the detour to **RENNES-LE-CHATEAU** ❽ (5km) climbs southeast up an unnumbered road off the D118 in the town.

Next drive north on the busy D118 beside the River Aude, turning right after 5km on to the D70 to go east through **Véraza** and across peaceful wooded countryside. Turn right again on to the D54. From the viewpoint just past **Valmigère**, you can see south on a clear day over the Corbières to the snowy top of the Canigou mountain with the Pyrenees beyond. As the road twists prettily down into **ARQUES** ❾, the castle (to the right of the village) is a notable landmark overlooking the dark green Rialsesse forest and cliffs with red gulleys behind it. The D613 then leads east through **Mouthoumet**. Two kilometres beyond it, turn right on to the D139 to join the D410 and go over the bleak Col du Prat (444m) to **Maisons**. The D123 follows the gentle gorge of the River Torgan past small vineyards to **Padern**, which is overlooked by its 17th-century ruined castle – and boasts a handy *cave coopérative* where you can sample and buy local wine. Return to Perpignan through Cucugnan and Maury.

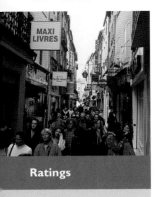

# Narbonne

## Ratings

| | |
|---|---|
| History | ●●●●● |
| Food and drink | ●●●●○ |
| Museums | ●●●●○ |
| Architecture | ●●●○○ |
| Entertainment | ●●●○○ |
| Shopping | ●●●○○ |
| Art | ●●○○○ |
| Children | ●●○○○ |

This small but vibrant city is bound to fire a sense of history in every visitor. In the centre you can even walk on the flat grey stones of a Roman road, the Via Domitia. Founded by the Romans as Narbo Martius in 118 BC, the city became capital of Gaul, their largest province. Its next great era came in the 12th century when it was a thriving port. The cathedral, founded then by its rich and powerful archbishops, was intended to be the biggest in Christendom. Though never completed, it remains a remarkable symbol of that time. The wars and plagues which followed brought the city to its knees for two centuries until the construction of the Canal de la Robine and later the railway helped revive its fortunes. Today, surrounded by vineyards and only a few kilometres from the Mediterranean, it is certainly a place to savour.

## Getting there and getting around

From the south, leave the A9 autoroute at Narbonne Sud, where the roundabout has an eye-catching centrepiece – a giant amphora (Roman vase). From the north, the D6009 and D6113 join straightforward routes along main roads into the city centre.

**Parking:** Car parks are well signposted and there are pay-and-display meters on the central streets; free on Sundays. South of the centre, parking is free on both sides of the Canal de la Robine, which is particularly convenient when driving in from Narbonne Plage, 10km away, and other beaches. In summer, traffic can be heavy along this route.

**Public transport:** The town centre is compact and all the sights are within a short walking distance. There are regular bus services to the

**Tourist Information** *31 rue Jean Jaurès; tel: 04 68 65 15 60; email: info@narbonne-tourisme.com; www.narbonne-tourisme.com. Open daily all year. Information also available at the* **town hall** *place de l'Hôtel de Ville.*

**Narbonne-Plage Office du Tourisme** *avenue des Vacances; tel: 04 68 49 84 86. Open daily Apr–Sept; Tue–Sun Oct–Mar.*

Narbonne

0                    100 metres
0                    100 yards

Legend:
○ Attraction
Important Building
Park
Main Road
Other Road
Railway

**Museum Information**
*tel: 04 68 90 30 54.*

beach at Narbonne-Plage in July and August. The railway station is in route de Montpellier, a 10-minute walk from the centre.

For boat trips on the canal, cruisers can be hired from Connoisseur Cruisers, *7 quai d'Alsace; tel: 04 68 65 14 55;* booking office: *The Port House, Port Solent, Portsmouth; tel: 02392 224252 (UK); email: sales@connoisseurafloat.com; www.leboat.co.uk*

Cycle hire is available on the beach at Narbonne-Plage, July–August.

# Sights

**Basilique St-Paul**
*rue Dupleix.*

**Cathédrale St-Just-et-St-Pasteur** *rue A Gauthier; tel: 04 68 32 09 52; email: culture@mairie-narbonne.fr*

### Basilique St-Paul
This lofty Romanesque building is notable for its soaring arches and elegant vaulting, on the Bourg side of the canal. Don't miss the small stone frog which sits on the font.

### Canal de la Robine
The canal cuts through the centre of the city, dividing the old Bourg district, where the lower classes lived, from the Cité, which was the home of the ecclesiastical authorities and the ruling *vicomtes* on the other. It was built in the 1680s along the bed of the River Aude (which had changed course 200 years earlier following massive floods) and joins the Canal du Midi, 15km and 10 locks to the north.

### Cathédrale St-Just-et-St-Pasteur
This massive building in the heart of the city was destined to be one of the biggest churches in Christendom, designed to chase away once and for all any thoughts of heresy which the local population might have been harbouring. However, only the chancel was completed before work stopped in 1340, 60 years after the first stone had been laid, because the municipal authorities refused to allow their clerical opposite numbers to pull down part of the city wall to make way for the nave. While the tussle was still dragging on, their resolve to keep the wall intact was strengthened when England's Black Prince stormed the city in 1355, overrunning the working-class Bourg district across the River Aude. (At that time, the river divided the city in two, though later, after it changed course, this section was turned into the canal.) By the time the walls were no longer needed for defence, the city could no longer afford to extend the cathedral.

The cathedral has superb stained-glass windows and Aubusson and Gobelins tapestries on its walls. The elaborately carved choir stalls date

## Via Domitia

In 118 BC, the Romans built a highway stretching over 250km from Beaucaire (75km east of Montpellier) to Le Perthus in the Pyrenees. They named it after Domitius Ahenobarbus, the proconsul of their Gallia Narbonensis province, which was governed from Narbonne and extended from Toulouse to Lake Geneva. Though originally intended to help their legions march between Rome and Spain, it quickly became an important commercial artery, facilitating trade within the Roman Empire and further afield by sea. Earlier Hannibal had used the same route on his way from Spain to Italy with his elephants in 218 BC. In Narbonne, the road joined up with another Roman highway, the Via Aquitania, which led northwest through Toulouse to Bordeaux. Some of the standing stones which once marked each mile are on show in local museums.

**L'Horreum** €€
7 rue Rouget de l'Isle;
tel: 04 68 32 45 30.
Open Wed–Mon all year.

**Musée Lapidaire** €€
Eglise de Lamourgier, place
Lamourguier; tel: 04 68 65
53 58. Open Wed–Mon
all year.

**Palais des Archévêques**
€€ place de l'Hôtel de Ville;
tel: 04 68 90 30 65. Open
Wed–Mon all year.
Entrance to the Gilles
Aycelin keep is through
the town hall.

The entrance ticket for
any of the above is valid
for three days and includes
entrance to the other
museums.

from the 16th century and the fine organ, also richly carved, from the 18th. The altar, designed by Jules Mansart, is made of local pink marble from Caune. What should have been the transept is now a courtyard with delicately vaulted 14th-century cloisters leading into the Archbishops' Palace.

## L'Horreum

This extraordinarily well-preserved underground Roman storehouse has a warren of vaulted stone cellars with grain chutes where perishable goods would have been kept. As Narbonne was an important port and also on the Via Domitia, it traded extensively with other parts of the Roman Empire, exporting meat and cheese from the Cévennes as well as oil, woad, wood and hemp. Stone containers and fragments of engraved stonework from Roman buildings are dotted along the galleries and in the small cubicles which open off them. An exhibition in the entrance area includes Roman objects and drawings showing what other buildings in Narbo Martius must have been like.

## Maison des Trois Nourrices

The 'house of the three wet nurses' in rue des Trois Nourrices gets its unusual name from the stone pillars shaped like curvaceous maidens, which support the lintel of its magnificent Renaissance façade. Actually, there are five of them, not three! The interior is not open to the public.

## Musée Lapidaire

This unusual museum in a deconsecrated church displays an extensive collection of stone fragments from sculptures and bas-reliefs dating back to Gallo-Roman times and the Middle Ages. The church, which in typical Southern Gothic style has a single nave, is all that remains of a Benedictine convent.

## Palais des Archévêques

The opulent Archbishops' Palace, built between the 12th and 14th centuries, is a grand and complicated complex of halls, passages, towers and courtyards. This is now attached to the neo-Gothic town hall, which was added under the auspices of Eugène Viollet-le-Duc, the famous military architect, in 1846. Within the complex, the **Palais Neuf** houses the **Musée d'Archéologie et de Préhistoire**, which has a fascinating collection of Roman objects and fragments of buildings. The **Chapelle de la Madeleine** houses amphorae (vases) and mosaics. The **Musée d'Art et d'Histoire** in the former archbishops' apartments has paintings by Canaletto and Brueghel. Steps lead to the top of the formidable Gilles Aycelin keep, which the archbishops had built to remind the town's *vicomtes*, who had a residence opposite, that they held the reins of power in the city. It also kept watch over the river port, which then existed directly below.

# Shopping

**Les Halles,** the turn-of-the-20th-century market hall, at cours Mirabeau, merits a visit whether or not you want to buy anything. Recently restored, it's an iron-framed glass building with elaborate stuccoed columns and a grand stone doorway crowned by a huge clock. Inside, the 80 stalls selling local produce and wine will certainly tempt you to stock up.

The most interesting small shops are to be found off place de l'Hôtel de Ville in rue Droite and rue de l'Ancien Courrier. **Monoprix,** on the place itself, is the only large store in the centre. A **Géant Casino** supermarket can be found on route de Perpignan and a **Carrefour** on the way to Narbonne-Plage.

# Entertainment

**Théâtre Narbonne**
*Scene Nationale de Narbonne, 2 avenue Domitius; tel: 04 68 90 90 00; email: le theatre@letheatre-narbonne.com; www.letheatre-narbonne.com*

Narbonne is justifiably proud of its **Théâtre** complex inaugurated in 1994, where concerts, conferences and exhibitions are staged as well as plays. **L'Espace de Liberté** (*route de Perpignan; tel: 04 68 42 17 89*) includes an Olympic-size pool, skating rink, bowling alley and a range of outdoor sports facilities. International sporting events take place at **Parc des Sports** (*tel: 04 68 90 90 68*).

# Accommodation and food

**Le Régent €** *13–15 rue Suffren; tel: 04 68 32 02 41; email: hotelleregent@wanadoo.fr; www.leregentnarbonne.com. Open all year.* A small family-run hotel in a quiet area, about a 10-minute walk from the centre. Free on-street parking. Fifteen rooms.

**Brasserie Co €€** *1 boulevard du Docteur Ferroul; tel: 04 68 32 55 25; email: brasserie.co@wanadoo.fr. Closed Sun Oct–Easter.* Trendy brasserie where the food matches the contemporary décor.

**Le Coq Hardi €€** *75 rue Droite; tel: 04 68 65 27 38. Open Thur–Tue all year.* Fresh fish and grills are always on the menu, but it is best known for its crème brûlée.

**Hôtel d'Occitanie €€** *23 avenue de la Mer; tel: 04 68 65 47 60; email: motel.occitanie@wanadoo.fr; www.hotel-occitanie.com. Open all year.* A modern hotel on the outskirts in the direction of the sea. Its excellent leisure facilities include a pool, fitness centre and tennis.

**Hôtel du Languedoc €€** *22 boulevard Gambetta; tel: 04 68 65 14 74; email: hotel.languedoc@wanadoo.fr; www.hoteldulanguedoc.com. Open all year.* Elegant city-centre hotel close to the train station and reached easily from the Narbonne Est exit on the A9 autoroute. Forty rooms.

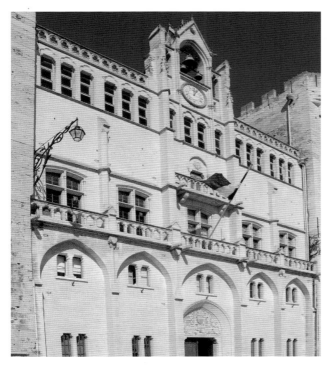

Le Petit Comptoir €€
4 boulevard M Joffre; tel: 04
68 42 30 35. Open Tue–Sat all
year. An attractive little
restaurant serving local
specialities, particularly fish and
duck.

La Résidence €€ 6 rue du 1er
Mai; tel: 04 68 32 19 41; email:
reservation@hotelresidence.fr;
www.hotelresidence.fr. Open all
year. Became a hotel in the
1960s when the Aiguille family
converted their splendid 19th-
century mansion. It's situated in
a quiet central street with garage
parking. Twenty-six rooms.

L'Alsace €€€ 2 avenue Pierre
Sémard; tel: 04 68 65 10 24.
Open Mon–Tue & Thur–Sat all
year. Opposite the railway
station, this is one of the best
restaurants in town for seafood.

**Above**
Town hall, Narbonne

# Suggested walk

**Length:** 2.5km.

**Duration:** Under an hour just to walk round, but allow a full day to
see all the sights.

Start in the steps of the Romans by treading the flat grey slabs of the
**Via Domitia** in the centre of **place de l'Hôtel de Ville**. There was a
huge outcry from the shopkeepers around the square when plans to
re-tile and pedestrianise it were announced, but the discovery of the
Roman road during the works changed all that. Now the square's well-
presented centrepiece, it attracts more people to the area.

To get your bearings, particularly as the layout of the **PALAIS DES
ARCHEVEQUES** (Archbishops' Palace) ❶ and the adjacent
**CATHEDRALE ST-JUST-ET-ST-PASTEUR** ❷ is complicated, climb the
162 steps to the upper terrace of the keep, whose entrance is through
the **town hall**. The views from the 43m-high tower stretch past
pinnacles and flying buttresses over the city rooftops and far beyond.
Another high spot is the cathedral's north tower.

The narrow rue Droite follows the straight route of the original Via Domitia past **L'HORREUM** ❸, whose entrance is now in the parallel rue Rouget de l'Isle. A little further up it, the pillars of a **Roman temple** stand in place Bistan as a reminder that it is the site where the Roman forum is thought to have been. On the way to place Lapeyrade, the 15th-century **Eglise St-Sébastian** is said to stand on the spot where the saint was born.

Narrow streets lead across rue Viollet le Duc and rue de l'Ancien Courrier to the busy **cours de la République**, which runs alongside a broad promenade shaded by plane trees beside the **CANAL DE LA ROBINE** ❹. Cruisers tie up along the quay below it.

Crossing the water by the wrought-iron footbridge, you will see the remains of the arched **Roman bridge** which once spanned the **River Aude** here. In summer, the **waterside gardens** with their fountains beside cours Mirabeau make a pleasant spot to sit and watch the comings and goings on the canal, but you might want to bear in mind that the nearby **market hall** closes at 1300. Behind it is the **MUSEE LAPIDAIRE** ❺ in the **Eglise Notre-Dame-de-la-Mourguié**.

Many of the old buildings in this area, particularly along rue de Belfort, have attractive façades, particularly the **MAISON DES TROIS NOURRICES** ❻ in the road of the same name. Just beyond it in rue Arago is the **BASILIQUE ST-PAUL** ❼.

The most interesting way to return to **place de l'Hôtel de Ville** is along rue Hoche and across the intimate old **place des 4 Fontaines**, which has a pretty fountain. The **Pont des Marchands** footbridge, a continuation of the Via Domitia, seems more like an arcade as there are shops on both sides. As an alternative, you can stroll along quai Dillon and take the footbridge next to a lock across to an old mill building now occupied by a library.

## Also worth exploring

Narbonne is divided from the sea and the busy resort of Narbonne-Plage by **Montagne de la Clape**, a rugged area of hills and ridges with rocky grey cliffs. Beneath them, narrow roads twist through pine woods and *garrigue* – moors of sweet-smelling thyme, rosemary and lavender. A poignant cemetery, **Cimetière des Marins**, occupies one of the two highest hilltops; its memorial stones are dedicated to sailors lost at sea. Small vineyards cover the lower slopes of the hills, producing good-quality la Clape Coteaux du Languedoc wines. There are few buildings around as it is a conservation area. The best way to explore is on foot or by bike.

**Abbaye de Fontfroide €€**

*Fontfroide (take the D6113 and D613 from Narbonne); tel: 04 68 45 11 08; www.fontfroide.com. Open daily for guided tours. Restaurant €€ in a former farm; tel: 04 68 45 02 26. Open daily Mar–mid-Nov.*

A 14km drive southwest from the city takes you into the Corbières hills where a huge 12th-century Cistercian abbey, **Abbaye de Fontfroide**, built in the local ochre and pink sandstone, nestles peacefully among cypress trees and terraced gardens in a small secluded valley. At its peak in the 15th century over 200 monks lived there, but it gradually declined until being abandoned altogether in 1791. The buildings, privately owned since 1908, have now been restored at vast expense. They include a perfectly proportioned Cistercian church with modern stained-glass windows, a pretty cloister, chapter house and monks' dormitory. A rose garden planted with over 3,000 bushes in 1990 has won awards for its design.

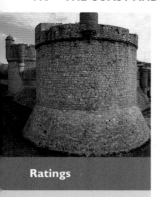

# The coast and lagoons

## Ratings

| | |
|---|---|
| Beaches | ●●●●● |
| Children | ●●●●○ |
| Outdoor activities | ●●●●○ |
| Wildlife | ●●●●○ |
| Castles | ●●●○○ |
| Coastal villages/ towns | ●●●○○ |
| Vineyards | ●●●○○ |
| Historical sights | ●●●○○ |

When this route moves away from the sea along the Golfe du Lion and heads into the Corbières hills, the atmosphere changes markedly – a happy combination. Within a few easy kilometres, the remote and often desolate countryside inland offers an interesting alternative to sun-worshipping resorts such as Leucate and Le Bacarès. Summer brings thousands of holidaymakers to them in search of a tan or to sail on either the shallow seawater lagoons or the Mediterranean itself.

The highlights inland include the mighty castle at Salses, which once guarded the border between France and the Kingdom of Aragon, and the cave at Tautavel, where the earliest remains of human existence in Europe have been found.

This is also the land of the famous Rivesaltes and Fitou vineyards, while children – and adults – will find plenty to interest them at the African safari park at Sigean.

## ETANG DE BAGES ET DE SIGEAN

**ⓘ Peyriac Tourist Information** *place Aubin Fabre; tel: 04 68 41 38 22; email: peyriac-de-mer@fnotsi.net. Open daily Jul–Aug.*

**ⓑ Musée Archéologique €** *rue de l'Etang, Peyriac-de-Mer. Open daily Jul–Aug by appointment through the tourist office.*

In Roman times, when Narbonne was a busy port, the shores of this lagoon were well populated. Ancient finds from that time are on show in the **Musée Archéologique** in the village of Peyriac-de-Mer. Subsequently, the area around the lagoon lay deserted for centuries because of the mosquitoes which infested it until coastal development started in the 1960s. Today the mosquitoes have gone from the lagoon but there are plenty of midges about in summer.

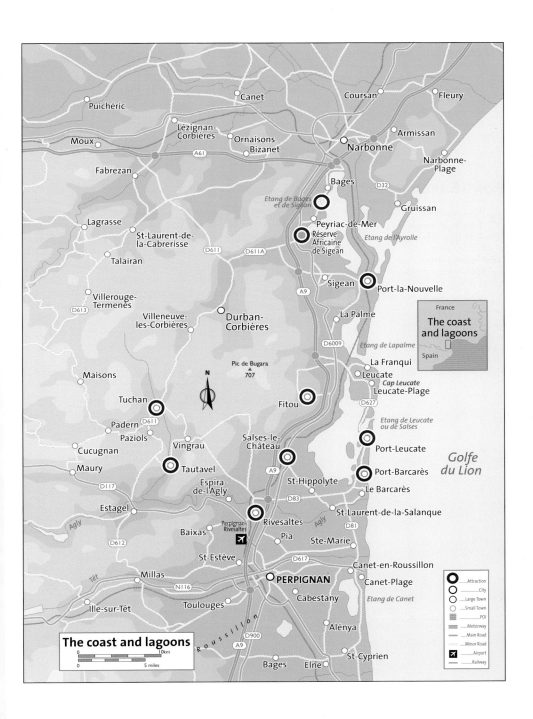

The coast and lagoons

Puichéric
Canet
Coursan
Fleury
Lézignan-Corbières
Moux
Ornaisons
Bizanet
Armissan
Narbonne
Narbonne-Plage
A61
Fabrezan
Bages
D32
Etang de Bages et de Sigean
Gruissan
Lagrasse
Peyriac-de-Mer
St-Laurent-de-la-Cabrerisse
Réserve Africaine de Sigean
Etang de l'Ayrolle
D611
D611A
Talairan
A9
Sigean
Port-la-Nouvelle
Villerouge-Termenès
D613
La Palme
Villeneuve-les-Corbières
Durban-Corbières
France
The coast and lagoons
Spain
Etang de Lapalme
D6009
Pic de Bugara
707
La Franqui
Maisons
Leucate
Cap Leucate
Leucate-Plage
N
Fitou
D627
Tuchan
Etang de Leucate ou de Salses
Padern
D611
Paziols
Vingrau
Salses-le-Château
Port-Leucate
Golfe du Lion
Cucugnan
Maury
Tautavel
A9
Port-Barcarès
D117
Espira-de-l'Agly
St-Hippolyte
Le Barcarès
Estagel
D83
St-Laurent-de-la-Salanque
Agly
Agly
Perpignan Rivesaltes
Rivesaltes
D81
Baixas
Pia
Ste-Marie
D612
St-Estève
D617
Canet-en-Roussillon
Millas
PERPIGNAN
Canet-Plage
Tèt
N116
Cabestany
Etang de Canet
Ille-sur-Têt
Toulouges
Alénya
The coast and lagoons
0                    10km
0              5 miles
Roussillon
D900
A9
Bages
Elne
St-Cyprien

Attraction
City
Large Town
Small Town
POI
Motorway
Main Road
Minor Road
Airport
Railway

# FITOU

**Fitou Tourist Information** 6 rue de la Mairie; tel: 04 68 45 69 11; email: tourisme@fitou.fr; www.fitou.fr. Open Mon–Sat all year.

This delightful winemaking village, overlooked by the ruins of a hilltop castle, has a distinct air of prosperity. Its quaint 800-year-old church is named – unusually – after a married couple, St-Julien and Ste-Basilisse.

# PORT-BARCARES

**Port-Barcarès Tourist Information** place de la République; tel: 04 68 86 16 56; email: tourisme@portbarcares.com; www.portbarcares.com. Open daily all year.

**Atlantide Marina** avenue du Roussillon; tel: 04 68 86 32 65. Open Jul–mid-Sept; Sat–Sun mid-Sept–Jun. Has a swimming pool, discos and laser show. There are also children's beach clubs Jul–Aug.

*Le Lydia*, a large white liner, was deliberately grounded in 1967 to become the centrepiece of the beach of this purpose-built resort and its near neighbour, Port-Leucate. All along the coast, pastel apartment and villa complexes with neat gardens and hotels have risen up on the flat sandbar between sea and lagoon, aiming to cater for every need of the 21st-century holidaymaker. A thalassotherapy centre offers to soothe away aches and stress, while watersports provide activity for those who want to do more than just lie in the sun. Bars and discos ensure that nobody needs to retire to bed early. Sardines have been fished locally for centuries and throughout the summer you can feast on them at stalls and restaurants, barbecued over vine twigs.

## Accommodation and food in Port-Barcarès

**Hôtel de la Mer €** *43 avenue Annibal; tel: 04 68 86 08 07; email: hoteldelamer.66@orange.fr; www.hoteldelamer.eu. Open daily Apr–Sept; Sat–Sun Oct–Mar.* Cheerful summer holiday hotel with 17 rooms, 100m from beach.

**Below**
Port-Leucate

Le Lydia *avenue de la Grande Plage; tel: 04 68 86 07 13. Open daily Jul–Sept; Sat–Sun Oct–Jun. The 'Paquebot des Sables' has a wide selection of entertainments, including a casino, bars and restaurants.*

**Le Relax'Otel €€** *avenue de Thalassa, Cap de Front; tel: 04 68 86 30 90; email: contact@relax-otel.com; www.relax-otel.com. Open Feb–Nov.* Located 100m from the beach with a seawater pool on the premises and a spa treatments centre next door. Forty-one en-suite rooms and a restaurant which serves traditional local dishes and caters for special diets.

## PORT-LA-NOUVELLE

**Port-la-Nouvelle Tourist Information**
*place Paul Valéry; tel: 04 68 48 00 51; email: officedetourisme. portlanouvelle@wanadoo.fr; www.portlanouvelle.com. Open daily Jun–Sept; Mon–Sat Oct–May.*

Unlike other towns along the Languedoc-Roussillon coast, Port-la-Nouvelle is not primarily geared to tourism. Instead, it is an industrial port handling oil supplies for the whole of Southwest France, and as such it has some rather unsightly refinery buildings, though the giant tankers which constantly come and go can be interesting to watch. The town also has a long beach, marina and canal basin where the Canal de la Robine reaches the sea. The nature reserve on Ile Ste-Lucie in the salt flats is a pleasant spot for walks.

## PORT-LEUCATE

**Port-Leucate Tourist Information**
*Espace Culturel; tel: 04 68 40 91 31; email: info@leucate. net; www.tourisme-leucate.net. Open daily Apr–Nov; Mon–Sat Dec–Mar.*

Like its neighbour, Port-Barcarès, this lively resort was purpose-built in the 1960s to cater for sun-loving holidaymakers. Together the two resorts now have the biggest marina complex on the French Mediterranean, fed by channels from the 10km-long Etang de Leucate ou de Salses lagoon, which stretches behind the sandbar on which they have been built. The winds, which frequently blow from either sea or land provide plenty of days when conditions are ideal for windsurfers. Sunset over the Etang de Leucate can be magical as the Corbières hills behind it become tinged with purple. The north end of the beach has a naturist village.

# RESERVE AFRICAINE DE SIGEAN

**ⓘ** **Tourist Information** *place de la Libération, Sigean; tel: 04 68 48 14 81; email: sigean@wanadoo.fr; www.sigean.org. Open daily Jul–Aug; Mon–Sat Sept–Jun.*

**ⓗ** **Réserve Africaine de Sigean €€€** *Off the N9; tel: 04 68 48 20 20; email: sigean@wanadoo.fr; www.reserveafricainesigean.fr. Open daily all year. Allow 30 minutes for the safari drive and 2 hours on foot for the nature trail.*

This large safari park (7km north of Sigean) is one of the few 'formal' attractions in this part of France. Ideal for families to visit, it has 3,000 animals including lions, bears and white rhinos. They roam freely in brushland that looks almost like their natural habitat. In addition, various exotic birds such as flamingos have joined the indigenous ones on the nearby lagoons. Cars drive round on a 5km route. Pedestrians can follow a nature discovery trail with observation posts for watching antelopes, zebras and cheetahs. Alligators bask in the warmth of a solar-heated house.

## Accommodation and food in Sigean

**Le Sainte Anne €€** *3 avenue de l'Hospital; tel: 04 68 48 24 38; email: contact@le-sainte-anne.com; www.le-sainte-anne.com. Open all year.* Picturesque nine-room hotel with restaurant, quietly situated on the edge of the town. Colourful garden with children's playground.

# RIVESALTES

**ⓘ** **Rivesaltes Tourist Information** *avenue Ledru-Rollin; tel: 04 68 64 04 04; email: contact@mairie-rivesaltes.fr; www.mairie-rivesaltes.fr. Open daily Jul–Aug; Mon–Fri Sept–Jun.*

**ⓗ** **Musée Maréchal Joffre €** *rue de la République; tel: 04 68 64 24 98. Open daily Jun–Sept.*

**ⓠ** **Trans-Vallées Express** *tel: 04 68 59 99 02; email: info@tpcf.fr; www.tpcf.fr. From Rivesaltes, a tourist train runs to Azat via St-Paul-de-Fenouillet. Using a former SNCF line, it twists and turns through magnificent scenery, climbing to over 500m high. The 40-mile journey takes about 2¼ hours. Tue–Sun Jul–Aug; Sun & Wed Sept–Oct & Apr–Jun.*

From the north you enter this little town, the centre of the area that produces the sweet Muscat de Rivesaltes aperitif wine, across a suspension bridge over the River Agly. A large plane tree, over a hundred years old, stands in the centre of the old quarter beside an elegant bell tower which – typical of the area – is built in brick and pebble. One of the narrow streets off it leads to the **Eglise St André**, which has a gilded altarpiece. On the church's exterior, notice how its olive-green glazed ceramic drainpipes each have a face at the bottom. The crenellations on the red-brick Portail Nef, one of the ancient fortified gateways into the old quarter, make it look like a small castle. An equestrian statue of Maréchal Joffre, one of France's famous World War I commanders, who was born in the town, stands in the modern part looking down a broad avenue of plane trees. His birthplace houses the **Musée Maréchal Joffre**, a museum dedicated to him. Don't miss a *dégustation* of the local muscat wine at one of the *caves*.

## Accommodation and food in Rivesaltes

**La Tour de L'Horloge €** *11 rue Armand Barbès; tel: 04 68 64 05 88; email: h.r.latour@wanadoo.fr; www.hotel-la-tour-horloge.com. Open Apr–Nov.* Small 17-room traditional hotel in centre of old quarter with restaurant serving Catalan dishes. Garage.

# Salses-le-Chateau

**Tourist Information**
*12 bis rue de la Poste;*
*tel: 04 68 38 66 13;*
*email: si.salseslechateau@*
*wanadoo.fr*

**Château de Salses**
*€€ tel: 04 68 38 60*
*13; www.monum.fr.*
*Open daily all year.*

When the narrow neck of land between the Corbières hills and the coastal lagoons formed the border between France and Spain, Salses-le-Château was an obvious place to have a castle. The king of Aragon built one in the 1300s. Today's **Château de Salses**, a vast building in yellow stone and pink brick, dates from 1497. Standing incongruously among vineyards, its 10m-thick walls – designed to withstand attack from the newly invented gunpowder – certainly look impregnable, though the moat around them has long since dried up. Constructed in just six years, the castle could house 1,500 men and 300 horses in vaulted stables. Its central courtyard was defended by an underground corridor with traps, which might have been how the term ha-ha (meaning 'sunken fence') originated (*see page 123*). The five-storey keep beyond the interior moat is where the governor and officers lived.

When the border was moved to the Pyrenees, the castle was handed over to France. Louis XIV's military architect Vauban improved its defences, but it was never attacked and subsequently became a prison.

# Tautavel

**Musée de Tautavel**
*€€ avenue Léon-Jean*
*Grégory; tel: 04 68 29 07*
*76; email:*
*contact@tautavel.com;*
*www.tautavel.com.*
*Open daily all year. Special*
*events, lectures and*
*exhibitions throughout the*
*year; also 'prehistoric'*
*banquets in Jul–Aug.*

Human bones estimated to be 450,000 years old, the oldest found in Europe, were discovered in 1971 in the **Caune de l'Arago**, a cave near the village which is situated in a vine-growing plain on the edge of the Corbières hills. The 40m-long cave, which opens out on to the plain from one of the surrounding cliffs, was excavated by Professor Henry de Lumley, who organised digs in the area and set up the Centre of European Prehistory in the village (visits by special arrangement).

In the excellent **Musée de Tautavel**, part of the centre, ancient objects found in the area bring prehistory to life. The highlight is a vivid life-size reconstruction of the cave made from castings. Videos depict the various stages of the cave's occupation, including prehistoric men returning from a hunt and hacking up game they have caught.

**Right**
Château de Salses

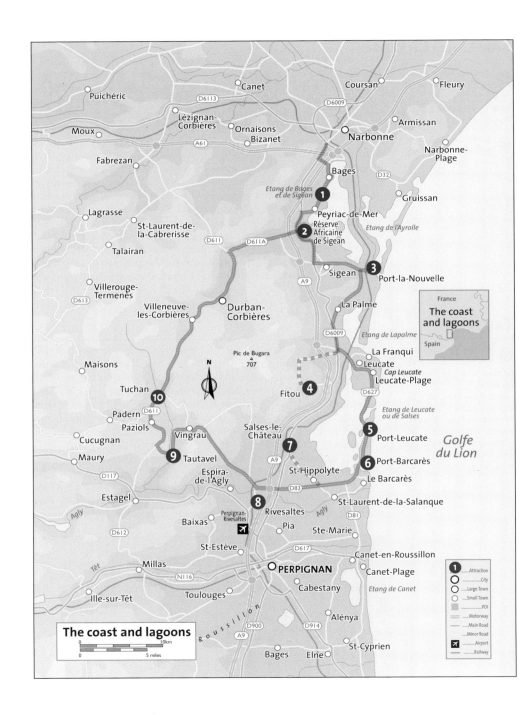

Puichéric

Canet

Coursan

Fleury

Moux

Lézignan-
Corbières

Ornaisons
Bizanet

D6113

D6009

Armissan

Narbonne

Narbonne-
Plage

Fabrezan

A61

Bages

D32

Etang de Bages
et de Sigean **1**

Gruissan

Lagrasse

St-Laurent-de-
la-Cabrerisse

**2** Réserve
Africaine
de Sigean

Peyriac-de-Mer

Etang de l'Ayrolle

Talairan

D611

D611A

A9

Sigean

**3** Port-la-Nouvelle

Villerouge-
Termenès

D613

Villeneuve-
les-Corbières

Durban-
Corbières

La Palme

France

**The coast
and lagoons**

Spain

Maisons

Pic de Bugara
707

N

D6009

Etang de Lapalme

La Franqui

Leucate

Cap Leucate
Leucate-Plage

Tuchan

**10**

Padern

D611

Fitou

**4**

D627

Paziols

Vingrau

Salses-le-
Château

Etang de Leucate
ou de Salses

Cucugnan

Maury

**9** Tautavel

**7**

A9

**5** Port-Leucate

Golfe
du Lion

D117

Espira-
de-l'Agly

St-Hippolyte

**6** Port-Barcarès

Le Barcarès

Estagel

Agly

D83

St-Laurent-de-la-Salanque

Baixas

Perpignan-
Rivesaltes

**8**

Rivesaltes

Agly

D81

D612

St-Estève

Pia

Ste-Marie

Millas

Tèt

N116

D617

Canet-en-Roussillon

**PERPIGNAN**

Canet-Plage

Ille-sur-Têt

Toulouges

Cabestany

Etang de Canet

Roussillon

D900

A9

Alénya

**The coast and lagoons**

0                    10km

0          5 miles

Bages

Elne

St-Cyprien

**1**  Attraction
○  City
○  Large Town
○  Small Town
▨  POI
━  Motorway
━  Main Road
━  Minor Road
✈  Airport
━  Railway

## Ha-has

The term ha-ha, meaning a sunken fence which forms a boundary without interrupting a view, is said to have originated at Salses castle – as they proudly tell you on a visit there. To aid its defenders, an underground corridor was built around the courtyard with water traps along it to catch spies. When they fell in, they would exclaim in surprise 'ah ah'. Those who did not drown were likely to knock themselves out on stone lintels which were deliberately set at different heights.

## TUCHAN

The village of Tuchan is brooded over by the Montagne de Tauch, an austere ridge of hills which makes this part of the Corbières feel wild and remote, especially if you happen to be driving through it at dusk. Surrounded by vineyards, it is the centre for the production of Fitou wine.

# Suggested tour

**Total distance:** 160km. The detour to Fitou adds 14km and the detour to Salses-le-Château adds 12km.

**Time:** 4 hours' driving. Allow about a day for the main route, or at least a full day with detours and time on the beach. Those with limited time should concentrate on Sigean and Tautavel.

**Links to other tours:** From Tuchan, the D611 and D14 lead southwest to Padern (*see page 107*), 7km away. From Port-Barcarès, the D81 leads south to Canet-Plage (*see page 51*), 15km away.

Leaving Narbonne south on the D6009 (towards Perpignan), turn left after 5km on to the D105. This hugs the shore of the **ETANG DE BAGES ET DE SIGEAN ❶** through **Bages** and then rejoins the D6009 just beyond **Peyriac-de-Mer**. After 5km on the D6009 (past the **RESERVE AFRICAINE DE SIGEAN ❷** safari park on the left), leave it again by turning left on to the D6139 to go through **Sigean** to the sea at **PORT-LA-NOUVELLE ❸**. Then take the D709 back to the D6009 again, through **La Palme** where the cliffs northwest of the village have a glorious view over the lagoon to the sea. Two kilometres after rejoining the N9, you come to its junction with the D627.

**Detour:** To visit **FITOU ❹**, stay on the D6009 for 5km beyond its junction with the D627. At **Les Cabanes-de-Fitou**, turn right on to the unnumbered road which goes over the A9 autoroute to Fitou (2km), then return north along the D6009 to rejoin the route at its junction with the D627.

The 20km train journey (30km by car) from Narbonne to Port-la-Nouvelle (on the line to Perpignan) takes 15 minutes. Frequent services. Boat trips on the Canal de la Robine also cross the lagoon.

At the D6009/D627 junction, take the D627 southeast towards the sea. It runs spectacularly along the narrow strip of land between the sea and the **Etang de Leucate ou des Salses** lagoon. The old village of **Leucate** overlooks the lagoon while **Leucate-Plage**, the original resort, is on the Mediterranean.

The new resorts of **PORT-LEUCATE** ❺ and **PORT-BARCARES** ❻ are unusual in having no seafront road. Instead, access to the beach is down cul-de-sacs, so unless you leave the D627 you will quickly sweep past them. Beyond Port-Barcarès, turn inland on the D83.

**Detour:** Turn right off the D83 on to the D11 through **St-Hippolyte** to visit **SALSES-LE-CHATEAU** ❼ (7km), and then pick up the route again by returning to the D83 along the D6009 (5km).

From the D83, continue inland over the A9 autoroute, turning left to go over a small suspension bridge into **RIVESALTES** ❽. From there, the D12 twists dramatically up beneath a ridge of white limestone cliffs into the Corbières hills and the village of **Vingrau** from where the D9 leads to **TAUTAVEL** ❾. Next take the D59 to join the D611, which goes through **TUCHAN** ❿ and past the **Château de Aguilar**, built on an isolated rocky outcrop. It was strongly fortified in the 13th century to guard the gorge below from Spanish attack. Now the hilly countryside covered in *garrigue* – sweet-smelling scrubby bushes – is wild and austere. The Montagne de Tauch broods over the lonely road as it makes its way through vineyards to **Villeneuve-les-Corbières** and **Durban-Corbières**. The latter is very much a southern wine village, with wineries along its plane-lined main street and the ruins of a castle on a hillock in the centre. The Fitou vineyards are all around and the countryside becomes much softer with cherry trees and pink outcrops as the D611 continues northeast to join the D6009 back to **Narbonne**.

## Getting out of the car I

The **Cap Leucate** cliffs, just north of Leucate-Plage, offer glorious views over the Golfe du Lion coastline. A scenic path leads from them down to **La Franqui**.

## Getting out of the car II

Although it is easy to drive to Port-la-Nouvelle from Narbonne, why not go by train? The line is one of the most scenic in France, running between two large lagoons, the **Etang de Bages et de Sigean** and the **Etang de l'Ayrolle**, on a narrow sandbar which it shares with the **Canal de la Robine**. Look out of the window and you seem to be almost floating as there is scarcely any 'land' on either side, just patches of dune – home to hundreds of seabirds – lapped by rippling water. Sunset, when the pink sky is reflected in the water, is the most beautiful time of all.

**Opposite**
Leucate-Plage on the Golfe du Lion coast

# Carcassonne

## Ratings

| | |
|---|---|
| History | ●●●●● |
| Architecture | ●●●●○ |
| Food and drink | ●●●○○ |
| Children | ●●○○○ |
| Entertainment | ●●○○○ |
| Museums | ●●○○○ |
| Shopping | ●●○○○ |
| Art | ●○○○○ |

The town has two distinct faces – La Cité and La Ville Basse – separated by the River Aude. Most visitors are attracted by La Cité, a formidable medieval citadel built on a high crag which looks particularly spectacular when floodlit at night. Across the river is the lower town, Bastide St-Louis, where the main offices and shops are to be found. Originally, the town thrived on cloth-making but now it is mainly an administrative centre.

It's easy to see why La Cité has become a museum piece. At the end of the 19th century it was saved from falling into complete decay by Viollet-le-Duc, the architect who specialised in military renovation. He restored it to its 12th-century form. In contrast, La Ville Basse, 'the new town', which King Louis IX had built in 1260, has the grid layout typical of a *bastide* (fortified town).

## Getting there and getting around

ℹ **Tourist Information**
*28 rue de Verdun;*
*tel: 04 68 10 24 30; email:*
*accueil@carcassonne-*
*tourisme.com;*
*www.carcassonne.org. Open*
*daily all year. Guided tours.*
*In La Cité: Porte*
*Narbonnaise; tel: 04 68 11*
*70 77. Open daily all year.*
Guided visits in English
available. Small charge.

**By air:** Carcassonne's small **Salvaza airport** (*tel: 04 68 71 96 46*) is 3km northwest of the town. It has flights from the UK and Ireland by Ryanair. There is a restaurant and car-hire desks, but no shops. A shuttle bus to La Ville Basse and La Cité operates daily. A coach service to and from Toulouse connects with the Ryanair flights.

**By train:** The **railway station** is on the northern edge of La Ville Basse, with parking opposite it across the Canal du Midi.

To reach La Cité by car, take exit Est from the A61 autoroute and follow signs to car parks. For La Ville Basse, exit Ouest is also convenient.

**Parking:** Access to La Cité by car is severely restricted. Cars are normally banned in mid-April–September. Instead, they have to be left in the well-signposted car park outside the walls with moderately priced day-long parking rates. Pedestrians walk in through the Porte Narbonnaise. Hotel guests should check parking arrangements with their hotel. There is also free on-street parking in the suburbs to the north of La Cité for those prepared to face the hilly walk up. Pay-and-display car parks are situated beside the boulevards surrounding La Ville Basse. The grid of narrow streets in the centre is all one-way. Pont-Vieux, one of two bridges over the river, is also one-way in the direction of La Cité.

**Public transport:** A shuttle bus operates every 15 minutes in high season from 0930 to 1230 and 1400 to 1930 between La Cité and square Gambetta on the edge of La Ville Basse (*tel: 04 68 47 82 22*) and also, more frequently and year-round, the No 4 bus. To walk between La Cité and La Ville Basse takes about 15 minutes. Go via the Pont-Vieux.

# Sights – La Cité

**Basilique St-Nazaire La Cité**
*Open daily all year.*

**Château Comtal €€**
*1 rue Viollet le Duc; tel: 04 68 11 70 70. Open daily all year.*

### La Cité
The citadel is a very convincing 19th-century restoration of the original medieval fortified town. Indeed, some say it is too perfect. Standing on a strategically sited hilltop first settled by the Romans, it was more or less abandoned when its position was no longer militarily useful and fell into serious disrepair until being restored, at enormous cost to the state, by Viollet-le-Duc. Now it is much as it was originally, with high double walls stretching for over 1km, 52 towers, a castle and basilica. Only 130 people actually live there, but its narrow streets are lined with small shops, mostly selling souvenirs. All summer it is a tourist honeypot.

### Basilique St-Nazaire
The outstanding feature is its 14th- to 15th-century stained glass, including two beautiful rose windows. The sun shining through them dapples the interior with colour. Only the barrel-vaulted nave is original from the 11th century. Viollet-le-Duc took it upon himself to put crenellations around the belfry wall outside.

### Château Comtal
Château Comtal, the inner bastion, was built in the 12th century by the viscounts of Carcassonne, the Trencavels. It has been knocked around extensively – though never by military attack – over the years,

**Below**
La Cité

**Musée de l'Ecole** €
3 rue du Plô; tel: 04 68
25 95 14; email:
musecole.carca@tele2.fr.
Open daily all year.

**Musée Mémoires
Moyen Age** €€ Espace
Pont Levis, chemin des
Anglais; tel: 04 68 71 08 65;
email: musee-memoires-
moyen-age@wanadoo.fr.
Open daily all year.

**Sightseeing tours** of
Carcassonne are possible
via a little train running
through the streets (tel: 04
68 24 45 70) or in a
horse-drawn carriage
(tel: 04 68 71 54 57; email:
spidatel@cegetel.net). Both
take about 20 minutes and
start from Porte
Narbonnaise (May–Sept).

ending up with five towers, two courtyards and wooden galleries, part
of its defences, along the outer walls. One of the towers contains the
**Musée Lapidaire**, which has a collection of Roman pottery and stone
fragments; also old prints showing what La Cité looked like before it
was restored.

### Les Lices
A 3km-long broad grassy bailey or ditch – Les Lices – runs round La
Cité between the high inner wall and lower outside one. It was
used for jousting tournaments and archery practice as well
as storage.

### Musée de l'Ecole
This nostalgic 1900 classroom is complete with old-fashioned desks,
blackboards and ink pens.

### Musée Mémoires Moyen Age
Mémoires Moyen Age is a 30-minute video presentation with music
and sound effects about the history of La Cité and its military
construction. The museum is situated just outside the walls.

### Porte Narbonnaise
The pedestrian gateway, which sports two huge towers, formerly
guarded the entrance to La Cité with a heavy chain backed up by
trapdoors and two portcullises. Today over a quarter of a million
visitors pass through it each year.

## Sights – La Ville Basse

### Bastide St-Louis (La Ville Basse)
'The new town' was built following the wholesale destruction of the
area during the Albigensian Crusade, which ended in 1240. Wide
boulevards shaded by plane trees have replaced the ramparts which
originally encircled its grid of straight narrow streets.

### Cathédrale St-Michel
The cathedral, in rue Voltaire, is typically Southern Gothic in style
with a single large nave. The altar is built in the local warm red/cream
marble from Caunes. The stained-glass windows are 19th century.

### Halle aux Grains
The town's open-sided corn market (rue du Dr Albert Tomey) dates from
the 17th century and has a lofty wooden roof. A circle (now often
covered by parked cars) marked on the square beside it is where traders
found guilty of cheating had to stand for an hour wearing a placard
proclaiming their misdemeanour.

**Musée des Beaux-Arts** *1 rue de Verdun; tel: 04 68 77 73 70. Open daily mid-Jun–mid-Sept; Tue–Sat mid-Sept–mid-Jun. Admission free.*

**Musée des Beaux-Arts**

The museum's collection ranges from 17th- to 19th-century French, Flemish and Dutch masters to local pottery and memorabilia from the Chéniers, a well-known local family who had strong Greek connections.

**Place Carnot**

This big square, the centre of the town, was originally surrounded by arcades, part of the traditional architecture of a *bastide*, but they disappeared long ago and the buildings are now a mixture of styles. Now traffic-free, it has a decorative Italian fountain in the centre depicting Neptune.

# Shopping

La Ville Basse is dotted with small shops, particularly in the pedestrianised streets across from the station, such as rue Georges Clemenceau and Courte Jaire. For pâtisserie and chocolate, such as the famous pavés de La Cité, head for place Carnot. There's also an open-air market there on Tuesday, Thursday and Saturday mornings. There's a daily market (fresh and cooked meat and fish) in the **Halle aux Grains**. **Monoprix** is the only department store, though several hypermarkets are situated on the outskirts near the autoroute. Most of the shops in La Cité are very touristy, though the **Comptoir des Vins** (*4 rue Compte Roger*) has an excellent selection of local wines.

# Entertainment

La Cité stages a summer festival during July and August when open-air concerts, plays and medieval re-enactments take place near the castle. On Bastille Day, 14 July, the town puts on one of the best firework displays in France, making the whole of La Cité look as if it is going up in flames. The best place to watch is on Pont-Vieux or the banks of the River Aude. This is not an evening to try driving through the town as both its bridges are closed to traffic.

# Accommodation and food

The three hotels in La Cité are handy if you enjoy being in the centre of the action but they charge for the privilege. There are many more just outside the walls and others lower down in La Ville Basse. The tourist offices can book accommodation but you have to go there in person. The streets of La Cité abound in eateries of varying quality, but you are much more likely to rub shoulders with local people in La Ville Basse.

## La Cité

**Auberge Dame Carcas** €€ *3 place du Château; tel: 04 68 71 23 23; www.damecarcas.com. Open Thur–Tue all year.* Reasonably priced menus in traditional surroundings.

**Auberge des Ducs d'Oc** €€ *6 place du Château; tel: 04 68 47 91 90; email: contact@auberge-des-ducs-doc.fr; www.auberge-des-ducs-doc.fr. Open all year.* Regional gastronomic dishes. Set meals include a house cocktail.

**Le Donjon Les Ramparts** €€ *2 rue du Comte Roger; tel: 04 68 11 23 00; email: info@bestwestern-donjon.com; www.hotel-donjon.fr. Open all year.* Medieval setting with modern comforts; transformed from an orphanage into a mid-priced hotel. Thirty-six rooms. Brasserie.

**Hôtel de La Cité** €€€ *place de l'Eglise; tel: 04 68 71 98 71; email: reservations@hoteldelacite.com; www.hoteldelacite.com. Open all year.* Everyone from Queen Elizabeth II to Walt Disney and Michael Jackson has checked into this exclusive wood-panelled, near-château which boasts a swimming pool and one of the few gardens in La Cité.

## La Ville Basse

**Hôtel du Pont Vieux** € *32 rue Trivalle; tel: 04 68 25 24 99; email: info@hoteldupontvieux.com; www.hoteldupontvieux.com. Open late-Jan–mid-Jan.* A quiet family-run hotel nestling in a small street in the oldest quarter of the town just below La Cité. Nineteen rooms.

**La Rotonde** € *13 boulevard Omer Sarraut; tel: 04 68 25 02 37.* A lively brasserie near the station which is popular with students, not least because its inexpensive menu includes a cinema ticket.

**Des Trois Couronnes** €€ *2 rue des Trois Couronnes; tel: 04 68 25 36 10; email: hotel3couronnes@wanadoo.fr; www.hotel-destroiscouronnes.com. Open all year.* A modern hotel boasting one of the best views of La Cité from its riverside position, particularly for diners in quai Bellevue, its terrace restaurant. Sixty-eight rooms.

**Hôtel Le Terminus** €€ *2 avenue du Maréchal Joffre; tel: 04 92 80 74 00; email: reservation@soleilvacances.com; www.soleilvacances.com. Open all year.* This hotel opposite the railway station is indeed grand. It has an imposing mirrored and marbled lobby in true *fin-de-siècle* style, yet surprisingly affordable rooms. One hundred rooms.

# Suggested walk

**Length:** 3km.

**Duration:** At least an hour, including 15 minutes from La Cité down to La Ville Basse.

Before heading into **LA CITE ❶** through the **PORTE NARBONNAISE ❷**, stroll around the broad ditch – **LES LICES ❸** – between the high inner wall and lower outside one, then walk along the walls and enjoy the view down over the **River Aude** and **LA VILLE BASSE ❹** with hills in the distance.

Inside La Cité, the narrow streets, jam-packed in summer, are lined with small shops and cafés occupying quaint old stone buildings. The most notable sights are the **CHATEAU COMTAL ❺** and **BASILIQUE ST-NAZAIRE ❻**.

Two routes lead down to La Ville Basse. Through the **Porte d'Aude**, a steep cobbled path named **Montée d'Aude** zigzags down to the **Eglise St-Pimer**; or the easier **Montée G Combéléran** leads down from the Porte Narbonnaise. Cross the 600-year-old **Pont-Vieux**, which has pointed recesses where pedestrians can stand to avoid vehicles, and turn left to walk down boulevard du Cdt Roumens past the grand 18th-century entrance gate, **Portail des Jacobins**, and on to the **CATHEDRALE ST-MICHEL**. Nearby is the covered marketplace, **HALLE AUX GRAINS ❼**.

Dotted around the narrow grid of streets within La Ville Basse, particularly rue de Verdun and rue Aimé Ramond, are a number of fine mansions dating from the 18th century when the town grew rich from cloth-making. Although they are closed to the public, you may pass open doorways where you can peep into their secluded courtyards. These invariably have attractive balconies and staircases and often a well with a palm tree beside it. To have such an exotic feature was regarded as a status symbol. The oldest is the **Maison du Sénéchal ❽** in rue du Dr Albert Tomey.

The traffic-free **PLACE CARNOT ❾** is the town's centre. Its red marble paving and cobbles provide a smart setting for a market on Tuesday, Thursday and Saturday mornings and pavement cafés at other times.

**Eglise St-Vincent** in rue du 4 Septembre has the second-widest nave in France (after the one at Mirepoix) and is topped by a flamboyant 54m-high tower with 47 bells. Nearby, the **Préfecture de Police** in rue Jean-Bringer occupies the former bishop's palace.

## Also worth exploring

The **Canal du Midi** passes through La Ville Basse in front of the railway station. Its wide basin and lock are a hive of industry in summer. Leafy Jardin Chenier beside it is an attractive spot for sitting or strolling and has a playground for children. You can walk along the towpath as far as you like in either direction.

The town's citizens made a serious mistake when they declined to contribute towards the cost of bringing the canal through the town centre, as Pierre-Paul Riquet suggested when he was building it in 1669 (*see page 197*). Instead, it followed the valley of the Fresquel, 2km north, which meant they missed out on the valuable trade it might have brought, unlike Castelnaudary – 32km west – which prospered from it. The canal was re-routed between 1786 and 1810, including a superb aqueduct over the Fresquel, but this was far too late for the town to benefit fully from water-borne business.

# The Corbières hills

## Ratings

| | |
|---|---|
| Scenery | ●●●●● |
| Food and drink | ●●●●○ |
| Villages | ●●●●○ |
| Castles | ●●●○○ |
| Churches | ●●●○○ |
| Vineyards | ●●●○○ |
| Walking | ●●●○○ |
| Spas | ●●○○○ |

The lively little town of Limoux is one of the highlights of this otherwise rural route around the Corbières hills, particularly during its entertaining carnival weekends.

To the west, this is Blanquette country where, nearly 500 years ago, the world's first sparkling white wine came to fruition in the monastery at St-Hilaire. To the east, around Lagrasse, the vineyards which produce Corbières wines stretch up the hillsides, dotted with *domaines* (estates) where you can sample and buy.

Everywhere the scenery is stunning, for this is hill country even though it lacks the drama of high mountain peaks. Limestone crags peep through wooded hillsides and there are long views to the distant Pyrenees. Ruined castles and the remains of ancient monasteries are forlorn reminders of its turbulent past.

Petrol stations – as well as shops and restaurants – are in short supply on this route so stock up before starting out.

## ALET-LES-BAINS

**ⓘ** **Alet-les-Bains Tourist Information** *avenue Nicolas Pavillon; tel: 04 68 69 93 56; email: info.aletlesbains@free.fr; http://info.aletlesbains.free.fr. Open daily mid-Jan–mid-Dec.*

True to the tradition of France's spa towns, Alet has a casino to complement its range of mineral waters, said to be helpful for gastric problems. Nostradamus, the French visionary, recommended them anyway. Situated in a sheltered spot beside the River Aude, the old quarter is a charming area with half-timbered and pink-stone buildings surrounded by ramparts. Its **Benedictine abbey**, burnt out during the Wars of Religion, is a forlorn ruin.

## CHATEAU DE TERMES

Termes castle is a crumbling ruin at the top of a wooded ridge surrounded by deep gorges. A steep track leads up to it from the bridge in the village; allow 15 minutes. Only parts of its thick walls survived

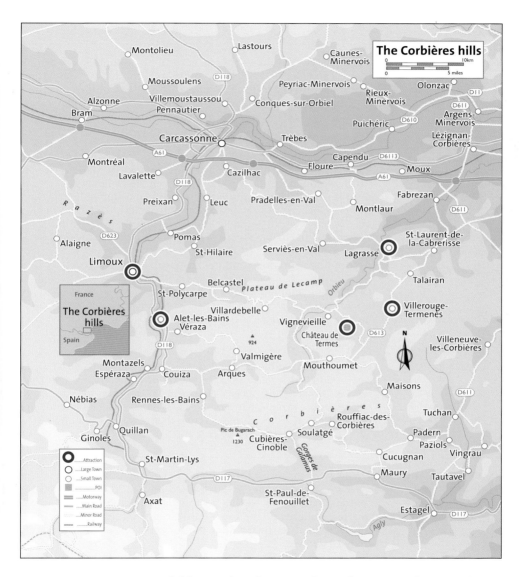

The Corbières hills

Montolieu
Lastours
Caunes-Minervois
Moussoulens
D118
Peyriac-Minervois
Rieux-Minervois
Olonzac
D11
Alzonne
Villemoustaussou
Pennautier
Conques-sur-Orbiel
Argens-Minervois
Bram
Puichéric
D610
D611
Carcassonne
Trèbes
Lézignan-Corbières
A61
Montréal
Capendu
D6113
Lavalette
Floure
Moux
Cazilhac
A61
D118
Preixan
Leuc
Pradelles-en-Val
Fabrezan
Montlaur
D611
Razès
Alaigne
D623
Pomas
St-Hilaire
Serviès-en-Val
Lagrasse
St-Laurent-de-la-Cabrerisse
Limoux
France
Belcastel
Plateau de Lecamp
Orbieu
Talairan
The Corbières hills
St-Polycarpe
Villardebelle
Villerouge-Termenès
Spain
Alet-les-Bains
Véraza
Vignevieille
Château de Termes
D613
Villeneuve-les-Corbières
D118
924
Valmigère
Montazels
Espéraza
Couiza
Arques
Mouthoumet
Maisons
Nébias
Rennes-les-Bains
Corbières
Tuchan
D611
Quillan
Ginoles
Pic de Bugarach
1230
Cubières-Cinoble
Soulatgé
Rouffiac-des-Corbières
Padern
Paziols
Vingrau
Gorges de Galamus
Cucugnan
St-Martin-Lys
D117
Maury
Tautavel
Axat
St-Paul-de-Fenouillet
Estagel
D117
Agly

Attraction
Large Town
Small Town
POI
Motorway
Main Road
Minor Road
Railway

**Château de Termes**
€€ *tel: 04 68 70 09*
*20; email:*
*info@payscathare.org;*
*www.payscathare.org. Open*
*daily Feb–Dec.*

its deliberate demolition in the 17th century after it had been occupied by brigands. Its position guarding the Sou Valley certainly merits the climb to the top. The castle played a large part in the first stages of the Albigensian Crusade (*see page 30*) when it sheltered a leading Cathar 'heretic', Ramon de Termes, but was finally taken by Simon de Montfort in 1210 after a 4-month siege.

# LAGRASSE

The capital of the Corbières is one of the most beautiful little towns in France – and that's official! It is classified as such. Certainly, its setting, beside the River Orbieu surrounded by hills, could scarcely be bettered. The quaint medieval centre within fortified walls has a maze of narrow streets with several fine houses dating from around the 14th century when the inhabitants made a good living from tanning leather and making cloth. There is also an attractive covered market.

An 11th-century humpbacked bridge across the River Orbieu links the town with the splendid Benedictine **Abbaye Ste-Marie d'Orbieu**, which was founded in 799, though the present buildings date from the 13th to the 18th centuries. They include a simple Romanesque church, cloisters, the abbot's chapel with a decorative tiled floor, a huge dormitory with a wooden ceiling and a bell tower – with a spiral staircase worth climbing for the view over the river and town.

## Accommodation and food in Lagrasse

**Le Clos des Souquets €€** *avenue de Lagrasse, Fabrezan (11km northeast of Lagrasse on the D212); tel: 04 68 43 52 61; email: clossouquets@free.fr; www.le-clos-des-souquets.com. Open Mar–mid-Nov. Restaurant open Mon–Sat.* Cosy inn with five individually decorated bedrooms, pretty gardens and pool.

**Hostellerie des Corbières €€** *9 blvd de la Promenade; tel: 04 68 43 15 22; email: hostelleriecorbieres@free.fr; www.hostelleriecorbieres.com. Open Feb–Dec.* Formerly the Auberge St-Hubert, this hotel on the edge of the village has been completely renovated and has a restaurant offering fine traditional local dishes with menus that change with the seasons.

# LIMOUX

The heart of this lively town on the River Aude is its arcaded square, place de la République. A 400-year-old bridge, Pont Neuf, links the central 'grande ville' to the 'petite ville', the more modern Aragou quarter. Sections of the town's 14th-century fortified walls, built following an attack by the Black Prince, son of England's King Edward III, have survived.

Limoux has several claims to fame. First and foremost it is the production centre for Blanquette de Limoux, the world's first sparkling white wine. Another is its fricassee, a tasty pork stew served with the local white beans. And the town is notable, too, for its carnivals, which take place every weekend from January to March on the place de la République, always a particularly jolly time to be there.

A small art gallery, **Musée Petiet**, displays 19th-century paintings by local artists, including Auguste and Léopold Petiet and Léopold's daughter Marie. The building was formerly their studio.

**Grand flea market** *avenue F d'Eglantine on first Sun of the month Oct–Aug.*

**Carnaval de Limoux** *from mid-Jan.*

**Below**
Pierrots at the Carnaval de Limoux

## Accommodation and food in Limoux

**Hôtel Moderne & Pigeon €€** *place du Général Leclerc; tel: 04 68 31 00 25; email: hotelmodernepigeon.wanadoo.fr; www.grandhotelmodernepigeon.fr. Open mid-Jan–mid-Dec.* Large stately town house converted to a hotel during the 19th century and now renowned for its restaurant (€€€). Grand staircase embellished by a large stained-glass window and frescoes painted by Italian pilgrims on their way to Santiago de Compostela. The hotel's unusual name results from the amalgamation of two businesses by the original owners.

**Left**
Traditional costumes, Limoux

## Carnaval de Limoux

Every weekend from January to Easter the centre of Limoux is filled with festive crowds. Three times each Saturday and Sunday (starting at 1100, 1700 and 2000), costumed revellers dance solemnly around the arcades of the place de la République accompanied by brass bands, pausing for refreshment at the five bars around it.

Men, women and children take part, all wearing either colourful Pierrot costumes or funny character masks with appropriate clothes. Some wave *la carabena*, a wand decorated with coloured strips of paper, while others carry sacks of coloured confetti to throw over the spectators.

The music is infectiously repetitive and the dance movements slow and precise. On the final evening a bonfire is lit in the centre of the square and everyone, both participants and spectators, dances around it.

Limoux's *carnaval* tradition dates back to the Middle Ages when the local millers celebrated after paying their dues to the monastery of Prouille. Then instead of confetti they threw sugared almonds and flour.

# VILLEROUGE-TERMENES

 **Château de Villerouge-Termenès €€**
*tel: 04 68 70 09 11; email: chateau.villerouge@wanadoo.fr; www.villerouge.fr. Open daily Feb–Dec.*

**Château de Villerouge-Termenès**, a square 800-year-old castle, has been completely restored. Inside you can see a vivid audiovisual about Cathar times seen through the eyes of the last *parfait*, Guilhem Bélibaste, who was burnt at the stake there. The castle's restaurant serves medieval fare only (*open Tue–Sun*).

## Suggested tour

**Total distance:** 110km. The detour to St-Hilaire adds 4km and the detour to Alet-les-Bains adds 16km.

**Time:** 3 hours' driving. Allow most of a day for the main route, a full day with detours. Those with limited time should concentrate on Limoux and Lagrasse.

**Links to other tours:** From Limoux, the D118 leads south to Couiza (*see page 103*), 15km away. From Villerouge-Termenès, the D613 leads southwest to Mouthoumet, 13km away. From Lagrasse, the D212 leads northeast to Lézignan-Corbières (*see page 193*), 20km away.

**ⓗ Abbaye de St-Hilaire**
*€ Information tel: 04 98
05 40 10; email:
contact@abbayedesthilaire.com;
www.abbayesainthilaire.com.
Open daily all year. Concerts
during the Fugue in
Romanesque Aude music
festival at end of Jul.*

**ⓒ Château du Floure**
*€€€ I rue Gaston
Bonheur, Floure (10km east
of Carcassonne, just off the
N113); tel: 04 68 79 11 29;
email: contact@chateau-de-
floure.com; www.chateau-de-
floure.com. Country
mansion, partly dating back
to the 12th century, with
impressive formal gardens.
Sixteen rooms, sun terrace,
tennis and pool. Restaurant:
open daily Apr–Dec.*

**Below**
The Corbières hills

From Carcassonne, take the D118 south beside the River Aude to **LIMOUX ❶**.

**Detour:** The birthplace of the famous sparkling white wine, Blanquette de Limoux, is the Benedictine abbey in the small village of **St-Hilaire** on the River Lauguer between Carcassonne and Limoux. To visit it, turn left off the D118 12km south of Carcassonne and go through **Pomas** (4km). Its pretty 600-year-old cloister is still in remarkably good condition, though the main attraction is the splendidly carved white marble tomb in the Romanesque church depicting St-Sernin's martyrdom. Afterwards, return to the route on the D104, which winds down to Limoux (12km).

**Detour:** To visit **ALET-LES-BAINS ❷**, continue south beyond Limoux for a further 8km on the D118.

From Limoux, the route goes east along the valley into quiet wooded countryside on the narrow D129 through **St-Polycarpe** and **Belcastel**. This winding, undulating road has extensive views over distant hills. At **Villardebelle**, turn left on to the D529 where a small plaque commemorates the planting of a tree by the local priest to mark the proclamation of France's First Republic. After a 2km descent, turn right on to the even narrower D40, which goes through farmland and woods to the lonely Col de la Louviéro (599m). This is a particularly peaceful part of the Corbières and civilisation seems far away. Turn left along the narrow Gorges du Terminèt where the **CHATEAU DE TERMES ❸** is on the right. Continue on the D40, enjoying the wide views on both sides, until it reaches the D613 where you turn left again. Now the vineyards which produce the famous Corbières wines make their appearance. Beyond **VILLEROUGE-TERMENES** ❹, you go over the Col de Villerouge (404m) and continue through vineyards. Next, turn on to the D23 to **LAGRASSE** ❺. Turn left there on to the D3 along the wide gorge of the River Alsou. Nine kilometres later, turn left again on to the D603 to **Serviès-en-Val** from where the D42 makes its twisting way with glorious views back to Carcassonne.

# Around the Montagne Noire

## Ratings

| | |
|---|---|
| Architecture | ●●●● |
| Nature | ●●●● |
| Scenery | ●●●● |
| Walking | ●●●● |
| History | ●●● |
| Outdoor activities | ●●● |
| Villages | ●●● |
| Art and craft | ●● |

The Montagne Noire, the most southerly part of France's Massif Central mountains, is a rolling rural landscape with breathtaking views over green valleys bordered by steep cliffs and dotted with sleepy little towns.

The mountain acts as a dividing line between the Atlantic and Mediterranean climates. The south-facing slopes are gentle, covered in gorse, sweet chestnuts and olives and their towns have a distinctly southern feel. By contrast, the northern side of the mountain, which reaches 1,211m at its highest point, the Pic de Nore, is steeper and thickly wooded with pine and beech. Here the houses, built in the local grey stone, look sombre, particularly as their walls are sometimes covered in black slate as protection from the weather.

The area gets a lot of rain – and snow in winter – as it catches winds from both east and west which bring over a metre per year.

## DOURGNE

 **Dourgne Tourist Information**
*1 avenue du Maquis; tel: 05 63 74 27 19; email: contact@paysdedourgne-tourisme.com; www.paysdedourgne-tourisme.com. Open daily all year.*

This small village where slate is quarried has the distinction of having a convent, Abbaye Ste-Scholastique, founded in 1890, and a monastery, Abbaye St-Benoît-d'En Calcat, founded six years later. Both are run by the Benedictine order. The monastery has a large ultra-modern bookshop which also sells pottery and religious pictures. The abbeys are north of the village in Calcat on the D85.

## HAUTPOUL

 **Tourist Information** *In Mazamet (see page 144).*

This quaint hilltop village is perched above the wooded valley of the River Arnette with Mazamet below. Its history as a fortress goes back to the 5th century but ended when Simon de Montfort stormed it during the Albigensian Crusade in the 13th century. The inhabitants

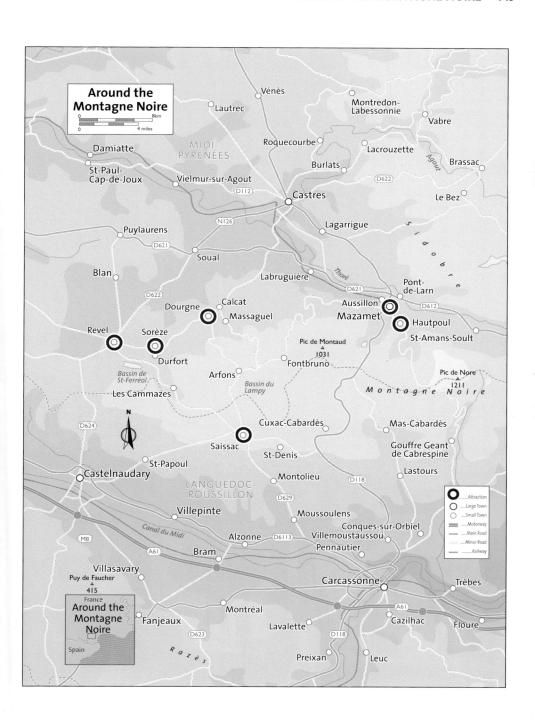

**Around the Montagne Noire**

0    8km
0    4 miles

Vénès
Lautrec
Montredon-Labessonnie
Vabre
Damiatte
MIDI-PYRÉNÉES
Roquecourbe
Lacrouzette
Brassac
St-Paul-Cap-de-Joux
Burlats
D622
Vielmur-sur-Agout
D112
Castres
Le Bez
Agout
N126
Lagarrigue
Sidobre
Puylaurens
D621
Soual
Blan
Labruguière
Thoré
Pont-de-Larn
D622
D621
Dourgne
Calcat
Aussillon
Mazamet
D612
Massaguel
Hautpoul
Revel
Sorèze
St-Amans-Soult
Durfort
Pic de Montaud
1031
Arfons
Fontbruno
Pic de Nore
1211
Bassin de St-Ferréol
Bassin du Lampy
Montagne Noire
Les Cammazes
D624
N
Cuxac-Cabardès
Mas-Cabardès
Gouffre Geant de Cabrespine
Saissac
St-Denis
St-Papoul
Montolieu
Lastours
Castelnaudary
D118
LANGUEDOC-ROUSSILLON
D629
Villepinte
Moussoulens
Conques-sur-Orbiel
Canal du Midi
Alzonne
D6113
Villemoustaussou
M8
Pennautier
A61
Bram
Villasavary
Puy de Faucher
415
Carcassonne
Trèbes
France
Around the Montagne Noire
Montréal
Cazilhac
Floure
Spain
Fanjeaux
Lavalette
A61
D623
D118
Razès
Preixan
Leuc

Attraction
Large Town
Small Town
Motorway
Main Road
Minor Road
Railway

**La Maison du Bois et du Jouet €€**
*Moulin de l'Oule, Val d'Hautpoul; tel: 05 63 61 42 70; email: jhb@hautpoul.org; www.hautpoul.org. Open daily Jul–Aug; Wed & Sat–Sun afternoons Sept–Jun.*

moved down into the valley, which actually proved to be more convenient for their occupation of making cloth.

The village's survival today depends largely on making wooden toys. Visitors can watch craftsmen at work in the Maison de l'Artisanat craft shop. In the valley, **La Maison du Bois et du Jouet** is a vivid modern exhibition about wood, including toys from around the world.

## MAZAMET

**Mazamet Tourist Information** *rue des Casernes; tel: 05 63 61 27 07; email: office-tourisme.mazamet@imsnet.fr; www.tourisme-mazamet.com. Open daily Jul–Aug; Mon–Sat Sept–Jun. Includes an exhibition about the Cathars.*

Gateway to the Montagne Noire, Mazamet is a comparatively large industrial town with a pleasant part-pedestrianised centre. It thrives on its textile industry, which was originally established in the Arnette Valley after the nearby hilltop village of Hautpoul was sacked.

Today the town is known particularly for dressing imported pelts. The process of separating wool from the hide of dead animals was developed locally during the 19th century and brought considerable prosperity. Grand mansions are dotted in the wooded hillsides around the town, owned by well-to-do families whose forebears made their

**Maison des Mémoires de Mazamet** € *rue des Casernes; tel: 05 63 61 31 52; email: contact@maison-memoires.com; www.maison-memoires.com. Open Tue–Sun Mar–Dec.*

**Market** *Tue & Sat mornings.*

Although there are bargain leather shops on the northeast side of the town along avenue de la Chevalière, few of the garments they sell are locally made.

**Below**
Revel's covered market

fortunes then. The museum in **Maison des Mémoires de Mazamet** covers the Cathars and the area's many ruined castles.

## Accommodation and food in Mazamet

**Le Boulevard** €€ *24 boulevard Soult; tel: 05 63 61 16 08; email: leboulevard@orange.fr. Open all year.* Long-established 14-room hotel on the edge of the town centre with traditional cooking.

### Mazamet

Mazamet's tanning and textile industries took off about 150 years ago by accident after some imported sheepskins went mouldy. This made the wool drop off the hide. No need to shear sheep if you can process the wool after the animals are dead – and you have the hide to tan as well. A group of local entrepreneurs perfected the technique and proceeded to buy up skins from around the world, importing them from as far afield as Australia and Argentina. The bonus was only having to pay knock-down prices as the sheep had been slaughtered for meat or because of disease.

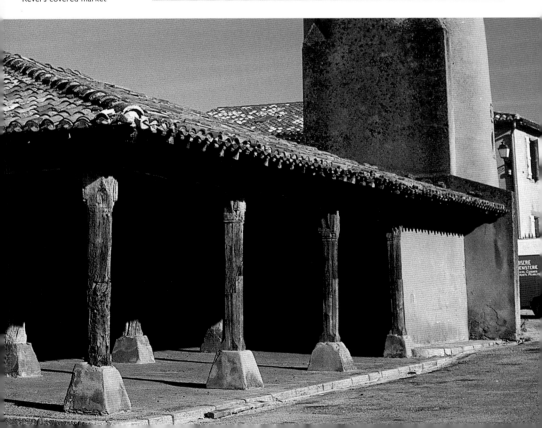

# REVEL

**Revel Tourist Information** *Le Beffroi, place Philippe VI de Valois; tel: 05 34 66 67 68; email: tourisme-revel@revel-lauragais.com; www.tourisme-revel.com. Open daily all year. Ask for the excellent town trail leaflet.*

**Market** *Sat morning* brims with local produce; around Christmas this is the place to buy ducks, geese and foie gras.

This attractive old town, laid out in *bastide* style, is one of the most striking in the area. Dating from 1342, it has a grid of straight streets around a large square surrounded by arcades supported by pillars of wood, brick or stone. Above them, the attractive old buildings have decorative wrought-iron balconies. The splendid 600-year-old market hall, each side 40m long, in the centre has a tiled roof topped by a neoclassical belfry (which replaced an earlier one in 1830). Today the town is famous for its cabinet-making, particularly marquetry and lacquerwork. This developed after Alexandre Monoury, a young craftsman from Versailles, set up a studio in 1888. Locally made furniture is on sale in workshops and shops. The museum at the **Conservatoire des Métiers du Bois**, where marquetry is taught, is open to the public.

**Conservatoire des Métiers du Bois €**
*13 rue Jean Moulin; tel: 05 61 27 65 50; http://cmbois.free.fr/fr/prestation.htm. Open daily all year.*

To buy furniture, try **Revel Art & Meuble** *(tel: 05 61 83 56 58)* at the roundabout on the road to Castelnaudary. *Open Mon–Sat all year.*

## Accommodation and food in Revel

**Auberge des Mazies €€** *route de Castres (on the D622 3km northeast of the town); tel: 05 61 24 04 38; email: bienvenue@mazies.com; www.mazies.com. Open all year.* Comfortably converted old farmhouse (seven rooms) with regional cooking which includes *cassoulet grillé au flambadou* and *confit de canard.*

# SAISSAC

**Saissac Tourist Information** *1 place des Tours; tel: 04 68 24 46 01; www.saissac.fr. Open daily Apr–Oct; Sat–Sun Nov–Dec & Feb–Mar.*

**Château de Saissac €** has an exhibition on medieval treasures and the history of the village. *Open daily Feb–Dec.*

Perched on a ridge above the River Vernassonne, this large grey hillside village straggles beside the ruins of its 15th-century castle. The terrace on the ramparts provides a wonderful view south over the river gorge.

## Accommodation and food in Saissac

**Hôtel de la Comtadine €€** *Lac de Saint Ferréol; tel: 05 61 89 73 03; email: contact@lacomtadine.com; www.lacomtadine.com. Open all year.* Delightfully situated, 8km northwest of Saissac, by the Saint Ferréol lake opposite the Montagne Noire, this nine-room hotel has a garden with outdoor pool.

# SOREZE

**Sorèze Tourist Information** *rue St-Martin; tel: 05 63 74 16 28; email: tourisme@ville-soreze.fr; www.ville-soreze.fr. Open daily all year.*

**L'Abbaye-Ecole €** *rue St-Martin; tel: 05 63 50 86 38; email: abbaye-ecole.soreze@cg81.fr; www.abbayeecoledesoreze.com. Open daily all year.*

This little town on the edge of the Haut Languedoc Regional Park is best known for **L'Abbaye-Ecole**, its abbey school, which was founded in 1638 by Benedictine monks. King Louis XVI turned it into an elite military academy in 1776 but after the French Revolution it reverted to being a school. After many ups and downs, it finally closed in 1991 but the opulent buildings, including cloisters, huge reception rooms and the church, are gradually being restored and some are open to the public. One wing has been transformed into a hotel. Only the bell tower of St-Martin, the original abbey nearby, survived the Wars of Religion in the 1570s. In the town centre, the rows of half-timbered houses with upper floors overhanging the narrow streets mostly date from the 17th century.

**Left**
L'Abbaye-Ecole of Sorèze

**Le Musée Municipal**
*Maison du Parc Régional, 4 allée de la Libération; tel: 05 63 74 11 58. Open Wed–Mon Jul–Sept; Sat–Sun Oct–Jun.* Exhibits local art and craft, especially artistic glass objects.

### Accommodation and food in Sorèze

**Hostellerie Abbaye Ecole de Sorèze €€** *18 rue Lacordaire; tel: 05 63 74 44 80; email: reception@hotelfp-soreze.com; www.hotelfp-soreze.com. Open all year.* Fifty-two rooms in the remarkable surroundings of the town's 17th-century former abbey school. Also a restaurant in the old refectory (*open Wed–Mon*). A further 17 simpler but equally tasteful rooms are available in the Pavillon des Hôtes annexe (€).

## Suggested tour

**Total distance:** 145km. The detour to Arfons adds 20km and the detour to Hautpoul adds 8km.

**Time:** 5 hours' driving. Allow at least a day for the main route, more with detours. Those with limited time should concentrate on the stretch between Revel and Fontbruno.

**Links to other tours:** From Revel, the D622 leads west to St-Félix-Lauragais (*see page 168*), 10km away. From Mazamet, the N112 leads northwest to Castres (*see page 182*), 17km away.

**Above**
Revel

**Opposite**
Sorèze

Head northwest through **Carcassonne**'s industrial outskirts on the
N113, forking right on to the D629 with the distant hills of
the Montagne Noire to the right. Pause in **Montolieu** to look in the
village church with its distinctive Stations of the Cross paintings. After
crossing the River Alzeau, you begin the scenic climb over rolling
farmland to **SAISSAC ❶**.

**Detour: Arfons**, a delightful mountain village of slate-roofed houses
(10km north of Saissac on the D4), was once owned by the Knights of
St John. The octagonal tower of its 17th-century church is unusual as
the four sides most exposed to the weather are covered by large slate
tiles. The village, in the heart of the Montagne Noire, is popular with
walkers – the GR7 long-distance footpath passes through it. On the
way there the D4 passes close to the **Bassin du Lampy**, a large
reservoir created between 1778 and 1782 to provide more water for
the Canal du Midi, which needed extra supplies after the opening of
the Robine branch to Narbonne. The beech woods around the Bassin
are ideal for a walk in the shade. At the start of the turn-off to Arfons,
look out for the deer farm/restaurant (on the right) at **Picarel le Haut**,
where 300 deer are reared in wooded parkland.

**La Renaissance €€**
*St-Ferréol; tel: 05 61
83 51 50; email: contact@
hotellarenaissance.fr;
www.hotellarenaissance.fr.
Open mid-Mar–Sept.*
Seventeen-room family-run
hotel scenically situated
near the lake and its beach.
Garden and playground.

From Saissac, the D629 continues northwest past the **Barrage des Cammazes**, a dam built across the River Sor to create a reservoir to supply drinking water and irrigate the fertile Lauragais plain east of Toulouse. Beyond it the D629 passes the pretty **Bassin de St-Ferréol** lake shortly before **REVEL**.

From Revel, take the D85 east to **SOREZE** ❷. **Durfort**, the neighbouring village, has revived the local tradition of copper-beating and you can call at one of the workshops making pots and pans. From Sorèze, the D85 continues to **DOURGNE** ❸ past a huge quarry which has made a real scar on the landscape. On the far side of Dourgne, just after passing the two monasteries at **Calcat**, turn right to go up an unnumbered road through **Massaguel** to **Fontbruno**. During World War II the Resistance was active in this hilly area, making full use of the thick cover provided by the beeches, oaks and firs of its forests. On reaching the D56, turn right briefly to see the big **Resistance memorial** which commemorates the heroism of the local men who died harassing the Germans. Turn round and follow the D56 to its junction with the D53 to go into **MAZAMET** ❹.

**Detour:** Leave Mazamet on the D54 and then turn right (as signed) past disused tanneries – somewhat depressing – and wind up to the hilltop village of **HAUTPOUL** ❺.

The D118 from Mazamet is a pleasingly quiet main road and very scenic, climbing through wooded hillsides. Beyond **Les Martys** the countryside opens out with views ahead to the Corbières hills. There's a southern feel to the vegetation and villages as the road runs south along the ridges back towards Carcassonne, before finally dropping down into the busy northern outskirts of the town.

**Below**
The Canal du Midi

## Getting out of the car

Surrounded by wooded hillsides, the Bassin de St-Ferréol is the main water source for the Canal du Midi. As the water is crystal clear, it is popular for swimming in summer as well as for sailing and windsurfing. A shaded footpath goes round its banks and across the 800m-long dam. The full circuit, passing a park with waterfalls, takes about an hour to walk round. At the eastern end, there is an attractive beach with sand and children's boats. There's a large car park on the D629 near the beach.

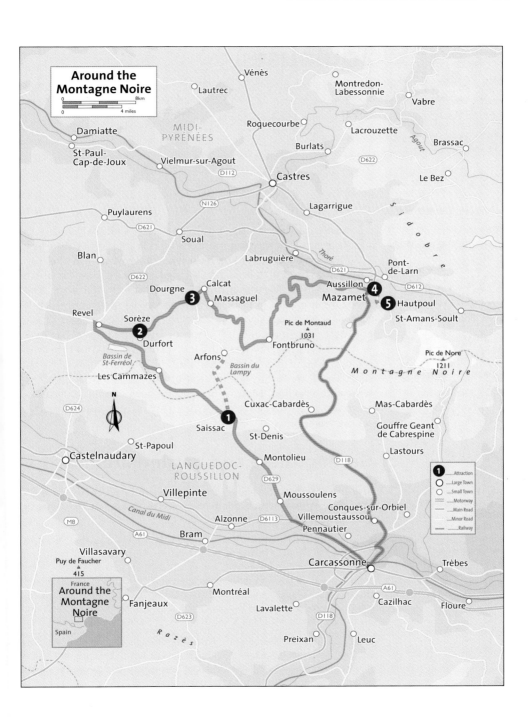

## Around the Montagne Noire

0          8km
0          4 miles

Vénès
Lautrec
Montredon-Labessonnie
Vabre
Roquecourbe
Lacrouzette
Damiatte
MIDI-PYRÉNÉES
Brassac
St-Paul-Cap-de-Joux
Burlats
D622
Vielmur-sur-Agout
Le Bez
D112
Castres
Agout
N126
Lagarrigue
Puylaurens
S i d o b r e
D621
Soual
Blan
Labruguière
Pont-de-Larn
D622
Calcat
Aussillon
D612
Dourgne
**3**
Massaguel
Mazamet
**4**
Revel
Sorèze
**5** Hautpoul
**2**
Durfort
Pic de Montaud
St-Amans-Soult
Bassin de St-Ferréol
Arfons
1031
Fontbruno
Pic de Nore
Bassin du Lampy
1211
Les Cammazes
M o n t a g n e   N o i r e
D624
N
Cuxac-Cabardès
Mas-Cabardès
**1**
Gouffre Geant de Cabrespine
Saissac
St-Denis
St-Papoul
Lastours
Castelnaudary
Montolieu
D118
LANGUEDOC-ROUSSILLON
D629
Villepinte
Moussoulens
Conques-sur-Orbiel
Canal du Midi
Alzonne
D6113
Villemoustaussou
M8
Pennautier
A61
Bram
Villasavary
Puy de Faucher
415
Carcassonne
Trèbes
France
Around the Montagne Noire
Montréal
Cazilhac
Fanjeaux
Lavalette
Floure
D623
A61
D118
Spain
R a z è s
Preixan
Leuc

**1** Attraction
○ Large Town
○ Small Town
Motorway
Main Road
Minor Road
Railway

# Toulouse

## Ratings

Architecture ●●●●●

Food
and drink ●●●●●

Art ●●●●○

Shopping ●●●●○

Entertainment ●●●○○

History ●●●○○

Museums ●●●○○

Children ●○○○○

T hanks largely to its highly successful aircraft industry, Toulouse is a thriving modern city – France's fourth largest. Woad production (to make blue dye) made it rich in the 17th century after 200 years of skirmishing, the plague and a disastrous fire. The magnificent residences that remain from that time are built in brick, giving the city its nickname – *la ville rose*. The colourful skyline is at its most vivid in the setting sun and best seen from the left bank of the broad River Garonne, which curves its way past the city centre. The Canal du Midi sweeps around it on the other side, linked to the river by the short Canal de la Brienne, so there's plenty of opportunity for waterside strolling. Months of sunshine also enable Toulousains to make the most of the terrace restaurants and the city's renowned cuisine.

## Getting there and getting around

**ⓘ Toulouse Tourist Information** *Donjon du Capitole, square Charles de Gaulle; tel: 05 61 11 02 22; email: infos@ot-toulouse.fr; www.toulouse-tourisme.com, www.ot-toulouse.fr. Open daily all year.*

The most straightforward routes into the city centre from the autoroute system which encircles it are from the west and north, particularly exit 30 (Ponts Jumeaux).

**By air**: Toulouse-Blagnac is 10km west of the city centre. There are flights to 20 domestic airports and various European ones including London Gatwick. Buses run every 20 minutes to the city centre Monday–Friday (weekend frequency depends on flights) with stops at the bus station (next to the Matibau railway station), allée Jean Jaurès, places Jeanne d'Arc and Compans Caffarelli. Information can be found on the ground floor of Hall 2; *tel: 01 70 46 74 74; www.toulouse.aeroport.fr*

Buses and the two Métro lines, with interchangeable zoned tickets, are run by Tisséo; *tel: 05 61 41 70 70*. Carnets of ten tickets are best value. A new tram line serving the north of the city is due to open in 2011 and later to be extended into the city centre.

**Toulouse**

| 0 | | 100 metres |
|---|---|---|
| 0 | | 100 yards |

PLACE ST-JULIEN

RUE DES SALENQUES

RUE E. CARTAILHAC

PLACE ST-SERNIN

Basilique St-Sernin

RUE BELLEGARDE

Musée St-Raymond

Canals

RUE D'ALSACE-LORRAINE

BOULEVARD DE STRASBOURG

RUE DENFERT-ROCHEREAU

ALLÉES JEAN JAURÈS

ALLÉES JEAN JAURÈS

N

RUE A. LAUTMANN

RUE DES LOIS

RUE DU TAUR

RUE DE RÉMUSAT

RUE GABRIEL

RUE D'AVILLE

RUE DE LA BASTIE

Eglise Notre-Dame du Taur

Hôtel de Ville

RUE LA FAYETTE

PLACE WILSON

RUE ROMIGUIÈRES

RUE PARGAMINIÈRES

Le Capitole

i

RUE LAPEYROUSE

RUE DU POIDS DE L'HUILE

Couvent des Jacobins

RUE LAKANAL

Musée du Vieux Toulouse

RUE ST-RÔME

RUE DE LA POMME

RUE D'ALSACE-LORRAINE

PLACE ST-GEORGES

Cité de l'Espace

RUE MALBEC

RUE PEYROLIÈRES

RUE ST-URSULE

RUE PEYRAS

RUE DES ARTS

RUE D'ASTORG

La Daurade

Hôtel d'Assézat

RUE DES CHANGES

Musée des Augustins

RUE DE METZ

Beaux Arts

PLACE ESQUIROL

Centre Municipale de l'Affiche

RUE DE METZ

Ch. de Commerce

Cathédrale St-Etienne

PONT NEUF

RUE CROIX BARAGNON

Galerie Municipale du Château d'Eau

RUE DES COUTELIERS

RUE DES PARADOUX

RUE DES FILATIERS

PLACE ROUAIX

PLACE ST-JACQUES

PLACE NINAU

COURS DILLON

Garonne

QUAI DE TOUNIS

RUE DE LA CARONNETTE

PLACE DES CARMES

RUE DU LANGUEDOC

RUE D'AUSSARGUES

RUE PERCHEPINTE

RUE VÉLANE

Prairie des Filtres

La Dalbade

RUE ST-JEAN

RUE DES PRÊTRES

PLACE DES CARMES

RUE DU PHARAON

GRANDE RUE NAZARETH

RUE OZENNE

RUE ESCOUSSIÈRES MONTGAILLARD

RUE JULES DE RESSÉGUIER

Musée Paul Dupuy

RUE DE LA DALBADE

O Attraction

Important Building

Park

Main Road

Other Road

i Information

PONT DE HALAGE DE TOUNIS

PLACE DU SALIN

RUE DU LANGUEDOC

ALLÉES JULES GUESDE

ALLÉES JULES GUESDE

Jardin des Plantes

Musée d'Histoire Naturelle

**By train:** The main railway station, Gare Matabiau, is in boulevard Pierre Sémard, just across the Canal du Midi from the centre. Facilities include car hire and showers. Four TGV trains a day connect with Paris (5 hours).

**Parking:** Though the city boasts 10,000 parking spaces, on-street places in the centre are hard to find (most are pay-and-display but free Sunday) so head for an underground car park. The handiest for sightseeing and shopping are at place Victor Hugo and place du Capitole from which the main sights are all within walking distance. Or you can park free at either end of the Métro underground line which crosses the city centre.

**Cycle hire:** Bikes can be picked up for rental at 250 cycle stations dotted around the city centre (over 13 years old only); *tel: 05 34 30 23 54; www.velo.toulouse.fr*

# Sights

ⓝ **Basilique St-Sernin**
*place St-Sernin;*
*tel: 05 61 21 80 45. Open*
*daily all year. Admission free.*

The city's most interesting sights are compactly gathered within the centre, which is encircled by grand boulevards and has the River Garonne cutting through its west side. Be prepared for a lengthy walk to see them all on foot. Allow time, too, for the distractions offered by the shops and pavement cafés on the way.

### Basilique St-Sernin
This massive Romanesque cathedral – all that remains of an 11th-century monastery on the pilgrimage route to Santiago de Compostela – is one of the most beautiful churches in France. Built in pink brick and yellow stone, it is crowned by a 65m-high octagonal bell tower which has five elegant tiers of arched windows topped by a spire.

**Below**
Basilique St-Sernin

Inside, honey-coloured stone sets off a high barrel-vaulted nave and prettily vaulted galleries. After much public debate, the 'improvements' made during the 19th century by Viollet-le-Duc were removed during repairs, so the building is now back to its superb original state.

### Canals
The first section of the Canal du Midi linking the city with the Mediterranean was opened in May 1681. Ninety years later it was linked to the River Garonne by the short Canal de la Brienne. Then in 1856 its second 'leg', the Lateral Canal, was completed, extending it to the Atlantic at Bordeaux. The twin bridges at the river basin, built in 1774, are decorated

River cruises aboard *Baladines*; tel: 05 61 80 22 26; email: contact@bateaux-toulousains.com; www.bateaux-toulousains.com. Lunch and dinner cruises aboard restaurant-boat *Occitania*: 4 boulevard Bonrepos; tel: 05 61 63 06 06; www.loccitania.fr; reservations essential.

**Le Capitole** place du Capitole; tel: 05 61 22 34 12. Interior rooms open daily by reservation only.

**Cathédrale St-Etienne** place St-Etienne; tel: 05 61 52 03 82. Open daily all year. Treasury in the crypt €.

**Centre Municipale de l'Affiche** €€ Espace St-Cyprien, 58 allées Charles-de-Fitte; tel: 05 61 59 24 64. Open Mon–Fri all year.

**Cité de l'Espace** €€ avenue Jean Gonord; tel: 08 20 37 72 23; www.cite-espace.com. Open daily Feb–Aug; Tue–Sun Sept–Jan. Twenty-minute journey by Métro to Jolimont, then bus No 37, or take exit 17 from the autoroute.

**Couvent des Jacobins** place des Jacobins; tel: 05 61 22 21 92. Refectory open daily all year.

with an elaborate bas-relief in white marble by François Lucas, a local sculptor. For a walk or cycle ride along the shaded towpath, head northwest rather than southeast where the countryside around is very flat.

## Le Capitole

The town hall, named after the *capitouls* – consuls – who once ran the city on behalf of the often absent count of Toulouse, is an impressive symmetrical 18th-century building in pink brick and white stone with three rows of windows and a balustrade along the top. Inside, several appropriately grand rooms, Salles des Illustres, hung with paintings depicting the city's history are open to the public. Across a courtyard, the tourist office occupies part of the original keep.

## Cathédrale St-Etienne

Red brick outside, grey stone inside, the city's other cathedral took several centuries to build because of financial problems – and it shows! The mixture of styles, starting in the 11th century, combine to make an interesting if rather odd unity and it now needs more money for restoration. Pierre-Paul Riquet (*see page 197*), who built the Canal du Midi, is buried in front of the massive stone pillar which stands between the unaligned chancel and gloomy nave where tapestries tell the story of Etienne (Stephen).

## Centre Municipale de l'Affiche

Posters and postcards are the subject of this unusual modern museum. Annual exhibitions are devoted to contemporary graphic artists.

## Cité de l'Espace

This exciting space park is a showcase for the city's aviation achievements during the 20th century. Its highlights are full-scale models of the Ariane 5 rocket on its launch pad and the Mir Space Station which shows the cramped conditions for the astronauts on board. There are plenty of buttons and computer screens, so budding young scientists – and adults – can experience what it's like to launch a rocket and 'post' a satellite. There's also a planetarium.

## Couvent des Jacobins

The only decorative feature of this huge fortress-like church, built in countless thin bricks with slits for windows, is its five-tier hexagonal belfry. Founded in honour of St Dominic's visit to preach in the city in 1230, it has a massive nave with two beautiful rose windows which is a Southern Gothic masterpiece. Huge grey columns rise along each side to ribbed vaults like palm trees; indeed, the most distinctive is known as the *palmier des Jacobins*. The tomb of St Thomas Aquinas, one of Toulouse University's first and most illustrious students, lies beneath the altar.

**① Eglise Notre-Dame du Taur** *rue du Taur.*

**Galerie Municipale du Château d'Eau €** *1 place Laganne; tel: 05 61 77 09 40; www.galeriechateaudeau. org. Open Tue–Sat afternoons all year.*

**Hôtel d'Assézat €€** *place d'Assézat; tel: 05 61 12 06 89. Open Tue–Sun all year, including Thur evening.*

**Jardin des Plantes** and **Musée d'Histoire Naturelle €** *35 allées Jules Guesde; tel: 05 67 73 84 84; www.museum.toulouse.fr*

**Musée des Augustins €** *21 rue de Metz; tel: 05 61 22 21 82; email: augustins@mairie-toulouse.fr; www. augustins.org. Open Wed–Mon all year (organ concert on Wed evening). Admission free on first Sun of the month.*

**Les Abattoirs €€** *76 allées Charles-de-Fitte; tel: 05 62 48 58 00; email: lesabattoirs@lesabattoirs.org; www.lesabattoirs.org. Open Wed–Sun all year 1100–1900. Métro: St Cyprien. Admission free on first Sun of the month.* Modern art gallery on the left bank of the Garonne, which now houses permanent and temporary exhibitions of experimental art.

The church and its convent buildings have had a considerably more diverse use than most. Napoleon gave it to one of his artillery regiments as a barracks. The soldiers and their 300 horses made themselves nicely at home, finding the beautiful arcaded cloisters ideal as a paddock and using the chapter house as a smithy. In the church itself they put in an extra mezzanine floor, blocked up the windows and demolished most of the side chapels. Not surprisingly, the restoration work after they left in 1864 took a lot of effort and time but finally the church was reconsecrated in 1974. The chapter house is used for concerts and the refectory for exhibitions.

### Eglise Notre-Dame du Taur

This old church is notable for its decorative brickwork, particularly its turret-like bell tower and façade of mitred arches in Southern Gothic style, which was subsequently copied in other churches throughout the area. It stands at the place where St Sernin, who brought Christianity to the city, died a martyr's death after denouncing paganism. He is reputed to have been dragged across the city attached to a bull.

### Galerie Municipale du Château d'Eau

The city's former water tower, built in 1822 to purify the local water, was adapted in 1974 to become a photographic gallery which regularly stages special exhibitions. It has also built up a unique archive on the history of photography.

### Hôtel d'Assézat

This is one of the most impressive of about 80 grand mansions built by wealthy merchants and lawyers during the boom times of the 16th century. Designed around a large courtyard by a well-known Renaissance architect, Nicholas Bachelier, it now houses the Fondation Bemberg art collection built up by Georges Bemberg, a local industrialist. On show there since 1995, it includes works by great masters such as Tintoretto, Canaletto and Gauguin.

### Jardin des Plantes

These formally laid-out gardens are an oasis of greenery with their avenues of flowerbeds and ponds. The **Musée d'Histoire Naturelle** in them is renowned for its collection of stuffed monkeys. One room is devoted to skeletons and it is fascinating to compare their shapes and sizes when you see all the bones but no skin.

### Musée des Augustins

The Musée des Augustins occupies another of Toulouse's former monasteries. The 600-year-old building itself is of interest as well as its contents. The rooms display decorative stonework, sculptures and paintings from the Middle Ages collected from various places, particularly churches, in the region. The large garden in the centre of

**Musée du Vieux Toulouse** € 7 rue du May; tel: 05 62 27 11 50. Open Mon–Sat afternoons mid-May–mid-Oct.

**Musée Paul Dupuy** €
13 rue de la Pleau (corner of rue Ozenne); tel: 05 61 14 65 50. Open Wed–Mon all year. Admission free first Sun of the month.

**Musée St-Raymond** €
place St-Sernin; tel: 05 61 22 31 44; www. saintraymond.toulouse.fr. Open daily all year.

the cloister is planted with vegetables and herbs that would have been grown in medieval abbeys. A row of gargoyles along one side of it provides a rare close-up of these decorative stone creatures which are normally at roof level serving as water spouts.

### Musée du Vieux Toulouse
Housed in a fine 16th-century mansion, L'Hôtel Dumay, this museum tells the story of Toulouse, its personalities, institutions, crafts and customs, mainly through paintings, sculptures and pottery.

### Musée Paul Dupuy
This small 17th-century mansion contains an exquisite collection of antique silver, china, scientific instruments and clocks (still keeping good time) donated to the city by M Dupuy, a local collector, in 1944. One section is a reconstructed pharmacy with old-fashioned medicine bottles and jars.

### Musée St-Raymond
One of France's most comprehensive collections of Greek, Roman and local antiquities including sculpture, stone carvings and pottery can be found in a medieval building, itself classed as a 'Monument Historique' having been built as a hospice for pilgrims at the same time as St-Sernin cathedral opposite.

# Shopping

The city has some memorable markets such as the one which sells food and wine in **Victor Hugo market hall** and the open-air **Marché des Boulevards** along the boulevard de Strasbourg whose stalls are colourfully piled with fruit and vegetables. Both operate *Tue–Sun*. Place du Capitole has markets on *Tue–Wed & Sat*. Bric-a-brac stalls surround St-Sernin at weekends. Place St- Etienne is taken over by books on Saturdays. In addition, place du Parlement is the scene of a seasonal garlic market from the end of August to mid-October.

**Below**
Hone your bartering skills at one of Toulouse's markets

The main shopping area, including several department stores, is along rue d'Alsace-Lorraine (**Galeries Lafayette** is at the northern end). The more exclusive clothes shops are off it in rue de la Pomme and rue des Arts. Crystallised violets are a local speciality; **Yves Thuriès** (*69 rue d'Alsace-Lorraine and 17 rue de la Pomme; tel: 05 61 29 02 82*) claims to have the best in France.

Rugby fans can invest in the local strip for men, women and children at **Éspace Stade Toulousain** (*75 rue d'Alsace-Lorraine; tel: 05 61 21 67 81*).

## Bricks galore

Toulouse, *la ville rose*, got its nickname from the colour of its many brick buildings, though they range from beige through pink to russet and red. The scarcity of stone available in the area first prompted the Romans to make the characteristic long thin bricks out of the local clay. Originally, these were made by hand, as in Italy, in wooden moulds, giving Toulouse the most Italian look of any city in France. In 1555, following a series of fires, a by-law required all new buildings to be built in brick or stone rather than wood. As brick is light and mortar sticks to it easily, masons were able to construct churches with wide vaults that could span a single nave. This became the main feature of the Southern Gothic style of architecture.

# Entertainment

The city boasts ten theatres including **Halle aux Grains** (*place Dupuy; tel: 05 61 63 13 13*), which stages opera and ballet, and **Théâtre du Capitole** (*place du Capitole; tel: 05 61 63 13 13; www.theatre-du-capitole.org*), the home of lighter music, particularly operetta and dance. **Stade Toulousain**, where the city's famous rugby club plays, is on an island in the River Garonne. The weekly listings magazine *Toulouse by Night* is on sale at newsagents.

In June, the **Garonna** is a one-day event on the river when up to a hundred home-made rafts are raced by costumed sailors to the Pont Neuf.

The four-day **Rio Loco Festival** (*enquiries tel: 05 61 32 77 28*) featuring riverside concerts is also in June, followed by **Toulouse d'Été** when music of all kinds is performed in various venues.

During October an **Organ Festival** highlights the importance of the town's historical organs.

# Accommodation and food

A good selection of centrally situated two-star hotels in smartly renovated old buildings is to be found around place du Capitole and place Wilson. Modern hotels, with the advantage of easier parking, are along allées Jean Jaurès or further out.

**Hôtel St-Sernin** € *2 rue St-Bernard; tel: 05 61 21 73 08; www.hotelstsernin.com. Open all year.* Small, impeccably furnished hotel in a quiet street near St-Sernin cathedral. Four rooms have splendid views of its tower. Eighteen rooms.

**Best Western Les Capitouls** €€ *29 allées Jean Jaurès; tel: 05 34 41 31 21; email: contact@hotel-capitouls.com; www.bestwestern-capitouls.com. Open all year.* A friendly but businesslike hotel – not at all grand – with typically French atmosphere. Situated on the edge of the main shopping area.

**Hôtel des Beaux Arts** €€ *1 place du Pont Neuf; tel: 05 34 45 42 42; email: contact@hoteldesbeauxarts.com; www.hoteldesbeauxarts.com. Open all year.* Overlooking the River Garonne, this is an exclusive little hotel with smart décor and attentive service. Nineteen rooms.

**Grand Hôtel de l'Opéra** €€€ *1 place du Capitole; tel: 05 61 21 82 66; email: opera@guichard.fr; www.grand-hotel-opera.com. Open all year.* The city's grandest hotel is centrally situated in a stately 17th-century building which began life as a monastery. Fifty rooms.

**Hôtel du Grand Balcon** €€€ *8 rue Romiguières; tel: 05 34 25 44 09; email: info@grandbalconhotel.com; www.grandbalconhotel.com. Open all* *year*. Luxuriously refurbished in 1930s style, this 47-room hotel in the heart of the city includes a suite dedicated to its most celebrated guest of that era, the writer and pioneer pilot, Antoine de Saint-Exupéry.

**Hôtel Pullman €€€** *84 allées Jean Jaurès; tel: 05 61 10 23 10; email: H1091@accor.com; www.decorhotels.com. Open all year.* All the comforts of a large modern hotel within a 5-minute stroll of the main shops and restaurants. Non-smoking floors and parking. One hundred and nineteen rooms.

The Toulousains have a reputation for being both gourmands and gourmets. Two hundred years ago they formed the first gastronomic association in France and you can always rely on eating copiously and well. Duck, goose and fish are served in abundance and the local sausages are without equal. So, too, is the foie gras spiked with truffles and baked in flaky pastry. Brasserie restaurants spill out on to most of the squares. Some, particularly around place du Capitole, are ideal for watching the world go by but others, such as those around place Wilson and place St-Georges, are more intimate.

**Le Bon Vivre €** *15 place Wilson; tel: 05 61 23 07 17; email: contact@lebonvivre.com; www.lebonvivre.com. Open daily all year.* A small friendly restaurant serving local specialities, popular with local people.

**Taverne de Maître Kanter €** *54 allées Jean Jaurès; tel: 05 62 73 16 16; www.tmk-toulouse.com. Open 24 hours.* Three hundred and fifty places, specialising in seafood, sauerkraut and regional dishes.

**Le Van Gogh €** *21 place St-Georges; tel: 05 61 21 03 15. Open daily all year.* Small brasserie in shaded square. Enormous salads.

**Brasserie des Beaux Arts Flo €€** *1 rue de la Daurade; tel: 05 61 21 12 12; email: accueil.tourisme@orange.fr; www.brasseriedesbeauxarts.com. Open daily all year.* Bustling Parisian-style brasserie with efficient service, plush bench seats and gilded mirrors. Strong on oysters and seafood, as well as local dishes.

**Below**
L'Hôtel d'Assézat

**Villa Tropezienne €€** *8–10 place Victor Hugo; tel: 05 61 22 58 58; email: info@jpgroup.com; www.villa-tropezienne.com. Open daily all year.* Matelot-dressed waiters scurry to serve Provençal dishes, especially fish, from a simple menu. Jolly atmosphere enhanced by photographs of sunny St-Tropez.

**Sept Place St-Sernin €€€** *7 place St-Sernin; tel: 05 62 30 05 30; www.7placesaintsernin.com. Open Mon–Sat all year.* Chic modern restaurant in a secluded setting opposite the cathedral. Its set menus are strong on seafood.

**Aérospatiale** *Usine Clément Ader, Colomiers.* Airbus factory visits are organised Mon–Sat by Taxiway, *tel: 05 34 39 42 00; email: reservation@taxiway.fr; www.taxiway.fr,* and foreign visitors must book eight days in advance with passport details.

**L'Aérothèque** *rue Montmorency; tel: 05 61 93 93 57; www.aerotheque.fr.* An aircraft museum next to the Airbus factory. *Visits Sat–Sun 1400–1700 all year.*

**Toulouse's canals**

The Canal du Midi was first filled with water on 19 May 1681. After being blessed by the archbishop of Toulouse, it was inaugurated by Pierre-Paul Riquet, the pioneering engineer who had the grand idea of linking the Mediterranean at Sète with the Atlantic at Bordeaux. He set off for Sète with his two sons in a large state boat followed by 23 others.

# Suggested walk

**Length:** 3km.

**Duration:** An hour just to go round, but allow a full day to see all the sights.

From the terrace café at the top of **Nouvelles Galeries**, on the corner of **rue Lapeyrouse** and **rue d'Alsace-Lorraine**, you can survey the whole city centre, so it makes a good starting point. Directly below is **place Wilson** with its fountains and shady park benches on one side and the **Donjon du Capitole** (information and maps at the tourist office) on the other. Admire the bronze **Occitan cross** surrounded by signs of the zodiac on the huge traffic-free square in front of **LE CAPITOLE** ❶ (unless it's market day), then head for the arcade on the west side where the city's history is depicted on the ceiling in 29 colourful panels painted by Raymond Moretti in 1997.

The straight narrow rue du Taur of small shops and cafés leads to **BASILIQUE ST-SERNIN** ❷, which stands in the centre of a leafy square. This area on the north side of the centre was originally the clergy district. As you make your way along the rue Cartailhac to place du Peyrou and place Anatole France, notice that it is now dotted with university buildings. Turn left along the rue de la Bastide, rue Pargaminières and rue Lakanal to the **COUVENT DES JACOBINS** ❸.

You are now in the 'merchant' district where several of the splendid Renaissance *hôtels particuliers* (mansions) built by the woad merchants are situated. Look out for **Hôtels de Bernuy** (now a school) in rue Peyrolières and **Assézat** (Fondation Bemberg gallery). Continue along rue des Paradoux and turn right. There are no fewer than 84 old mansions dotted around the city centre including about 10 along rue de la Dalbade, the lawyers' district. Turning along rue St-Jean, you come to one of the most impressive, the **Hôtel du Vieux Raisin**. Continue along rue Ozenne until you reach rue Perchepinte.

Rue Perchepinte and rue Ferma, elegant quiet streets with antique shops, lead to **CATHEDRALE ST-ETIENNE** ❹. After you cross the busy rue de Metz, rue d'Astorg will take you to **place St-Georges** where you might want to linger at a pavement café before facing the temptations of the haute-couture shops along rue de la Pomme.

## Also worth exploring

A tour of the Airbus company's Jean-Luc Lagardère site is not just for aircraft enthusiasts. Looking down from a viewing platform above the factory floor where the world's biggest passenger airliner, the Airbus A380, is assembled is mind-boggling. A conducted tour also takes you to see the final assembly line of other Airbus products, including the long-haul A340 aircraft and the massive Beluga.

Toulouse

0      100 metres
0      100 yards

PLACE ST-JULIEN
RUE DES SALENQUES
PLACE ST-SERNIN
RUE BELLEGARDE
Basilique St-Sernin
Musée St-Raymond
RUE E. CARTAILHAC
RUE DU TAUR
RUE DES LOIS
RUE DEVILLE
RUE DE LA BASTIDE
Canals
BOULEVARD DE STRASBOURG
RUE DENFERT ROCHEREAU
RUE D'ALSACE-LORRAINE
RUE DE RÉMUSAT
ALLÉES JEAN JAURÈS
ALLÉES JEAN JAURÈS
RUE GABRIEL
Eglise Notre-Dame du Taur
Hôtel de Ville
RUE ROMIGUIÈRES
RUE LA FAYETTE
PLACE WILSON
RUE PARGAMINIÈRES
Le Capitole
RUE LA PEYROUSE
Couvent des Jacobins
RUE GAMBETTA
RUE DU POIDS DE L'HUILE
RUE MALBEC
Musée du Vieux Toulouse
RUE ST-ROME
RUE STE-URSULE
RUE DES CHANGES
RUE D'ALSACE-LORRAINE
RUE DE LA POMME
PLACE ST-GEORGES
Cité de l'Espace
RUE D'ASTORG
RUE PEYRAS
Musée des Augustins
RUE DES ARTS
La Daurade
RUE DES PUITS-CLOS
Hôtel d'Assézat
PLACE ESQUIROL
RUE DE METZ
Beaux Arts
Centre Municipale de l'Affiche
PONT NEUF
RUE DE METZ
Ch. de Commerce
RUE CROIX BARAGNON
Cathédrale St-Étienne
RUE NINAU
PLACE ST-JACQUES
Galerie Municipale du Château d'Eau
RUE DES COUTELIERS
RUE DES FILATIERS
PLACE ROUAIX
Garonne
QUAI DILLON
QUAI DE TOUNIS
RUE DE LA DALBADE
RUE DE LA GARONNETTE
RUE DES PRÊTRES
PLACE DES CARMES
PLACE DES CARMES
RUE DU LANGUEDOC
RUE D'AUSSARGUES
RUE PERCHEPINTE
RUE VÉLANE
Praire des Filtres
La Dalbade
RUE ST-JEAN
RUE DU PHARAON
Musée Paul Dupuy
RUE OZENNE
RUE ESCOUSSIÈRES MONTGAILLARD
RUE JULES DE RESSÉGUIER
GRANDE RUE NAZARETH
PLACE DU SALIN
RUE DU LANGUEDOC
PONT DE PALACE DE TOUNIS
ALLÉES JULES GUESDE
ALLÉES JULES GUESDE
Jardin des Plantes
Musée d'Histoire Naturelle

N

1 Attraction
Important Building
Park
Main Road
Other Road
i Information

## Ratings

| | |
|---|---|
| Canals | ●●●●● |
| Churches | ●●●●● |
| Architecture | ●●●●○ |
| Food | ●●●●○ |
| History | ●●●●○ |
| Restaurants | ●●●○○ |
| Scenery | ●●●○○ |
| Shopping | ●●●○○ |

# The land of milk and honey

This is an easy and relaxing route to drive as the area is mainly flat. The roads are often straight and quiet, with long lines of plane trees on both sides. The Canal du Midi, however, and a few gentle hills ensure plenty of variety.

During the 16th century, the area became known as the Pays de Cocagne – the land of milk and honey – as the demand for *pastel* (woad) to make blue dye, then the fashionable colour, brought it considerable prosperity. Local farmers grew the plant in profusion, but now the rich soil is mainly devoted to vegetables.

Although Pamiers is the largest town, with good shops, the gem of the route is Mirepoix with its colourful half-timbered houses and arcades. St-Félix-Lauragais is another highlight, particularly in April when its Foire de la Cocagne (*see page 168*) turns back the clock to celebrate the great times of woad.

## CASTELNAUDARY

**ⓘ Castelnaudary
Tourist Information**
*place de Verdun; tel: 04 68
23 05 73; email: ot@ville-
castelnaudary.fr; www.ville-
castelnaudary.fr. Open daily
all year.*

This is very much a canal town, having thrived since the **Canal du Midi** was cut through it in the 1660s. The council's decision to contribute 30,000 francs to bring it to the foot of the town proved to be a very far-sighted move.

The canal's Grand Bassin, actually more a lake than a basin, used to be a busy commercial port. Now it is used by pleasure craft and there is a constant coming and going of boats all summer. At any time of year the banks are a pleasant place to stroll, especially when the spire of Eglise St-Michel and the red-tiled roofs of the houses round it are reflected in the water.

The canal's arrival enabled the town to build up pottery and brick industries. Several workshops are open to visitors and sell 'seconds'. Among the items to look out for are *cassoles*, the shallow terracotta bowls which gave their name to cassoulet, the town's famous thick pork and bean stew (though both Toulouse and Carcassonne also

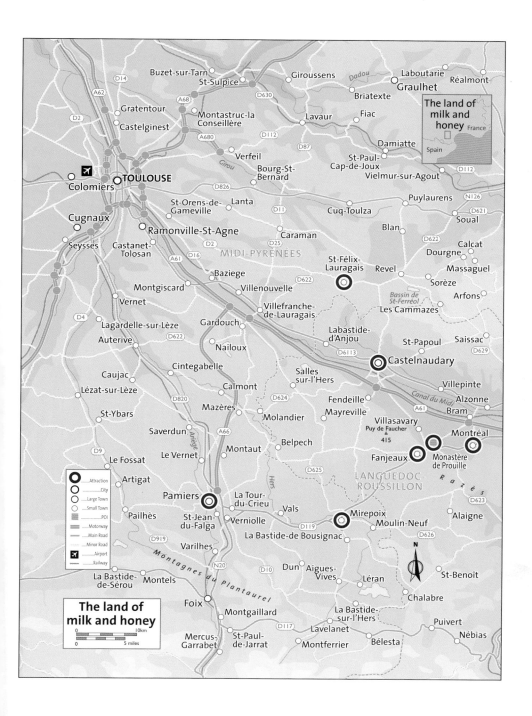

The land of milk and honey France
Spain

Buzet-sur-Tarn
St-Sulpice
Giroussens
*Dadou*
Laboutarie
Graulhet
Réalmont
Briatexte
Gratentour
Montastruc-la Conseillère
Lavaur
Fiac
Castelginest
Damiatte
Verfeil
St-Paul-Cap-de-Joux
Bourg-St-Bernard
Vielmur-sur-Agout
TOULOUSE
Colomiers
Puylaurens
St-Orens-de-Gameville
Lanta
Cuq-Toulza
Soual
Cugnaux
Blan
Calcat
Seysses
Castanet-Tolosan
MIDI-PYRÉNÉES
Dourgne
Massaguel
Ramonville-St-Agne
Caraman
St-Félix-Lauragais
Revel
Sorèze
Baziege
Arfons
Montgiscard
Villenouvelle
*Bassin de St-Ferréol*
Les Cammazes
Vernet
Villefranche-de-Lauragais
Lagardelle-sur-Lèze
Gardouch
Labastide-d'Anjou
St-Papoul
Saissac
Auterive
Nailoux
Castelnaudary
Caujac
Cintegabelle
Salles sur-l'Hers
Villepinte
Lézat-sur-Lèze
Calmont
Fendeille
Alzonne
St-Ybars
Mazères
Mayreville
Bram
Molandier
Villasavary
Puy de Faucher
415
Saverdun
Montréal
Le Fossat
Le Vernet
Montaut
Belpech
Fanjeaux
Monastère de Prouille
Artigat
LANGUEDOC-ROUSSILLON
*Razès*
Pamiers
La Tour-du-Crieu
Vals
Pailhès
St-Jean-du-Falga
Verniolle
Mirepoix
Alaigne
La Bastide-de-Bousignac
Moulin-Neuf
Varilhes
*Montagnes du Plantaurel*
La Bastide-de-Sérou
Montels
Dun
Aigues-Vives
Léran
St-Benoît
Foix
Chalabre
Montgaillard
La Bastide-sur-l'Hers
Puivert
Mercus-Garrabet
St-Paul-de-Jarrat
Lavelanet
Nébias
Montferrier
Bélesta

Attraction
City
Large Town
Small Town
POI
Motorway
Main Road
Minor Road
Airport
Railway

The land of milk and honey

0          10km
0        5 miles

**Canal du Midi** holiday cruisers can be hired from **Le Boat**; *tel: 0844 463 6413 (UK); email: sales@leboat.co.uk; www.leboat.co.uk*. Short trips on *Le Saint-Roch* cruiser from the quai du Port, *daily Apr–Oct*. A website describes, in English, the facilities for enjoying the canal: *www.canal-du-midi.org*

**Moulin de Cugarel** € *Open Jul–Aug*. To organise a visit, contact the tourist office; *tel: 04 68 23 05 73*.

There is a market on Mon.

**Below**
Mirepoix: covered arcades

claim to have invented it). Two other local specialities, *Alleluias* and *Glorias*, are found, not in a church, but at the Pâtisserie Belloc (*48 rue du 11 Novembre*). They are small cakes flavoured with *cédrat*, a kind of grapefruit, which were named in honour of Pope Pius VII's Easter visit shortly after one of Napoleon's soldiers imported the recipe in 1800.

The town has few major sights, though the Eglise St-Michel has a 56m-high belfry, beautiful rose windows and an 18th-century organ built by the Cavaillé-Colls, a Gaillac family who were responsible for installing more than 600 instruments in the area between 1709 and 1889. The **Moulin de Cugarel**, a 300-year-old restored windmill complete with milling machinery, stands on a breezy hillside on the northern edge of the town overlooking flat farmland. Originally, it was one of a ring of flour mills round the town powered by water from the canal.

## Accommodation and food in Castelnaudary

**Hôtel de France** €€ *2 avenue Frédéric Mistral; tel: 04 68 23 10 18; email: hotel@hdefrance.com; www.cassoulet.com. Open all year*. Comfortable family-run 17-room hotel well placed in town centre. Guests who enjoy the chef's award-winning cassoulet and other local dishes can buy them tinned to take home.

**Cassoulet** A website describes the delights of cassoulet, including recipes, in English at *www.cassoulet.com*

## Cassoulet

Pork, mutton, sausage and haricot beans are the key ingredients of cassoulet, which has been described as *le dieu occitan* (the Occitan God). One of the area's most famous and filling dishes, it is a thick stew whose distinctive flavour owes much to goose fat and the local pink garlic.

Traditionally prepared and served in a *cassole* (the shallow terracotta bowl glazed only on the inside from which it got its name), it is by no means straightforward to cook as several lengthy stages are involved, including soaking, boiling and frying.

Castelnaudary is generally regarded as being its birthplace, though Carcassonne and Toulouse also claim the honour. Restaurants throughout the area feature it on their menus, but it can also be enjoyed at home without effort as supermarkets and butchers sell it in tins – usually the meat and juices in one and the beans in another.

# FANJEAUX

**Fanjeaux Tourist Information** *place du Treil; tel: 04 68 24 75 45; email: tourisme@piege-lauragais.fr. Open daily Apr–Sept; Mon–Fri Oct–Mar.*

Enjoying a magnificent view of the Montagne Noire (Black Mountain), this little hilltop town of narrow streets clusters around a covered market hall and the Notre Dame de l'Assomption church. The hill was a sacred place for the Romans; hence the town's name, which is derived from the Latin for 'Temple of Jupiter'. The town also has close connections with St Dominic, who founded the Dominican order. You can visit his 'bedchamber', now a chapel but originally the saddlery of a castle which has long gone. In the church, be sure to look at the *miracle du feu* beam in the St-Dominic, chapel. It was scorched in 1203 when Dominic de Guzman, as he then was, settled a theological dispute between Catholics and Cathars. To test their opposing views, he burnt their texts. The Cathar version ended up as ashes but the Catholic one flew up intact, scorching the beam. Park your car on the edge of the old quarter and walk as the streets are very narrow.

# MIREPOIX

**Mirepoix Tourist Information** *place Maréchal Leclerc; tel: 05 61 68 83 76; email: contact@tourisme-mirepoixcom; www.tourisme-mirepoix.com. Open daily Jul–Aug; Mon–Sat Sept–Jun.*

This attractive little town is a typical *bastide*, built in the shape of a grid around a central square which has a covered market hall with a splendid 19th-century cast-iron roof. Many of the other buildings, 500–600 years old, are half-timbered with sturdy carved beams jutting over ground-floor arcades. With its pavement cafés, the square is a pleasant spot to pass the time of day. The **Cathédrale St-Maurice** was built from 1327 onwards but not consecrated until 1506. Even then its elegant spire had not been completed and the rib vaulting was not

There is a market *Mon & Thur mornings.*

**Festivals** include an Easter jazz festival, medieval re-enactments in *Jul*, a puppet festival in *Aug*, and St-Maurice in *Sept*.

added until the 1860s. Southern Gothic in style, it has the widest nave in France (some say too wide for its length and height), frescoes and a series of rose windows, another late addition, high along the sides.

The town's speciality is Mirepoix sauce, made from onions, carrots and celery. The recipe was first concocted for the duke of Lévis-Mirepoix in the 18th century.

### Accommodation in Mirepoix

**La Maison des Consuls €€€** *6 place des Couverts; tel: 05 61 68 81 81; email: hotel@maisondesconsuls.com; www.maisondesconsuls.com. Open all year.* Small hotel converted from the most beautiful of the buildings which surround the town's 14th-century arcaded square. Perfect vantage point for watching the busy Monday and Thursday morning markets. No restaurant. Garage. Eight rooms, including one suite with a private terrace.

## MONASTERE DE PROUILLE

St Dominic established a community of nuns here in 1206, having spotted the site from Fanjeaux. The large church in the present pink stone monastery, built in 1886, is now bare. Instead, worship takes place in a modern chapel created at one end.

## MONTREAL

**Montréal Tourist Information** *rue de la Mairie; tel: 04 68 76 20 05. Open Mon–Fri all year.*

France has no fewer than five towns called Montréal (meaning 'royal mount') and they have recently formed an association to foster links between each other and their rather bigger sister in Canada. This one has a collegiate church, **St-Vincent**, built in the austere Southern Gothic style – very big and very dark with a single nave decorated with frescoes. The church's fine 18th-century organ was built by Aristide Cavaillé-Coll, a member of the famous organ-building family.

## PAMIERS

**Pamiers Tourist Information** *boulevard Delcassé; tel: 05 61 67 52 52; email: info@ot-pamiers.fr; www.ot-pamiers.fr. Open Mon–Sat all year.*

Markets on *Tue, Thur & Sat.*

The largest town on the route, this is the place to head for to go shopping, particularly as it is not at all 'touristy'. Its most distinctive features are the towers of its four monastery churches and the large red-brick Cathédrale St-Antonin, which has a 49-bell carillon in its octagonal belfry, which once served as a watchtower. The canal which skirts the town centre near the tourist office is one of the few hangovers from the Middle Ages when it was built for defence and to provide water for mills; it linked with the nearby River Ariège, which was then navigable.

**Previous page**
Pamiers, Notre Dame du Camp

**Opposite**
St-Félix-Lauragais

The town's role as the base of the dreaded anti-Cathar Inquisition in the 13th century is a piece of its history that today's occupants prefer to forget. Much more creditable was its bishop's grant in the 1860s to a local lad, Gabriel Fauré, which enabled him to study music in Paris; he subsequently became a famous composer. *Cocos* – the white haricot beans used for making cassoulet – are grown on the flat farmland all around; however, the town's speciality dish is *azinat* (cabbage soup).

# ST-FÉLIX-LAURAGAIS

ⓘ **St-Félix-Lauragais
Tourist
Information** *place
Guillaume de Nogaret;*
tel: 05 62 18 96 99.
*Open daily Jul–Aug.*

☉ **La Foire de la
Cocagne** at Easter
evokes the time when
woad brought prosperity
to the area. People dress
up in period costumes and
take part in medieval
processions. Old country
crafts are demonstrated
and a traditional country
market sells local
specialities like foie gras.

There is a major pottery
fair *during the third weekend
in Sept.*

This hillside village is scenically situated overlooking the Lauragais plain, the so-called Pays de Cocagne. The centre is laid out in typical 13th-century *bastide* style. Half-timbered buildings with brown brick and stone line the square which has a small market hall topped by a belfry. The 14th-century church nearby, painstakingly restored, is notable for its sculpted tableaux of the Stations of the Cross and *trompe l'œil* frescoes. The view from the terrace of the castle stretches from the Montagne Noire to the Pyrenees.

## Accommodation and food in St-Félix-Lauragais

**Auberge du Poids Public €€** *Faubourg St-Roch; tel: 05 62 18 85 00; email: poidspublic@wanadoo.fr; www.auberge-du-poidspublic.fr. Open Feb–Dec.* Named after the public weighbridge outside, this smart country hotel is considered by many to be the area's top hotel. Thirteen rooms. Michelin-starred restaurant (€€€).

### Woad

In the 16th century, the flat countryside in the 'golden triangle' between Toulouse, Albi and Carcassonne was famous throughout Europe for its woad (which the French call *pastel*). The plant, which belongs to the mustard family and has small yellow flowers on a tall stem, was then in great demand for dyeing cloth blue, the fashionable colour of the period.

The dye was produced by letting the leaves dry in piles – *cocagnes* – and then grinding them into powder in mills. At the height of the trade, 500 mills were in operation and the area became known as the Pays de Cocagne – the 'land of milk and honey'.

Eventually woad was superseded by indigo, imported from India, though a few local people still grow it to make their own dye. It is also grown at the Château de Magrin near Lavaur, north of Albi, where a museum is devoted to its history.

## Suggested tour

**Total distance:** 220km. The detour to St-Papoul adds 16km and the detour to Vals adds 3km.

**Time:** 5 hours' driving. Allow at least a day for the main route, a full day with detours. Those with limited time should concentrate on Castelnaudary (for a trip on the Canal du Midi) and Mirepoix.

**Links to other tours:** From St-Félix-Lauragais, the D622 leads east to Revel (*see page 146*), 10km away. From Pamiers, the N20 leads south to Foix (*see page 93*), 20km away.

Take the A61 autoroute southeast from Toulouse (towards Carcassonne). Turn off it at **Villefranche-de-Lauragais** and follow the D622 to **ST-FELIX-LAURAGAIS ❶** where the terrace of the castle provides a good view over the Lauragais plain (Pays de Cocagne). Today, instead of woad, the farmers have turned to more familiar crops, including the white beans which are an essential ingredient of cassoulet, and poultry. So many chickens are reared in the area that there is also a thriving industry in making feather duvets. Five kilometres beyond St-Félix-Lauragais, turn right on to the D624 to **CASTELNAUDARY ❷**.

**Abbaye de St-Papoul €€**
*tel: 04 68 94 97 75;*
*email: mairie.saint-papoul@libertysurf.fr;*
*www.saintpapoul.free.fr.*
*Open daily Apr–Oct; Sat–Sun Nov–Dec & Feb–Mar.*

**Detour:** The village of **St-Papoul** (8km east of Castelnaudary on the D103) boasts a 14th-century church which was elevated to the status of a cathedral in 1317 when Pope John XXII, keen to restore orthodoxy to the Catholic church in the area, installed a bishop there. Much rebuilt over the centuries, it has an attractive cloister and some fine stone carvings.

Leaving Castelnaudary, take the D6113 towards Carcassonne. A fast road across farmland, it runs parallel with the Canal du Midi, railway and the A61, the 'Autoroute des Deux Mers'. After 16km, turn right on to the D4, which takes you across the canal to **Bram**, a village with an unusual layout. It is built in concentric circles around its church. Beyond Bram, cross the autoroute and turn left following the signs up the gentle climb to **MONTREAL ❸**. From there, the D119 passes the **MONASTERE DE PROUILLE ❹** (on the right) just before **FANJEAUX ❺**. Continue along it across rolling farmland to **MIREPOIX ❻** and then towards Pamiers, enjoying views of the snow-topped Canigou mountain in the distance.

**Detour:** Ten kilometres after Mirepoix, turn right off the D119 on to the D206 to visit **Vals** (4km), a hamlet whose tiny 11th-century chapel, Ste-Marie, is – amazingly – built into a cliff. One of the oldest in the Midi, it has three tiers and a belfry. Steps in its cave-like entrance lead through a crevice to the crypt and then to the apse, which is decorated with simple 12th-century frescoes of scenes from the life of Christ. From Vals, return to the D119 on the D40 (3km).

The D119 takes you to **PAMIERS ❼**, then take the D820 north (towards Toulouse) but turn right at **Le Vernet** where the D624, a long straight road bordered with plane trees, runs across flat countryside to **Mazères**. Most of this pleasant town, with its red-brick parish church and market hall, dates from the 17th century (it was largely destroyed during the area's Wars of Religion). Pause in the church to admire the paintings around the altar. From Mazères, the D14 and then the D16 enable you to join the A61 autoroute just before **Villefranche-de-Lauragais** to return to Toulouse. On the way, look back and enjoy the wide views over the huge fields of the plain, punctuated by villages and a lonely water tower.

**Below**
Fanjeaux

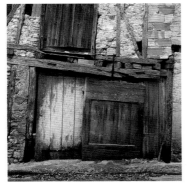

## Getting out of the car

In Castelnaudary, it's worth considering taking a boat trip on the **Canal du Midi**. By way of introduction, there are 30-minute ones around the Grand Bassin, or you can take a 2-hour one towards Toulouse and through La Planque lock. Like many of the roads in the area, the peaceful water is lined by plane trees which Napoleon had planted to provide shade.

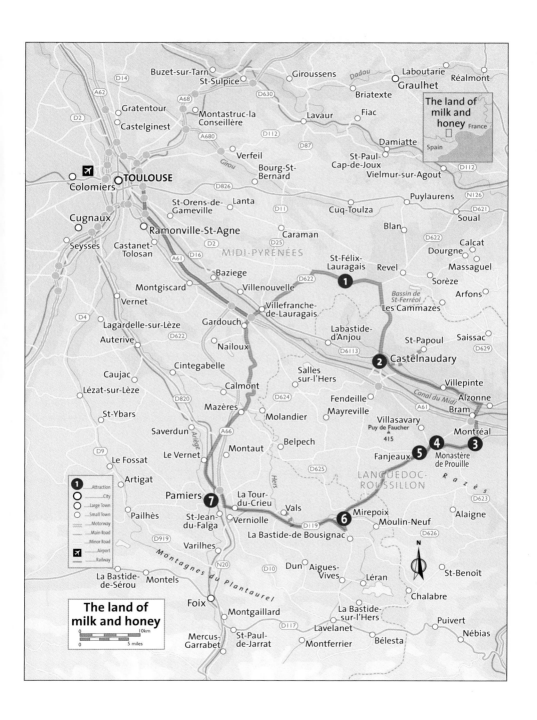

The land of
milk and
honey France

Spain

MIDI-PYRÉNÉES

Bassin de
St-Ferréol

LANGUEDOC-
ROUSSILLON

Razès

**The land of
milk and honey**

| | |
|---|---|
| **❶** | Attraction |
| ◯ | City |
| ◯ | Large Town |
| ◯ | Small Town |
| | Motorway |
| | Main Road |
| | Minor Road |
| ✈ | Airport |
| | Railway |

0 ——————— 10km
0 ——————— 5 miles

Buzet-sur-Tarn
St-Sulpice
Giroussens
Dadou
Laboutarie
Réalmont
Graulhet
Briatexte
D14
D630
A62
Gratentour
A68
Montastruc-la-
Conseillère
Lavaur
Fiac
Damiatte
D2
Castelginest
A680
D112
D87
St-Paul-
Cap-de-Joux
Vielmur-sur-Agout
D112
Verfeil
Bourg-St-
Bernard
Girou
✈
TOULOUSE
D826
Colomiers
Lanta
Puylaurens
N126
St-Orens-de-
Gameville
D11
Cuq-Toulza
D621
Soual
Cugnaux
Ramonville-St-Agne
Caraman
Blan
D622
Calcat
Seysses
Castanet-
Tolosan
D2
D25
Dourgne
Massaguel
A61
D16
St-Félix-
Lauragais
Revel
Sorèze
Baziege
D622
❶
Arfons
Montgiscard
Villenouvelle
Les Cammazes
Vernet
Villefranche-
de-Lauragais
D4
Lagardelle-sur-Lèze
Gardouch
Labastide-
d'Anjou
St-Papoul
Saissac
Auterive
D622
Nailoux
D6113
St-Papoul
D629
Caujac
Cintegabelle
Salles
sur-l'Hers
❷ Castelnaudary
Villepinte
Lézat-sur-Lèze
Calmont
D624
Fendeille
Alzonne
Canal du Midi
A61
Bram
St-Ybars
D820
Mazères
Mayreville
Villasavary
Puy de Faucher
Montréal
Saverdun
A66
Molandier
415
❹
❸
D9
Le Vernet
Montaut
Belpech
Fanjeaux ❺
Monastère
de Prouille
Le Fossat
Ariège
D625
Razès
Artigat
Pamiers ❼
La Tour-
du-Crieu
Vals
D623
Pailhès
St-Jean-
du-Falga
Verniolle
Mirepoix
❻
Alaigne
Moulin-Neuf
D919
Varilhes
D119
La Bastide-de-Bousignac
D626
Montels
N20
D10
Dun
Aigues-
Vives
Léran
St-Benoît
La Bastide-
de-Sérou
Montagnes du Plantaurel
Foix
Montgaillard
La Bastide-
sur-l'Hers
Chalabre
Puivert
D117
Lavelanet
Nébias
Mercus-
Garrabet
St-Paul-
de-Jarrat
Montferrier
Bélesta

N

# Albi

## Ratings

| | |
|---|---|
| Architecture | ●●●●● |
| Art | ●●●●● |
| Food and drink | ●●●●○ |
| History | ●●●●○ |
| Entertainment | ●●●○○ |
| Museums | ●●●○○ |
| Shopping | ●●○○○ |
| Children | ●○○○○ |

**ⓘ Tourist Information**

*Palais de la Berbie, place Ste-Cécile;* tel: 05 63 36 36 00; *email: accueil@albitourisme.com; www.albi-tourisme.com. Open daily all year.* Hotel reservation service, currency exchange and a selection of publications in English.

Built in brick, this vivacious little city straddling the River Tarn is known as Albi la Rouge (Albi the Red), though in fact it is an attractive mixture of soft yellows and browns as well as reds. Two major features bring tourists flocking in – the fortress-like Cathédrale Ste-Cécile, which dominates the skyline and the Musée Toulouse-Lautrec where you can see the world's largest collection of the famous artist's work. There is much else for visitors to discover too: how in the 13th century the city lent its name to the bloody Albigensian Crusade when Catholics wiped out Cathars in the area; how in the 16th it grew rich from woad; and how the fiery socialist Jean Jaurès founded France's first trade union at the local glass factory in 1896. A busy calendar of events, including many outdoor ones in summer, helps keep everyone entertained.

## Getting there and getting around

By car, the A68 autoroute from Toulouse leads straight on to the D888 and into the city centre. From the north, you cross the Pont du 22 Août 1944 over the river to it. In high season, traffic can be heavy, particularly on both river bridges and on the one-way system around the cathedral and pedestrianised old quarter. The railway station, place de Stalingrad (10-minute walk from the centre) has a direct nightly service to and from Paris. Other national and international connections are via Toulouse or Montauban.

The old town quarter is small and easily walkable. Three walking tours, signed in purple, blue and yellow, lead around it. Explanatory plaques (in French) are sited at points of interest complemented by a leaflet showing the routes (available in English) from the tourist office. Street signs show their names in the old Occitan language beside their

**Tarn département Information** *Moulins Albigeois, 41 rue Porta; tel: 05 63 77 32 10; email: documentation@ cdt-tarn.fr; www.tourisme-tarn.com*

modern ones. A road-train operates daily from the tourist office. There are 35-minute boat trips on the Tarn daily every half-hour June–September.

**Parking**: The streets on the hill below the cathedral are the best place to try to find a space and parking is free at the bottom. There are various car parks on the edge of the old quarter to the south, including place du Vigan, Jardin National, place Jean-Jaurès and avenue Général de Gaulle, or cross the river to the Base de Loisirs de Pratgraussals park area (15 minutes' walk back to the centre).

# Sights

**Cathédrale Ste-Cécile** *boulevard Général Sibille; tel: 05 63 43 23 43; email: paroisse.ste-cecile@wanadoo.fr. Open daily all year. Small charge to go through the rood screen into the choir. Guided tours. Free organ recitals Wed 1700 & Sun 1600 Jul–Aug.*

**Centre d'Art le Lait** *Moulins Albigeois, 41 rue Porta; tel: 05 63 38 38 91. Open Wed–Sun afternoons.*

**Eglise St-Salvi** *place du Cloître. Concerts are given on its 400-year-old organ, which was originally installed in the cathedral.*

**Hôtel de Bosc** *14 rue Toulouse-Lautrec. Not open to the public.*

**Hôtel de Ville** *rue de l'Hôtel de Ville. Not open to the public.*

## Cathédrale Ste-Cécile

This forbidding fortress-like building is visible from miles away, as indeed it was meant to be, having been built at the end of the bloody anti-Cathar Albigensian Crusade. The idea was that no one should be in any doubt about the power of Catholicism and should tremble in their boots if they even thought about challenging it again. Work on it started in 1282 and took over 200 years to complete. Built using long, thin pink bricks, it is a masterpiece of Southern Gothic, with a single nave, tiny windows and a huge bell tower like a castle keep. In contrast to the brickwork, it had an ornate stone porch added in the early 16th century.

The interior comes as such a surprise. Beautiful frescoes, mainly royal blue and pale yellow, cover the huge vaulted roof, which is 100m long and 20m wide, and also the walls of the side chapels. The work of Italian artists, they were the first Renaissance paintings to be done in France and depict scenes from the New Testament. Remarkably, their vivid colours have never been retouched. Other unique treasures include a delicately sculpted limestone rood screen which looks like a lace curtain, 120 carved choir stalls and a 3,500-pipe organ, France's biggest.

## Centre d'Art le Lait

Art centre displaying the work of contemporary artists, housed in a former watermill.

## Eglise St-Salvi

The church of St-Salvi is dedicated to a 6th-century bishop who introduced Christianity to the area. Despite six centuries of alterations – work began in the 12th century but was constantly interrupted – the interior forms a harmonious though gloomy whole. Tour de la Gâche, its unusual three-tiered stone and brick belfry, used to double as a watchtower.

**Below**
Cathédrale Ste-Cécile

## Hôtel de Bosc

This attractive creeper-covered mansion has been in the Toulouse-Lautrec family for over 300 years. The artist Henri de Toulouse-Lautrec was born there in 1864 and lived in it until leaving for Paris when he was 18.

## Hôtel de Ville

Built as a private home in the 17th century, this large mansion was later bought by the council to be the town hall. Its features include a pretty courtyard and a ceiling in the Salle des Etats Albigeois painted with the emblems of the old diocese of Albi.

🏛 **Hôtel Reynès** *14 rue Timbal. Not open to the public.*

**Maison du Vieil Alby** € *Corner of rue de la Croix Blanche and rue Puech Bérenguier; tel: 05 63 54 96 38. Open Mon–Sat all year.*

**Musée Lapérouse** € *Moulins Albigeois, place Botany Bay, which is across the river from the town centre; the entrance is in rue Porta; tel: 05 63 46 01 87. Open daily Jul–Oct; Tue–Sun Nov–Jun.*

**Musée Toulouse-Lautrec** €€ *Palais de la Berbie, next to the cathedral; tel: 05 63 49 48 70; www.museetoulouselautrec.net. Open daily Apr–Oct; Wed–Mon Nov–Mar. Guided tours available. Special exhibitions during summer.*

## Hôtel Reynès

Now occupied by the Chamber of Commerce, Hôtel Reynès is one of the town's many splendid Renaissance mansions built by merchants who made their fortunes from trading in woad (or 'blue gold' as it was nicknamed) in the prosperous 16th century. It has a small Italianate courtyard.

## Maison du Vieil Alby

This medieval half-timbered brick house has been painstakingly restored. Like many of Albi's old buildings, it has a *solehièr* under the eaves – a room with an open balcony where woad would have been dried. Many balconies have now been glassed in.

## Musée Lapérouse

This museum is dedicated to the local explorer who set off on a scientific expedition in 1785 but never returned. After leaving Botany Bay, he was shipwrecked in a storm on the reefs of Vanikoro. Remains from the wreck are on show, together with navigation instruments and models of Lapérouse's ship, the *Boussole*, and Cook's *Endeavour*.

## Musée Toulouse-Lautrec

The Musée Toulouse-Lautrec is housed in the Palais de la Berbie, originally the bishops' palace, next to the cathedral. The building's name derived from *bisbia*, the Occitan word for bishop. Constructed in the same formidable style as the cathedral, it is more a citadel than a residence, though later additions and alterations have softened it somewhat. These include formally laid-out gardens which blaze with colour in summer and an attractive riverside promenade.

The museum is almost entirely devoted to works by Toulouse-Lautrec, the city's most famous son. The collection, donated by his family, consists of 1,000 works and documents ranging from early drawings to all 31 of his well-known posters and some of his sombre last paintings. Paintings and sculptures by contemporary artists are also on show and there is an archaeological gallery.

## Place du Vigan

Place du Vigan, a large bustling square built in the 18th century, separates the medieval and modern quarters of the town. Its many pavement cafés and bars where crowds congregate on warm summer evenings are now even more popular since its pedestrianisation.

## Pont-Vieux

This 900-year-old bridge with six uneven brick arches is one of France's oldest. It had houses on it until 1766 when flooding swept them away. You get a classic view of the cathedral from it and also from its newer twin just upstream, which is named after the day, 22-Août (22 August), when Albi was liberated from the Germans in 1944.

## Shopping

The main shopping street, the pedestrianised rue Mariès, leads off place Ste-Cécile. There are no large stores in the town centre. Hypermarkets on the outskirts include **Géant Casino** (on the road to Millau) and two **Leclercs** (on the roads to Toulouse and Rodez).

**Confidences du Terroir** (*1 place Ste-Cécile*) has a wide selection of local specialities including Gaillac wines produced in the neighbouring vineyards which are little known outside the area. Local wines are sold by the litre at **La Petite Cave** (*just across Pont-Vieux*). In pâtisseries, look out for little aniseed-flavoured cakes called *jeannots* and *gimblettes*.

The town's covered market at place Lapérouse is *open Tue–Sun mornings*. On Saturday mornings there are also food markets at place Fernand Pelloutier and boulevard de Strasbourg, and a flea market in the Halle du Castelvieil.

## Entertainment

Throughout the summer months, there is plenty of informal entertainment on the streets. Tickets for events are sold at the tourist office, including the **Jazz festival** during May and June which has outdoor concerts as well as groups performing in bars.

**Theatre festival:** early July.

**Grand Prix:** first weekend in September.

**Base de Loisirs de Pratgraussals** (*tel: 05 63 60 64 06*), a large park on the north bank of the Tarn, has picnic areas, tennis courts, adventure playgrounds and a mountain-bike area.

### Toulouse-Lautrec

Born in 1864, Henri de Toulouse-Lautrec enormously enjoyed riding as a child, like his mother, and the family frequently visited their estate at Celeyran. While there, he also began to sketch and paint. Sadly, when he was 14, he fell from a chair at his home, the Hôtel du Bosc, damaging one of his legs. A similar accident the following year left him permanently disabled when his legs failed to grow properly, compounding genetic problems arising from the fact that his parents were cousins.

Increasingly unable to join in outdoor activities – a cause of much frustration to him – he enjoyed cooking and came up with a range of recipes. Some of these are now featured by Albi restaurants on their menus.

Henri left home at 18 for the seedy bohemian lifestyle of Montmartre where he painted the singers, dancers and prostitutes who were his neighbours, becoming friends with many of them. His best money-spinners were the posters he began to design in the late 1880s. But ten years on, his health had severely deteriorated, mainly due to alcohol, and he died at another family residence, the Château de Malromé in the Gironde, when he was only 36.

# Accommodation and food

**Le Clos Sainte-Cécile €** *rue du Castelvieil; tel: 05 63 38 19 74. Open Thur–Mon all year.* Local cuisine served in a former school beside the cathedral. Large garden.

**Le Goulu €** *1 place Stalingrad (in the Grand Hôtel d'Orléans); tel: 05 63 54 16 56. Closed Sat midday & Sun.* Classic restaurant featuring local dishes at moderate prices.

**Hôtel La Régence George V €** *29 avenue Maréchal-Joffre; tel: 05 63 54 24 16; email: info@hotelgeorgev.com; www.laregence-georgev.fr. Open all year.* Small hotel near the railway station with outdoor breakfast terrace. Nine rooms.

**Grand Hôtel d'Orléans €€** *1 place Stalingrad; tel: 05 63 54 16 56; email: hoteldorleans@wanadoo.fr; www.hotel-orleans-albi.com. Open all year.* Friendly rather than grand, this comfortably updated turn-of-the-20th-century hotel has always been run by the same family. Eight of the fifty-six rooms are family-size. Breakfast terrace beside outdoor pool. Quietly situated opposite the station with parking.

**Below**
Albi's Pont-Vieux

**Hôtel Chiffre €€** *50 rue Séré-de Rivières; tel: 05 63 48 58 48; email: contact@hotelchiffre.com; www.hotelchiffre.com. Open all year.* This old coaching inn with stables, over a hundred years old, has been thoroughly modernised. Now smart décor complements impressive facilities (such as air conditioning and twin washbasins) in the 35 bedrooms. Situated in a quiet street in the town centre, it has plenty of parking space.

**La Table du Sommelier €€** *20 rue Porta; tel: 05 63 46 20 10. Open Tue–Sat all year.* Rustic-style wine bar and bistro owned by one of the region's leading wine experts, with some tables outdoors in summer.

**Vieil-Alby €€** *25 rue Toulouse-Lautrec; tel: 05 63 54 14 69; email: levieilalby@wanadoo.fr.* A charming small hotel (nine rooms) in the centre of the old quarter. Its restaurant features a wide range of local dishes including Albi's special starter, *salade de radis au foie de porc salé* (radishes with salted liver).

# Suggested walk

**Length:** 2km.

**Duration:** 45 minutes just to walk round, but allow at least half a day to visit the cathedral and the Toulouse-Lautrec museum.

The **CATHEDRALE STE-CECILE** ❶ is the obvious place to start as the oldest part of the town radiates from its square on the south bank of the **River Tarn**. Also explore the adjoining citadel, the ramparts and **Palais de la Berbie**, which houses the **MUSEE TOULOUSE-LAUTREC** ❷ inside; the tourist office also occupies a corner of it on the square.

**Cordes-sur-Ciel Tourist Information** *Maison Fonpeyrouse, place Jeanne Ramel Cals; tel: 05 63 56 00 52; www.cordessurciel.eu. Open daily all year.*

**Cordes-sur-Ciel** There are two car parks at the bottom of the town and another at the top for anyone unable to negotiate the steep cobbled climb up.

**Maison du Pays Cordais** *8 place Jeanne Ramel Cals; tel: 05 63 56 00 52. Open daily all year.* Located at the entrance to the village, Maison du Pays Cordais is a showcase of the work of artists and local craftsmen and the agricultural products of the area. *Open daily.*

Rue Mariès leads from the square past an interesting selection of small shops. Appropriately, the street is named after Jean-François Mariès, a local town planner who succeeded in overruling suggestions that the cathedral should be pulled down when plans were afoot to completely redesign the town centre after the French Revolution. Instead, he had wide boulevards built around the old quarter – a much better idea.

The **HOTEL REYNES ❸** is situated in rue Timbal, where the 16th-century half-timbered **Maison Enjalbert** is also noteworthy. Now a pharmacy, it has criss-cross timberwork on its façade. Continue to the **Jardin National** where you can stroll amid beautifully laid-out gardens with fountains. Head back, via the quaint old **Patus Cremat** district, which has recently escaped developers' bulldozers, to the **Palais de Justice**, formerly a Carmelite convent, which has a small cloister. Then continue on to rue de l'Hôtel de Ville, which used to be the city's most prestigious street. The mansions at Nos 13, 14 and 17, and the **HOTEL DE VILLE ❹** itself at No 16, are very impressive. At the top of rue Toulouse-Lautrec, No 14 is the attractive creeper-covered **HOTEL DE BOSC ❺** where the artist was born and lived until he was 18. The former home of the explorer Lapérouse is nearby. Narrow cobbled streets take you back to the pretty **MAISON DU VIEIL ALBY ❻** and then on to **EGLISE ST-SALVI ❼**, whose cloister tucked behind the shops of rue Mariès is a quiet haven.

**Detour:** For the best view of the old town and its red rooftops, cross the **PONT-VIEUX ❽** to the north bank. This is a particularly worthwhile stroll at sunset when swallows dip over the water and the bricks of the mighty cathedral seem to glow.

## Also worth exploring

The walled town of Cordes-sur-Ciel, huddled around a hilltop 25km northwest of Albi, is reached on the D600, which leads along a high ridge overlooking the vineyards of Gaillac. Protected by three lines of ramparts and scarcely changed in 800 years, it is as scenic from a distance as when you explore it on foot. Steep cobbled streets wind past cottages trailing flowers, leading to flights of steps. These go up through stone arched gateways into the heart of the town, a large tree-shaded square surrounded by cafés which is taken over by a market on Saturdays.

The long straight grande rue Haute is lined with grand houses built by the Cathar nobility when they had to take refuge in Cordes during the 13th and 14th centuries. Now many artists have studios in the quaint narrow streets; over 50 artists and craftsmen live and work in Cordes-sur-Ciel and the tourist office website lists those who accept visitors to their studios and workshops. They range from painters, sculptors and potters to glass-blowers, jewellery designers, makers of musical instruments and many other crafts.

# The Tarn Valley

## Ratings

| | |
|---|---|
| Rivers | ●●●●● |
| Scenery | ●●●●● |
| Villages | ●●●○○ |
| Art | ●●●○○ |
| Geology | ●●●○○ |
| Outdoor activities | ●●●○○ |
| Shopping | ●●●○○ |
| Historical sights | ●●○○○ |

Why is the Tarn Gorge in the Cévennes so much more famous than the Tarn Valley, a few miles downstream? The answer is that the gorge is so dramatic, yet the valley is certainly as beautiful. From Brousse-le-Château to Albi, the river meanders gently between its wooded hillsides and charming villages.

This route then runs south through the valley of the Rance to the Monts de Lacaune where the scenery becomes mountainous with grey-stone villages and thick forests.

By way of contrast, Castres offers worthwhile sightseeing and smart shopping in congenial riverside surroundings. Réalmont is also a tempting place to pause, particularly on market days.

Bear in mind, however, that the route is comparatively long and has stretches that twist around hillsides as well as the fast final stretch from Castres to Albi, so allow plenty of time.

## AMBIALET

🛈 **Tourist Information** *Le Bourg; tel: 05 63 55 39 14; email: postmaster@si-ambialet.fr; www.si-ambialet.fr. Open Tue–Sun Jul–Aug.*

🏛 **Notre-Dame de l'Oder** Although you can drive to the church and priory, an attractive walk marked by the Stations of the Cross leads up to them from the car park (and adjoining picnic tables) by the river in the village.

The village of Ambialet is distinctive for its unusual position in a noose-shaped loop of the River Tarn, with a hydroelectric station (disguised as a small mansion) at the neck, which is only 23m across. **Notre-Dame de l'Oder**, an 11th-century church which is all the more beautiful for its simple undecorated interior, overlooks it from a high cliff top. The church is part of a Benedictine priory which still functions. The village church, Eglise St Gilles, also dates back to the 11th century.

### Accommodation and food in Ambialet

**Hôtel du Pont €€** *tel: 05 63 55 32 07. Open mid-Feb–mid-Nov.* Twenty-room hotel above river beside bridge with lovely view. Restaurant serves local fare (*closed Sun evening*).

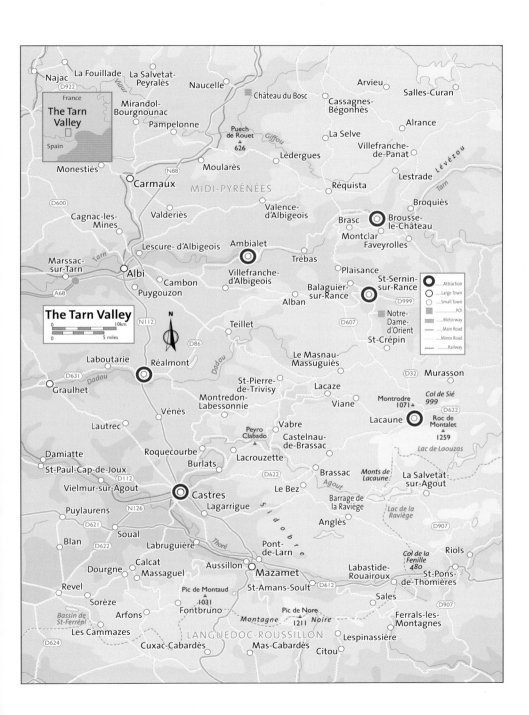

The Tarn Valley

France
Spain

**The Tarn Valley**

Najac
La Fouillade
La Salvetat-Peyralès
Naucelle
D922
Mirandol-Bourgnounac
Pampelonne
Monestiés
Carmaux
Cagnac-les-Mines
Valderiès
Lescure- d'Albigeois
Marssac-sur-Tarn
Albi
Cambon
Puygouzon
Laboutarie
Réalmont
Graulhet
D631
Lautrec
Damiatte
St-Paul-Cap-de-Joux
Vielmur-sur-Agout
Puylaurens
D621
Blan
Soual
Calcat
Labruguière
Dourgne
Massaguel
Aussillon
Revel
Sorèze
Fontbruno
Arfons
Bassin de St-Ferréol
Les Cammazes
D624
Cuxac-Cabardès

Château du Bosc
Puech de Rouet 626
Moularès
MIDI-PYRÉNÉES
D600
Valence-d'Albigeois
Ambialet
Villefranche-d'Albigeois
Trébas
Alban
Teillet
St-Pierre-de-Trivisy
Montredon-Labessonnie
Vénès
Peyro Clabado
Vabre
Castelnau-de-Brassac
Roquecourbe
Lacrouzette
Burlats
Castres
Lagarrigue
Le Bez
Brassac
D622
Pont-de-Larn
Mazamet
St-Amans-Soult
D612
Pic de Montaud 1031
Pic de Nore 1211
Montagne Noire
LANGUEDOC-ROUSSILLON
Mas-Cabardès
Citou
Lespinassière

Lédergues
Giffou
Arvieu
Cassagnes-Bégonhès
La Selve
Villefranche-de-Panat
Réquista
Brasc
Montclar
Faveyrolles
Plaisance
Balaguier-sur-Rance
St-Sernin-sur-Rance
D999
Notre-Dame-d'Orient
St-Crépin
Le Masnau-Massuguiès
Lacaze
Viane
Montrodre 1071
Lacaune
Roc de Montalet 1259
Lac de Laouzas
Monts de Lacaune
Agout
La Salvetat-sur-Agout
Barrage de la Raviège
Anglès
Lac de la Raviège
Angès
Col de la Fenille 480
Sales
Ferrals-les-Montagnes
St-Pons-de-Thomières
Riols
Labastide-Rouairoux
D907

Salles-Curan
Alrance
Lestrade
Broquiès
Brousse-le-Château
Murasson
D32
Col de Sié 999
D622
D907

Tarn
Lévézou
Viaur
N88
A68
N112
D86
Dadou
Sidobre
Thoré
N126

**The Tarn Valley**
0        10km
0        5 miles

Attraction
Large Town
Small Town
POI
Motorway
Main Road
Minor Road
Railway

# BROUSSE-LE-CHATEAU

**Château de Brousse** € *Le Bourg; tel: 05 65 99 45 40; email: brousselechateau@ wanadoo.fr. Open daily Feb–Nov. Visits can include a 15-minute video on its history and the surrounding area.*

Tiny alleyways bordered by old stone cottages lead steeply up to the village's partly ruined 14th-century **castle**, which occupies a commanding position on a ridge between the River Tarn and its small tributary, the Alrance. With its sturdy curtain walls and turrets, it is a classic example of medieval military architecture. The small church inside is prettily decorated with frescoes which have recently been restored.

## Accommodation and food in Brousse-le-Château

**Le Relays du Chasteau** €€ *tel: 05 65 99 40 15; email: contact@ lerelaysduchasteau.com; www.le-relays-du-chasteau.com. Open mid-Feb–mid-Dec.* Nestling in the village street in a row of old buildings below the castle, this traditional 12-room hotel has been in the Senegas family for four generations.

# CASTRES

**Castres Tourist Information** *2 place de la République; tel: 05 63 62 63 62; email: otcastres@wanadoo.fr; www.tourisme-castres.fr. Open daily all year. Organises guided tours.*

Take a 45-minute boat trip (€€) aboard the *Miredames*, a replica wooden barge, from the Pont-Vieux to the Parc de Gourjade to see the waterfront at its best; *tel: 05 63 71 58 58; daily Jun–Oct.*

**Musée Goya** €€ *Hôtel de Ville; tel: 05 63 71 59 27; email: goya@ville-castres.fr. Open Tue–Sun all year.*

**Centre National et Musée Jean Jaurès** € *2 place Pélisson; tel: 05 63 62 41 83; email: jaures@ville-castres.fr. Open Tue–Sun all year. A Goya festival is held each Jul and a folklore festival in Aug.*

Castres is well placed as a base for exploring the Sidobre hills. A sizeable industrial town, it also offers sightseeing, shopping and entertainment. The oldest part spreads along the banks of the River Agout. Along the quai des Jacobins, a row of tall clapboard houses painted white and green, once occupied by weavers and dyers, is reflected picturesquely in the water with arched doorways and overhanging balconies.

**Cathédrale St-Benoît**, on the site of a 9th-century abbey, looks rather forbidding but its interior is brightened by a huge altar supported by pillars of local red marble. There are some fine paintings in its side chapels. The Hôtel de Ville is a grand 17th-century building designed by Jules Hardouin-Mansart as the bishops' palace. On the second floor, the **Musée Goya** displays an outstanding collection of the artist's work, collected by a local painter, Marcel Briguiboul. Its formal gardens, laid out by the famous landscape architect Le Nôtre, are a work of art too. One of the best examples of a *jardin à la française* (French garden), they feature a tapestry of low box hedges and tall yew trees, each neatly clipped to a different shape.

**Centre National et Musée Jean Jaurès** is devoted to the famous French socialist politician who was born in the town in 1859 (*see page 185*). A statue of him occupies the place of honour on the main square.

**Parc de Gourjad** (*tel: 05 63 72 27 06*), a leisure complex on the northeast side of town, includes indoor and outdoor pools, a skating rink, nine-hole golf course, horse riding and children's playground with a gigantic spider's web for climbing on. The town's industrial area, built up in the 17th century on textiles, but now including chemicals, meat-curing and mechanical engineering, is on the south side and does not intrude on the centre.

**Market** *place Jean-Jaurès; Sat morning.* Look out for regional specialities such as *melsat* (white sausage) and *boudin de Languedoc* (black pudding).

Opera season at the **Théâtre Municipal** *rue de l'Hôtel de Ville; in Castres Sept–Jul. Reservations tel: 05 63 71 56 58; email: spectacle.vivant@ville-castres.fr*

**Hôtel Rivière €€** *10 quai Tourcaudières; tel: 05 63 59 04 53; email: hotelriviere@orange.fr. Open Jan–mid-Dec.* Fifteen rooms. Conveniently situated hotel in the town centre overlooking old tanners' houses across the river.

**Right**
Ambialet

# LACAUNE

**ⓘ** **Lacaune Tourist Information** *place du Général de Gaulle; tel: 05 63 37 04 98; email: office-tourisme@lacaune. com; www.lacaune.com. Open daily Jul–Aug; Mon–Sat Sept–Jun.*

**ⓑ** **Raymond Mill** € *Open daily by appointment through the tourist office.*

**◔** **Market** *Sun morning and 21st of the month.*

**◉** Free organ recitals in the **Eglise Notre-Dame** *Thur Jul–Aug.*

Grey-slate roofs make this little town look rather sombre – the slate is quarried locally. Until the 1930s, its small spa attracted many visitors. Tiny statues of four well-endowed men on top of the Fontaine des Pisseurs (erected in 1559) in front of the town's old open-air stone wash house demonstrate the diuretic qualities of *l'eau de Lacaune* (Lacaune water).

The charcuterie for which the Monts de Lacaune area is famous – salamis, sausages and air-dried ham – is made at several small factories around the town. Visits to some of them can be arranged through the tourist office. This industry, however, has declined in recent years as mass-production has taken over.

Another hangover from the past are seven hand-operated looms, still in working order, at the **Raymond Mill**, a rambling old mill run by the Raymond family from 1841 to 1992 and still fully equipped.

## Accommodation and food in Lacaune

**Calas** €€ *4 place de la Vierge; tel: 05 63 37 03 28; email: hotelcalas@wanadoo.fr; www.pageloisirs.com/calas. Open mid-Jan–mid-Dec.* Centrally placed old-fashioned hotel with 16 rooms, outdoor pool and gourmet restaurant.

## Jean Jaurès

Almost every town in France seems to have a square or street named after him. But who was he?

The answer: a leading socialist politician and pacifist who was assassinated by a nationalist youth in Paris in 1914. Born in Castres in 1859, he studied to be a teacher and worked in a school at Albi before becoming a philosophy lecturer at Toulouse University. When he was 26 he entered politics as the Republican member of parliament for Tarn, later becoming the Socialist member for the mining town of Carmaux. A skilful orator and writer, he argued passionately for social change, notably the introduction of accident compensation for workers and retirement pensions. He also demonstrated his independence by publicly supporting Alfred Dreyfus, the Jewish soldier whom the French High Command convicted of being a German spy in 1894, but pardoned 12 years later.

# REALMONT

**Left**
Lacaune

This is a typical *bastide* – fortified town – created in 1271 by King Philippe III with the characteristic grid layout of straight streets with a large square at the centre, place de la République. This is surrounded by arcades, some supported by sturdy wooden beams, others by stone

**① Réalmont Tourist Information**
8 place de la République;
tel: 05 63 79 05 45; email:
office-tourisme-
realmont@wanadoo.fr;
www.realmont.fr.
Open daily Jun–Sept;
Mon–Sat Oct–May.

columns. Market days are definitely the liveliest time to visit as the stalls brim with the local pink garlic, poultry and other fresh produce from this essentially agricultural region.

Take time off from shopping to drop into the parish church, Notre-Dame-du-Taur, to see its splendid Baroque altarpiece. On the edge of the old quarter, which was originally encircled by ramparts, the communal wash house and Fontaine de la Fréjaire, a fountain where villagers came for water until 1950 when pumps were installed, are also worth seeing.

# ST-SERNIN-SUR-RANCE

**① St-Sernin-sur-Rance Tourist Information**
avenue d'Albi; tel: 05 65 99
29 13; email: info.st-
sernin@Roquefort.com;
www.tourisme-
saintsernin.com. Open daily
Jul–Aug; Mon–Fri Sept–Jun.

Built on a rocky spur high above the rivers Rance and Merdanson, this medieval stronghold has a jumble of old houses and a 300-year-old bridge. The film director François Truffaut put the town on the map in 1968 when he made *L'Enfant Sauvage*, based on the story of a local boy who was captured nearby on 8 January 1800 after being raised by wolves. The boy's statue stands on the place du Fort.

### Accommodation and food in St-Sernin-sur-Rance

**Hôtel Carayon €€** *place du Fort; tel: 05 65 98 19 19; email: contact@hotel-carayon.fr; www.hotel-carayon.com. Open all year.* Sixty rooms, many with balcony overlooking garden. Large restaurant. Tennis, mini-golf and pool with slides.

The town's speciality is *gimblettes* (small doughnut-shaped caraway seed biscuits) sold at the **Maison Nespoulous** pâtisserie *(tel: 05 65 99 60 06. Open Tue–Sun all year)*. The women used to bake them on Sundays and take them to church, threaded on a stick, to be blessed.

# Suggested tour

**Total distance:** 230km. The detour to Notre-Dame d'Orient adds 4km, the detour to St-Crépin adds 6km and the detour on to the Sidobre adds 24km.

**Time:** 6 hours' driving. Allow up to two days for the main route, and a full two days with detours. Those with limited time should concentrate on the Tarn Valley between Albi and Brousse-le-Château.

**Links to other routes:** From St-Sernin-sur-Rance, the D999 leads northeast to Roquefort-sur-Soulzon (*see page 242*), 45km away. From Lacaune, the D907 leads south to La Salvetat-sur-Agout (*see page 203*), 20km away. From Castres, the N112 leads southeast to Mazamet (*see page 144*), 17km away.

Head east from **Albi** on the D999 (signposted Millau), which passes through the town's industrial outskirts. After 11km, the scene changes welcomingly when you turn left on to the D77 as it zigzags down through old oak woods to join the D172. This takes you along the south bank of the River Tarn to **AMBIALET** ❶. Gentle wooded slopes frame the serene blue water on each side, making the valley here as scenic as any stretch on the river's varied journey from Mont Lozère; it is definitely a pleasant place for a waterside picnic. Leave Ambialet on the D700 (signposted to Couris) but fork left off it almost immediately to cross the Tarn and drive along its north bank to Trébas.

You will notice that this road is flat, curves only gently and occasionally goes through short tunnels. The reason is that it was part of a railway line between Millau and Albi, built by German prisoners during World War I. No trains ever ran on it as it was never completed.

**Below**
Castres: the quai des Jacobins

**Trébas**, a tiny spa town with a Sunday market, claims to have the most copper-rich thermal waters in Europe. Beyond it, the D172 continues along the north bank of this beautiful stretch of the Tarn to

BROUSSE-LE-CHATEAU ❷; you cross the river and then re-cross it on your way there. From Brousse-le-Château, continue east on the D902 leaving the 'railway road' where it crosses the river and disappears into a tunnel. Shortly afterwards, you have to leave the Tarn too. Then, 3km later, turn sharp right just before **Faveyrolles** on to the D60, which climbs up to **Montclar**, providing increasingly splendid views over distant farmland and woods. The D552 (which becomes the D33) leads along a ridge with wide views of farmland on both sides through **Brasc**. It winds down to the wide wooded valley of the River Rance at **Plaisance**, following the river through the tiny village of **Balaguier** (which has a surprisingly large church) to **ST-SERNIN-SUR-RANCE** ❸. As you climb out of the town, be sure to look back to see the backs of its houses clinging to the hillside.

**Detour:** Five kilometres beyond St-Sernin-sur-Rance on the D33, the D91 on the left leads (2km) to the church of **Notre-Dame-d'Orient**, part of a Benedictine convent, which has a beautiful wooden carved and painted altarpiece from the 17th century.

## Pigeon-houses

In the Tarn countryside, look out for pigeon-houses. These small windowless buildings were mostly built between the 17th and 19th centuries when pigeons were particularly valued for their ability to carry messages, their tasty meat and the fertiliser value of their droppings. The houses were often raised above the ground on pillars or arches to protect the birds from rats and other animals. As they were regarded as status symbols by the landowners, many have elaborate brick- or stonework, elegant roofs and often a decorative pinnacle on top. Because pigeons prefer to live in tranquil surroundings and like to be able to watch out for predators, the houses tend to be isolated from other buildings.

**🅑 St-Crépin**
    **Musée Damien Bec**
€ *Open Apr–Oct afternoons;*
*daily Nov–Mar.* Local
tourist offices have details
of walking trails leading to
standing stones.

**Château du Bosc €€**
*Naucelle; tel: 05 65 69 20*
*83. Open daily all year for*
*guided tours.* The childhood
home of the artist
Toulouse-Lautrec, with the
painter's bedroom kept
almost in its original
condition.

**Detour:** Twelve kilometres beyond St-Sernin-sur-Rance on the D33, a left turn up the D554 leads (3km) to the village of **St-Crépin** where the **Musée Damien Bec** has a section devoted to the area's menhirs. Many of these prehistoric standing stones with mysterious markings are scattered around the Monts de Lacaune hills.

After the turn to St-Crépin, continue south (now on the D607) along a panoramic ridge which climbs past farmland and woods over the Col de Sié (999m) before dropping down to **LACAUNE ❹**, a little town of grey-slate roofs in the heart of the Monts de Lacaune. From there, take the D81 west, which winds through beech woods (glorious in autumn) to **Lacaze**, followed by the D171 to **Vabre**, another small grey-slate town, which has some attractive 16th- and 17th-century houses. Its isolated position surrounded by lonely hillsides is probably one of the reasons it became a hippy haunt in the 1970s. At Vabre, join the D55, which winds through woods beside the River Agout to **Roquecourbe**.

**Detour:** From Roquecourbe, the D30 leads to the **Peyro Clabado** (10km). This massive, precariously balanced boulder is one of many 'rocking stones' on the **Sidobre**, a wide granite plateau averaging 650m in height. Just beyond it is the **Chaos de la Resse**, a 'river' of rocks covering a real river, and the wooded **Lac du Merle**, a lake whose surface is broken by boulders.

From Roquecourbe, continue to **CASTRES ❺**, then take the N112, a fast flat road, north through **REALMONT ❻** to **Albi**.

### Also worth exploring

If you're a Toulouse-Lautrec fan, **Château du Bosc**, the country house where the painter spent childhood holidays, is at Naucelle, just off the N88, 45km north of Albi. It's a small red-shuttered 19th-century castle with sturdy towers, lavishly furnished in *fin-de-siècle* Parisian style.

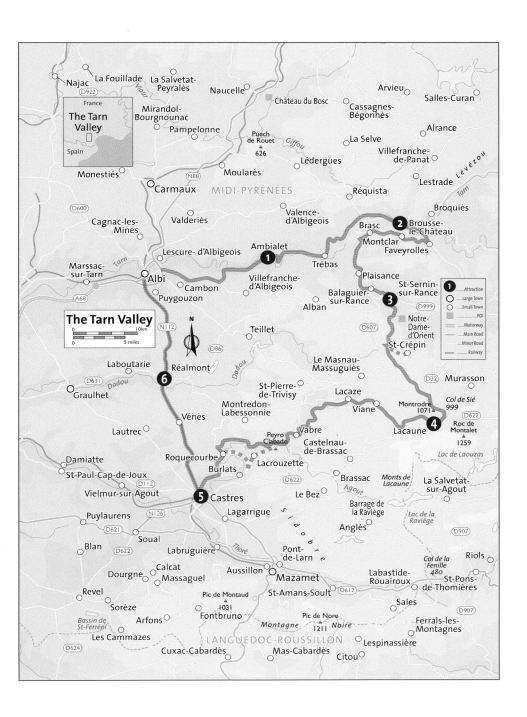

The Tarn Valley

France
Spain

Najac
La Fouillade
La Salvetat-Peyralès
Naucelle
Arvieu
Salles-Curan
Château du Bosc
Cassagnes-Bégonhès
Mirandol-Bourgnounac
Alrance
Pampelonne
Puech de Rouet 626
La Selve
Villefranche-de-Panat
Giffou
Lédergues
Lestrade
Lévezou
Monestiés
Moularès
N88
Carmaux
MIDI-PYRÉNÉES
Réquista
Tarn
D600
Broquiès
Cagnac-les-Mines
Valderiès
Valence-d'Albigeois
Brasc
**2** Brousse-le-Château
Marssac-sur-Tarn
Lescure- d'Albigeois
Ambialet
Montclar
Faveyrolles
Tarn
Albi
Cambon
**1**
Trébas
Plaisance
St-Sernin-sur-Rance
A68
Puygouzon
Villefranche-d'Albigeois
Balaguier-sur-Rance
**3**
D999
**1** Attraction
Large Town
Small Town
POI
Motorway
Main Road
Minor Road
Railway
Alban
Notre-Dame-d'Orient
**The Tarn Valley**
0        10km
0     5 miles
N112
N
Teillet
D607
St-Crépin
Laboutarie
D86
Le Masnau-Massuguiès
Murasson
D631
Dadou
Réalmont
**6**
D32
Graulhet
St-Pierre-de-Trivisy
Lacaze
Montrodre 1071▲
Col de Sié 999
Dadou
Montredon-Labessonnie
Viane
**4**
Vénès
Roc de Montalet ▲ 1259
D622
Lautrec
Vabre
Lacaune
Damiatte
Peyro Clabado ▲
Castelnau-de-Brassac
Lac de Laouzas
St-Paul-Cap-de-Joux
Roquecourbe
Lacrouzette
D112
Burlats
Vielmur-sur-Agout
Brassac
Monts de Lacaune
La Salvetat-sur-Agout
**5** Castres
Le Bez
Agout
Puylaurens
Lagarrigue
D622
Barrage de la Raviège
Lac de la Raviège
N126
Anglès
D907
Blan
D621
Soual
Sidobre
Pont-de-Larn
Thoré
Col de la Fenille 480
Riols
D622
Labruguière
Labastide-Rouairoux
St-Pons-de-Thomières
Dourgne
Calcat
Massaguel
Aussillon
Mazamet
D612
Sales
D907
Revel
Pic de Montaud ▲ 1031
St-Amans-Soult
Ferrals-les-Montagnes
Sorèze
Arfons
Fontbruno
Pic de Nore ▲ 1211
Montagne Noire
Bassin de St-Ferréol
LANGUEDOC-ROUSSILLON
Lespinassière
D624
Les Cammazes
Cuxac-Cabardès
Mas-Cabardès
Citou
Viaur
D922

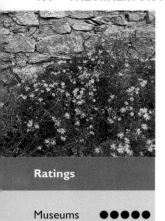

# The Minervois and its vineyards

## Ratings

| | |
|---|---|
| Museums | ●●●●● |
| Vineyards | ●●●●● |
| Caves | ●●●●○ |
| Churches | ●●●●○ |
| History | ●●●●○ |
| Villages | ●●●●○ |
| Scenery | ●●●○○ |
| Canals | ●●○○○ |

The Romans knew the flat countryside around Narbonne well – and left some fascinating traces of their occupation. It was they who first planted the Minervois vineyards on the sunny dry slopes which rise gently from it towards the hills of the Haut Languedoc. Today 61 villages produce the highly drinkable red, white and rosé Minervois wines – and the quality is improving all the time. With frequent opportunities to sample them, this is a route on which it pays not to be the driver.

South of the rugged hills which are covered in *garrigue* and vines, the River Aude and the Canal du Midi, often distinctively bordered by plane trees, follow peaceful courses across a flat band of countryside planted with yet more vines. The museums along the route help explain the area's history and winemaking from Roman times.

## CAPESTANG

 **Capestang Tourist Information**
*5 boulevard Pasteur;*
*tel: 04 67 93 34 23; email:*
*ot-capestang@wanadoo.fr;*
*www.capestango-t.com,*
*www.ville-capestang.fr. Open*
*Mon–Sat May–Oct; Mon–Fri*
*Nov–Apr.*

 **Tower** € Visits by arrangement with the tourist office.

This little canal-side town has an imposing Gothic church, Collégiale St-Etienne. It had the same architect as the cathedral at Narbonne (*see page 110*) but neither was completed as he committed suicide. Climb its **tower** for a splendid view of the Aude plain as far as Narbonne.

### Food in Capestang

**La Galinière €€** *37 rue Gambetta; tel: 04 67 26 14 77; www.restaurantlagaliniere.com. Open Wed–Sun all year.* Traditional French restaurant with convivial atmosphere, extensive menu and terrace.

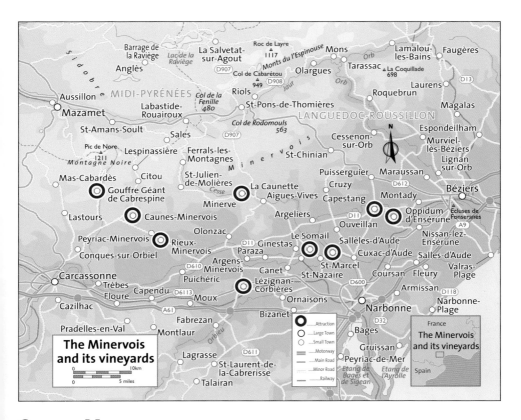

**The Minervois and its vineyards**

0          10km
0          5 miles

## CAUNES-MINERVOIS

**ⓘ Abbaye de Caunes-Minervois**
€€ *tel: 04 68 78 09 44; email: otsi@ caunesminervois.com; www.paysathare.org.* Has tourist information.

A striking modern pillar-like sculpture in the famous local red and white mottled marble (which was quarried nearby until the 1980s) welcomes you to this quaint village on the edge of the Montagne Noire. Narrow streets with some fine medieval and Renaissance mansions – *hôtels particuliers* – slope up to the honey-coloured stone **Abbaye de Caunes-Minervois**, around which the village developed over 1,200 years ago. Parts of the Romanesque abbey church, resplendent with lots of the red marble, date from the 11th century. The other abbey buildings include a basement, now converted into a wine cellar, and newly restored cloister.

### Accommodation and food in Caunes-Minervois

**Hôtel d'Alibert** €€ *rue Saint Genes; tel: 04 68 78 00 54; email: frederic.dalibert@wanadoo.fr. Open Apr–Oct.* Small eight-room hotel in one of the town's historic mansions on the tiny square in the centre.

# GOUFFRE GEANT DE CABRESPINE

**ⓘ Gouffre Géant de Cabrespine €€**
tel: 04 68 26 14 22; email: cabrespine11@orange.fr; www.grottes-de-france.com. Open daily Mar–Nov. Tours last 45 minutes.

This huge cave in the Montagne Noire is known as Les Balcons du Diable ('the balconies of the devil'). Inside, you walk along a balcony to view its various chambers – the largest is a phenomenal 250m high – and its intricate crystal formations. Serious cave explorers can book a five-hour tour off the normal tourist route, through **Safari Souterrain**, *tel: 04 67 66 11 11*.

# LE SOMAIL

**ⓘ Le Musée de la Chapellerie €€**
3 rue Bergerie; tel: 04 68 46 19 26. Open daily all year.

**Right**
Le Somail

**Left**
Capestang's Gothic church

Bargemen used to stop overnight at this delightful old canal-side village where their old stables and inn provide reminders of a slower age. Two recent unusual additions are a large second-hand bookshop, **Le Trouve-Tout du Livre** (*tel: 04 68 46 21 64. Open Wed–Mon all year*) and **Le Musée de la Chapellerie**, a hat museum displaying 6,500 examples dating back to the 1850s. Collected by Antoine Ramoneda, whose family worked in Limoux's hat-making industry for six generations, they include everything from wedding bonnets and bishops' mitres to soldiers' helmets from a succession of wars.

# LEZIGNAN-CORBIERES

**ⓘ Lézignan-Corbières Tourist Information**
9 cours de la République; tel: 04 68 27 05 42; email: officedetourismelezignan-corbieres@wanadoo.fr; www.lezignan-corbieres.fr/ tourisme. Open daily Jul–Aug; Mon–Sat Sept–Jun.

Though not very picturesque, this bustling small town at the heart of the Minervois wine area dates back to pre-Roman times and has a 13th-century church, some notable old houses and a popular Wednesday market. The pine woods and *garrigue* surrounding it are pleasant for walking and cycling, though the majority of visitors tend to be wine lovers. Sadly, its rambling old wine museum is currently closed while a new home is sought for its extensive collection of objects, large and small, related to viticulture and winemaking.

# MINERVE

**ℹ Minerve Tourist Information** *rue des Martyrs; tel: 04 68 91 81 43; email: minervois.accueil@ orange.fr; www.minerve-tourisme.com. Open Tue–Sun Apr–Sept.* Guided tours include **St-Etienne church**, which is closed otherwise.

**P** Access to the village by car is for residents only; there are car parks before the bridge.

**🏛 Musée Hurepel €** *5 rue des Martyrs; tel: 04 68 91 12 26. Open daily Apr–Sept.*

For its dramatic setting and poignant history, this small village is the jewel of the Minervois – and justifiably thronged by visitors all summer. Its sandy-coloured old houses with red roofs cluster along a rocky ledge with deep river gorges on either side. The main access is over a triple-arched bridge from which narrow streets lead up to the chimney-like tower of its ruined castle, past the 900-year-old **St-Etienne church** whose white marble altar dates from the 5th century. Several of the handful of shops, cafés and *caves* offer tastings of Minervois wines.

A Cathar stronghold during the Albigensian Crusade, the village held out for five weeks in 1210 in searing summer heat when besieged by Simon de Montfort and 7,000 men. After running out of water when de Montfort managed to destroy the only well, Puits St-Rustique, in the ramparts at the bottom of the village, the Cathar villagers finally gave in. Threatened with slaughter or Catholicism, about 180 stood by their faith and were burnt alive. Their courage is commemorated by a memorial stone on place de la Mairie. The story of the Crusade is portrayed by miniature tableaux in the **Musée Hurepel**.

# OPPIDUM D'ENSERUNE

**Oppidum d'Ensérune** tel: 04 67 37 01 23; email: enserune@monuments-nationaux.fr; www.oppidumdenserune.com. Admission free.

**Museum** €€ Open daily May–Aug; Tue–Sun Sept–Apr.

Standing on a hillock surrounded by flat countryside just outside the village of Nissan-lez-Ensérune, the pre-Roman site of Oppidum d'Ensérune enjoys distant views as far as the Canigou mountain to the west and the Cévennes to the north. Today it resembles an abandoned garden, as the remains of its ancient columns and walls are mixed with cypress trees and pines. Excavations in 1915 revealed that the hill was inhabited from the 6th century BC until the 1st century AD. The earliest settlement was probably destroyed by Hannibal around 300 BC when 10,000 people may have been living there. It was rebuilt by the Romans in 118 BC when they settled in Narbonne. Pottery, coins, jewellery and even an egg (found intact in one of the graves) are on show in a small **museum**.

# RIEUX-MINERVOIS

**Rieux-Minervois Tourist Information** place de l'Eglise; tel: 04 68 78 13 98; email: rieux-minervois@fnotsi.net. Open daily all year. Ask for the free leaflet about the church.

There is a very good reason to pause in this small town as a wonderful surprise awaits you inside **Eglise Ste-Marie**, part of a row of unprepossessing houses, though recognisable as a church from its sturdy bell tower. The interior is a 14-sided polygon surrounding a circular sanctuary whose dome is supported by seven arches made up of three pillars and four columns with carved capitals. It's unusual and a real gem.

# SALLELES D'AUDE

**Sallèles d'Aude Tourist Information** rue du Marché; tel: 04 68 46 81 46; email: mairie@sallelesdaude.fr; www.sallelesdaude.fr. Open Mon–Fri all year 1000–1800.

**Amphoralis** €€ allée des Potiers (off the D1626 beside the canal 1km north of town); tel: 04 68 46 89 48. Open daily Jul–Sept; Tue–Sun Oct–Jun.

**Musée du Vieux Sallèles** €€ 5 avenue Marcellin Albert; tel: 04 68 46 95 53; www.museeduvieuxsalleles.com. Open Sat–Sun May–Sept.

The reason for going to this small town is to visit its two museums. **Amphoralis (Musée des Potiers Gallo-Romains)**, a striking modern construction, has been built over an old Roman pottery where amphorae – huge storage pots – and domestic items were made. The amphorae, each holding six gallons, were used to transport wine across Europe to the edges of the Roman Empire, a reminder that Languedoc has been an important wine-producing area for many centuries. The other museum, **Musée du Vieux Sallèles**, has three sections, covering old crafts, vines/wines and everyday life from the late 19th century to the end of the German occupation in 1945.

## Food in Sallèles d'Aude

**Les Ecluses** € 20 grand'rue; tel: 04 68 46 94 47. Open Thur–Tue all year. This small homely restaurant, renowned for its cuisine, specialises in fresh local produce.

**Left**
The Oppidum d'Ensérune

**Canal holiday boat hire: Minervois Cruisers** 38 chemin des Patiasses, Le Somail; tel: 04 68 46 28 52; www.minervoiscruisers.com. Bookings (in UK): tel: 01926 811842; email: enquiries@minervoiscruisers.com. Canal open daily Apr–Oct.

**Auberge Lou Somaillou €€** I chemin de Halage; tel: 04 68 46 19 41. Open Wed–Mon Apr–Oct. Cosy canal-side inn serving home-cooked fish dishes and meat from a wood-fire grill. Tables on a terrace overlooking the canal.

## Canal du Midi

The 240km-long canal between **Sète** and **Toulouse**, designated by UNESCO as a World Heritage Site, was the brainchild of a prosperous salt-tax inspector, Pierre-Paul Riquet. In 1667, he persuaded Louis XIV to support his ambitious idea of linking the Mediterranean and the Atlantic to enable boats to avoid the long voyage around Gibraltar, which was notorious for pirates. Some 15,000 labourers worked on the canal's wandering course but by the time it was completed, after 14 years, Riquet himself was bankrupt. Fed by a complicated system of smaller canals and reservoirs and punctuated by locks, aqueducts and tunnels, it remains a remarkable engineering achievement, enhanced by the elegance of its many bridges and the long lines of trees on its banks. Boats can be hired at several places along the canal.

# Suggested tour

**Total distance:** 170km. The detour to Sallèles d'Aude adds 6km, the detour to Lézignan-Corbières adds 10km and the detour to the Gouffre Géant de Cabrespine cave adds 20km.

**Time:** 4 hours' driving. Allow a day for the main route, more with detours. Those with limited time should concentrate on the stretch between Caunes-Minervois and Minerve.

**Links to other tours:** From Caunes-Minervois, the D620 leads to Carcassonne (see page 126), 20km away. From Sales, the D920 leads to St-Pons-de-Thomières (see page 205), 25km away. From Capestang, the D16 leads to Puisserguier (see page 204), 5km away, and the D11 leads to Béziers (see page 200), 15km away. From Lézignan-Corbières, the D611 and D212 lead to Lagrasse (see page 136), 20km away.

Leave Narbonne northwest on the D607 across the flat countryside to **St-Marcel**.

**Detour:** From St-Marcel, the D1118 leads to **SALLELES D'AUDE ❶** (3km), passing its ruined abbey and crossing the **Canal du Midi** on the way to the **Amphoralis**, which is to the left beyond the village centre.

From St-Marcel, continue on the D607 and cross the Canal du Midi again in the picturesque hamlet of **LE SOMAIL ❷**. Then take the D207 through **St-Nazaire** to join the D124, which goes through **Paraza** beside the canal to **Argens-Minervois**.

**Detour:** At Argens-Minervois, cross the canal and the River Aude to join the D611, which goes to **LEZIGNAN-CORBIERES ❸** (5km).

From Argens-Minervois, the D124 continues between the canal and river to **Olonzac**. Despite being the 'capital' of the Minervois, this

**Left**
The Canal du Midi

**Above**
Minerve

small town has a rather neglected feel, particularly in the maze of narrow streets in the centre. However, it has a pleasant municipal park with ducks and swans on a pond. Leave on the D610 (towards Carcassonnne), but turn right off it after 5km on to the D11 to go to **RIEUX-MINERVOIS ❹** and then towards **CAUNES-MINERVOIS ❺**. Immaculately straight lines of vines cover almost every inch of the flat landscape.

**Detour:** Six kilometres after Rieux-Minervois, turn left on to the D620 and then right on to the D111 to visit the **GOUFFRE GEANT DE CABRESPINE ❻** cave (10km).

North from Caunes-Minervois the scenery changes as you wriggle along the D620 beside the River Argent-Double. The vineyards are now replaced by apple, cherry and peach orchards as the road climbs through **Citou**, below its castle ruins, and **Lespinassière**, whose square castle tower is a landmark high on the edge of its steep terrace. Approaching **Sales**, the road continues to climb through forests over the Col de Salette (886m) where you come to a sad reminder of World War II. From the road, a short flight of steps leads down to the Stèle de la Résistance, a memorial to two local men killed there by the Germans in July 1944.

At Sales, turn right on to the D920, which soon passes the **Roc Suzadou** (720m) viewpoint. The rock itself, jutting out above the countryside, is a good spot for a picnic – and fun for children to clamber over. After 5km, turn right again on to the D12 through **Ferrals-les-Montagnes**, dropping down all the time. Just after **St-**

**◖ La Bastide de Cabezac €€**
*18–20 Haneau de Cabezac, Bize-Minervois (just north of D5); tel: 04 68 46 66 10; email: contact@la-bastide-cabezac.com; www.la-bastide-cabezac.com. Open all year.* Twelve-room hotel and restaurant in a renovated 18th-century *relais de poste* between Béziers and Carcassonne. Swimming pool. Disabled access.

**Hôtel du Parc €**
*18 avenue Hompes,
Olonzac; tel: 04 68 91 14
55. Open all year.* Small,
very French hotel above a
busy bar. Next door to a
large school and opposite
a pleasant park.

**Hôtel du Résidence €€**
*35 avenue de la Cave,
Nissan-lez-Ensérune; tel: 04
67 37 00 63; email:
reservations@hotel-
residence.com; www.hotel-
residence.com. Open mid-
Jan–mid-Dec.* Comfortable
family-run hotel with 17
rooms, garden, pool and
garage.

**Julien-de-Molières**, turn left on to the D182, which runs above the **Canyon de la Cesse** (on the left), a deep winding ravine of white rocks below a plateau topped by brush and heather. Don't expect to see the river in this extraordinary canyon as it runs for several miles underground except after winter storms. Just before **MINERVE** ❼ are two natural bridges, the 30m-high **Grand Pont** and 15m-high **Petit Pont**, created as the river carved its way through the white cliffs. To visit the village, you have to park on the edge and walk. The landscape all around is wild and barren and on the plateaux of sweet-smelling *garrigue* you can find dolmens, Bronze Age burial chambers made of huge stone blocks whose entrances mysteriously face east or south. Continuing down the Cesse Valley, the D907 takes you past the village of **La Caunette** whose pale limestone buildings almost merge with the enormous cliff behind it. Arriving at the D5 (which becomes the D11), turn left to **CAPESTANG** ❽ and **OPPIDUM D'ENSERUNE** ❾ . From there, return to Narbonne through **Coursan** (whose large Gothic church has a Romanesque bell tower) on the D37 and then the D6009, which has long straight stretches lined with plane trees to provide shade in the heat of summer.

# Roman Languedoc

## Ratings

| | |
|---|---|
| Scenery | ●●●●● |
| Churches | ●●●●○ |
| History | ●●●●○ |
| Walking | ●●●●○ |
| Wine | ●●●●○ |
| Museums | ●●●○○ |
| Shopping | ●●●○○ |
| Villages | ●●○○○ |

The quiet wooded hillsides of the Monts de l'Espinouse, where this route takes you, are another world compared with the busy streets of Béziers where it begins. In between, it crosses that characteristic feature of the Languedoc plain, a seemingly endless patchwork of neatly planted vineyards. Along the way you have the choice of shopping, drinking or walking – or why not indulge in all three?

Plenty of roadside *caves* offer the opportunity to sample and buy wine. On reaching the Haut Languedoc Regional Park, shortly before St-Pons-de-Thomières, you will be tempted to leave your car and head into the hills along one of the many marked footpaths. Here the lush Monts de l'Espinouse have gloriously wide views dotted with lakes, waterfalls and prehistoric standing stones. For shopping, Béziers is well endowed with hypermarkets, but be prepared for its congested traffic in summer.

## BÉZIERS

**ⓘ Tourist Information**
*29 avenue Saint Saëns; tel: 04 67 76 84 00; email: accueil.tourisme@beziers-agglo.org; www.beziers-tourisme.fr. Open daily Jul–Aug; Mon–Sat Sept–Jun.*

**Ⓑ Château de Raissac**
*route de Murviel; tel: 04 67 49 17 60; email: info@raissac.com; www.raissac.com. Open Tue–Sat all year. Ceramics artist Christine Viennet's workshop and collections on display; wine cellar visit and tasting.*

Surrounded by vineyards, this lively town enjoys an attractive hillside setting above the River Orb and Canal du Midi. Its centrepiece is allée Paul Riquet, an acacia-shaded promenade created in honour of the famous engineer who built the canal in the 1660s. People gather there to gossip, stroll and browse among the stalls selling flowers and bric-a-brac. The top end slopes up to the town's grand 150-year-old theatre. At the other end is Plateau des Poètes, a park with ornate sculptures and a small lake surrounded by trees.

Narrow streets punctuated by intimate squares lead to the fortress-like **Cathédrale de St-Nazaire**, a landmark for miles around. It was rebuilt in its original distinctive Romanesque style with a beautiful rose window after being burnt down, when thousands of people had taken refuge inside, during the start of the Albigensian Crusade in 1209. Its 14th-century cloister leads into formal gardens, the Jardin de l'Evêché. The views down across the countryside from the cathedral's wide terrace are superb. You can see over the River Orb to the Oppidum d'Ensérune, with the Canigou mountain in the distance.

Map: Roman Languedoc

**Cathédrale de St-Nazaire** €€
*Open daily all year.*

**Musée du Biterrois** €
*Rampe du 96ème, Caserne Saint-Jacques; tel: 04 67 36 71 01; email: musee@ville-beziers.fr. Open Tue–Sat all year.*

**Musée des Beaux Arts** €
*place de la Révolution; tel: 04 67 28 38 78; email: musee@ville-beziers.fr. Open Tue–Sat all year.* The Fine Arts Museum comprises two mansions, Hôtel Fabregat and Hôtel Fayet near the cathedral. They hold works by Flemish and German masters.

The **Musée du Biterrois** (also called St-Jacques) in the former Royal Barracks covers the town's history from Roman times. Its exhibits include milestones that once lined the Via Domitia and the Trésor de Béziers, three silver platters from the 2nd, 3rd and 5th centuries, discovered in a local vineyard in 1983. It also has sections devoted to the building of the Canal du Midi and to local wines.

Today the town's highly successful rugby team, ASB, keeps it prominently on the European map. Bullfights are another sporting love.

## Accommodation and food in Béziers

**Le Cep d'Or** € *2 Impasse Notairie; tel: 04 67 49 28 09. Open Tue–Sun all year.* Tucked away in an old narrow street, this small restaurant offers a tapas plate of 18 different starters, though they might prevent your doing justice to its delicious pâtisserie.

**Imperator** €€ *28 allée Paul Riquet; tel: 04 67 49 02 25; email: info@hotel-imperator.fr; www.hotel-imperator.fr. Open all year.* Centrally located 45-room hotel in 200-year-old mansion overlooking the lively allée Paul Riquet promenade, but with garden and garage. No restaurant.

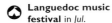 **Languedoc music festival** in *Jul.*

**Feria** including street entertainment and bullfights in *Aug.*

**Château de Lignan €€€** *Lignan-sur-Orb (7km northwest of Béziers on the D19); tel: 04 67 37 91 47; email: chateau-lignan@wanadoo.fr.com; www. chateaulignan.fr. Open all year.* Handsome, white three-storey mansion whose 6-hectare grounds beside the River Orb include several 300-year-old trees. Forty-nine rooms. Piano bar, swimming pool and whirlpool. Top-class restaurant (€€€) specialising in seafood and regional cuisine such as baked pigeon.

## ECLUSES DE FONSERANES

**Below**
Béziers by night

On the southwest edge of Béziers, just beyond the railway, this staircase of seven locks is one of the most remarkable features of the Canal du Midi, lifting the water 21.5m uphill. Boats pass through in convoy under the guidance of a lock-keeper, alternating the direction each hour. A parallel hydraulic lift-slope was built in 1983 but has never worked properly.

# FRAISSE-SUR-AGOUT

**ⓘ Fraisse-sur-Agout Tourist Information** *route de la Salvetat; tel: 04 67 97 53 81; email: ot-espinouse@wanadoo.fr; www.ot-espinouse.fr. Open daily Apr–Oct; Mon–Fri Nov–Mar.*

Nestled on the leafy banks of the River Agout, which fishermen rank highly, this mountain village got its name from the tall ash trees which have bordered it for centuries (*fraïsse* is the Occitan word for ash). Here, trout with mushrooms is a local speciality. During World War II the villagers were heavily involved with Resistance fighters based in the nearby Château de les Syères.

# LA SALVETAT-SUR-AGOUT

**ⓘ La Salvetat-sur-Agout Tourist Information** *place des Archers; tel: 04 67 97 64 44; email: salvetat-sur-agout.ot@wanadoo.fr; www.lasalvetatot.com. Open daily all year.*

Built on a promontory high above two rivers, the Vèbre and Agout, this little town, a maze of hilly narrow streets, traces its roots back to the Knights Templar, who founded 'new towns' in the 11th and 12th centuries to increase the value of their land. The 11th-century Chapelle St-Etienne de Cavall, below the town near the 800-year-old three-arch bridge, was a stop on the Via Tolosana, one of four routes which pilgrims used on their way to Spain.

# OLARGUES

**ⓘ Olargues Tourist Information** *avenue de la Gare; tel: 04 67 23 02 21; email: otsi.olargues@ orange.fr; www.olargues.org. Open daily Jul–Aug; Mon–Sat Sept–Jun.*

**ⓜ Musée d'Art et Traditions Populaires** € *rue de la Place Escalier de la Commanderie; tel: 04 67 97 70 79. Open Sun–Fri Apr–Oct; rest of year by arrangement.*

Olargues, one of the prettiest villages in the area, perches above the River Jaur on a rocky outcrop with a mountain ridge, Le Caroux, as its backdrop. The best view of it is from the quaint 800-year-old humpback bridge, Pont du Diable, over the river. A medieval bell tower, all that remains of its 11th-century fort, looks down on the red rooftops of the old houses. Through a stone gateway opposite the tourist office, steep narrow streets lead past the 17th-century church up to the tower which enjoys a spectacular view down to the bridge and river with the mountains beyond. The **Musée d'Art et Traditions Populaires** in the old Commandery building traces the village's history.

# PUISSERGUIER

**ⓘ Puisserguier Tourist Information** *7 boulevard Victor Hugo; tel: 04 67 93 85 27; email: ot.puisserguier@free.fr; www.ot-puisserguier.com. Open Mon–Sat all year.*

It's easy to hurry along the modern main street of this little town without realising that its medieval centre is only a few steps away. Be sure to park your car and turn up the narrow rue de la République to the intimate place de l'Eglise, which is surrounded by a 12th-century castle, a Romanesque church and other ancient buildings, some now occupied by small shops.

# ROQUEBRUN

**ⓘ Roquebrun Tourist Information** *avenue des Oranges; tel: 04 67 89 79 97; email: office-tourisme-roquebrun@wanadoo.fr; www.roquebrun.org. Open daily Jul–Aug; Mon–Sat Sept–Jun. Guided tours available.*

Beneath its distinctive old tower, this little town spreads down a sunny hillside to the River Orb. Known as the 'little Nice of the Hérault' because of its luxuriant vegetation, it benefits from a microclimate thanks to its sheltered position and 300 days of sunshine a year. The exotic **Jardin Méditerranéen** (*tel: 04 67 89 55 29. Open daily mid-Feb–mid–Nov*) features 200 varieties of cactus on riverside terraces. Canoeing is a popular pursuit on the river as it is navigable for 37km, including 11km of rapids.

# ST-CHINIAN

**ⓘ St-Chinian Tourist Information** *I grand rue; tel: 04 67 38 02 67; email: ot.saint.chinian@ gmail.com; www.ot-saint-chinian.com. Open daily Jul–Aug; Mon–Sat Sept & May–Jun; Mon & Wed–Thur Oct–Apr.*

Surrounded by the vineyards, St-Chinian is a busy wine town with a long shaded square. Shepherds used to bring their wool to be spun in its mills here, but now it is notable for its **Cave Coopérative de Vinification** where you can sample and buy the wines produced by the 20 villages which belong to the St-Chinian Appellation d'Origine Contrôlée. Wine has been produced in this area for centuries, as it has a favourable climate and geological setting. St-Chinian wines are among the best of the Languedoc region. Vineyard tours, market visits and wine tastings are organised by the **Maison des Vins**, which is an information centre and shop window of local products, and wine festivals are held in the villages in the spring.

## St-Pons-de-Thomieres

This old mountain town grew up around a Benedictine abbey founded in 936 by Count Raymond Pons of Toulouse. It stood on the site of the present cathedral, which dates back to the 12th century and is richly decorated with sculptures, including a huge red and white marble altar. Though an impressive building, it was originally very much bigger as the choir used to stretch over the car park which is now in front of it. This was destroyed by Protestants in 1567, which accounts for the irregular layout and subsequent additions.

Being situated at the head of the Jaur Valley in the centre of the Haut Languedoc Regional Park, the town is a good base for enjoying the great outdoors, whether by walking, riding or mountain biking. A network of footpaths and trails radiates from it into the hills. The landscape all around is dotted with caves and prehistoric megaliths and menhirs. They include some of the oldest in Europe as the **Musée Municipal de Préhistoire** shows.

**Musée Municipal de Préhistoire** €€
rue du Barry; tel: 04 67 97 22 61. Open Tue–Sun Jul–mid-Sept; Thur–Sun mid-Sept–Jun.

**Pig festival** in Feb and **Chestnut festival** in Oct.

**Below**
La Salvetat-sur-Agout

## Accommodation and food in St-Pons-de-Thomières

**Bel Horizon** €€ *9 chemin d'Artenac; tel: 04 67 97 33 51; email: belhorizon34@orange.fr; www.belhorizon34.com. Open Tue–Sun (reservations essential).* Smart, peacefully located hotel-restaurant with five rooms, terrace and panoramic views.

**Les Bergeries de Pondérach** €€ *route de Narbonne; tel: 04 67 97 02 57; email: bergeriesponderach@wanadoo.fr; www.les-bergeries-de-ponderach.abesalles.com. Open mid-Mar–mid-Nov.* A 300-year-old farmhouse on the edge of the town with seven rooms and a large garden. The restaurant features local produce such as chicken from the Montagne Noire and lamb from the Cévennes.

## The Albigensian Crusade

Although named after Albi, this fierce crusade to stamp out Catharism started in Béziers. In 1209, the French king, Philippe Auguste, saw it as his chance to subjugate the powerful counts of Toulouse, who were tolerating this new creed which had spread throughout the Languedoc. The king was supported by Pope Innocent III, who was also keen to see the 'heresy' stamped out.

In Béziers, the Roman Catholics stood loyally beside the comparatively few Cathars when the crusaders arrived from the north down the Rhône Valley and started to rout them out. Many fled for shelter to the cathedral and the Madeleine church where they burnt to death when the buildings were set on fire. Afterwards, the papal legate proudly reported that they had 'only killed 20,000'.

Initially, the crusade was led by Simon de Montfort, but he was killed laying siege – for the second time – to Toulouse. The final bloody slaughter took place in Montségur in 1244, though 80 more years were to pass before the Inquisition succeeded in stamping out Catharism completely.

# Suggested tour

**Total distance:** 145km. The detour to the Saut de Vésoles waterfall adds 10km and the detour to the Lac de la Raviège adds 24km.

**Time:** 4 hours' driving. Allow at least a day for the main route, more with detours. Those with limited time should concentrate on the stretch between St-Pons-de-Thomières and Olargues for scenery or the stretch between Béziers and St-Chinian for wine and shopping.

**Links to other tours:** From Béziers, the D11 leads west to Capestang (*see page 190*), 15km away, the D612 leads east to Agde (*see page 268*), 23km away, and the N9 leads northeast to Pézenas (*see page 274*), 22km away. From Puisserguier, the D16 leads south to Capestang, 5km away. From St-Pons-de-Thomières, the D920 leads southwest to Sales (*see page 198*), 25km away. From La Salvetat-sur-Agout, the D907 leads north to Lacaune (*see page 185*), 20km away.

Before leaving **BÉZIERS ❶**, pause at the **ECLUSES DE FONSERANES ❷** on the **Canal du Midi**, reached along a track on the southern edge of the town. In summer, the queues of boats going up and down this staircase of locks are always entertaining to watch. The flat N112 then takes you northwest towards **PUISSERGUIER ❸** through the St-Chinian vineyards which stretch along the gently rounded ridges making the most of the abundant sunshine. The reddish soil is poor, almost rocky, and seems to glow in the setting sun. After **ST-CHINIAN ❹**, you soon leave the vineyards behind as the road climbs into

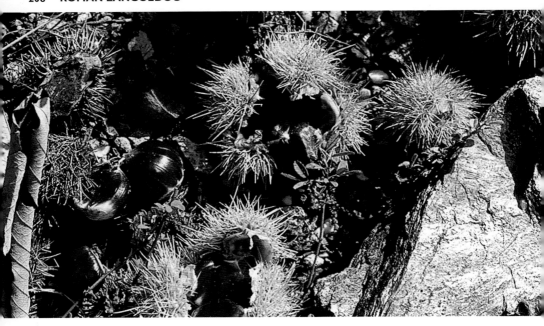

**Above**
The soil in the Somail area is ideally suited to chestnuts

wooded hills, snaking up the Défilé de l'Llouvre to **ST-PONS-DE-THOMIERES** ❺ in the heart of the **Haut Languedoc Regional Park**. The D907 winds up picturesquely out of the town with pretty views back over its rooftops before it climbs over the Col de Cabarétou (949m). This has a splendid view over the sea to the southeast and of the Somail hills stretching away to the north. The Somail area, which rises to 1,000m above the Jaur Valley, is the lushest and most fertile part of the Monts de l'Espinouse. The hillsides are mainly covered with chestnut and beech trees, though these sometimes give way to expanses of moorland patched with heather.

**Detour:** To see the 200m-high **Saut de Vésoles** waterfall, a noted beauty spot, turn right at the Col de Cabarétou on to the D169 and then, after 4km, right again for a further 1km. The water tumbles over massive granite boulders to the River Jaur. The D907 then winds down to **LA SALVETAT-SUR-AGOUT** ❻.

**Detour:** From La Salvetat-sur-Agout, a pleasant 24km drive, mostly in woods, on the D14, leads round the **Lac de la Raviège** reservoir, part of the River Agout. The road crosses the dam at the far end and passes **Les Bouldouires**, a beach popular for swimming and watersports.

Leave La Salvetat-sur-Agout on the D14, which follows the river through gently rolling countryside to **FRAISSE-SUR-AGOUT** ❼.

The D14 climbs over the Col de Fontfroide (972m) where a roadside memorial commemorates the Resistance and De Gaulle's leadership of

● **Roc Fourcat €**
*Mons la Triviale,
near Tarrasac; tel: 04 67
97 71 83; email:
didier.granier@neuf.fr.*
Open all year. Simple
eight-room family-run
hotel beside the River Orb
with scenic terrace.
Located 3km from the
Héric Gorges and close to
a former railway track that
now serves as a green path
for exploring the mountain
landscape on foot, bicycle
or horseback.

the Free French in World War II. An urn beneath it contains the ashes of concentration camp victims.

Ahead the road zigzags dramatically over the Espinouse hills before dropping down into **OLARGUES** ❽. Follow the D908 (towards Clermont l'Hérault), turning sharp right after 8km on to the D14 over the decorative white suspension bridge built in 1928 at **Tarassac** to go to **ROQUEBRUN** ❾. As the road wriggles along the wooded Gorges de l'Orb beneath rocky ridges, the scenery becomes distinctly 'southern'. There are red-roofed villages and increasing numbers of vineyards as it flattens out on the way back through **Cessenon-sur-Orb** to Béziers.

### Getting out of the car

To stretch your legs, a gentle hour's walk is marked out from the church in Fraisse-sur-Agout. It leads beside the River Agout, showing how the force of the water is used to create hydroelectricity through simple examples such as driving a musical wheel and a piston. Nearby there are picnic tables on a pretty island shaded by ash trees.

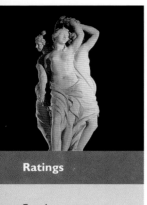

# Montpellier

## Ratings

| | |
|---|---|
| Food and drink | ●●●●○ |
| Shopping | ●●●●○ |
| Architecture | ●●●○○ |
| Entertainment | ●●●○○ |
| History | ●●●○○ |
| Museums | ●●●○○ |
| Art | ●●○○○ |
| Children | ●○○○○ |

T he citizens of Montpellier have a reputation for being sociable and good-tempered, perhaps because they have the benefit of the place de la Comédie. This enormous square, surrounded by cafés and restaurants, is a popular spot for chatting over the local Languedoc wine. A high proportion of those who gravitate there each evening are young, as the city has a student population of nearly 50,000. It is also swelled by an influx of visitors throughout the hot summer months.

Montpellier first made its mark on the world through its medical school, which was founded over 1,000 years ago and is still the most prestigious in France. This has also led to the development of a strong research base, particularly in biochemistry. Today the city prides itself on being forward-looking, epitomised by the construction during the 1980s of Antigone, a daring postmodern housing development in pseudo-classical style.

## Getting there and getting around

ⓘ **Languedoc-Roussillon regional information office** 20 rue de la République; tel: 04 67 22 81 00; email: contact.crtlr@sunfrance.com; www.tourisme-languedoc-roussillon.com. Open Mon–Fri all year.

**By air:** Montpellier Méditerranée is 8km southeast of the city centre on the D21 or D66. Information: *tel: 04 67 20 85 00; email: accueil.aerogare@montpellier.aeroport.fr.* Facilities include car hire, hotel reservations, restaurants, nursery and local products shop. As you come in to land, watch out for the view over the lagoon, Etang de Mauguio, home to 4,000 flamingos. Buses to the city centre run every 30 to 50 minutes (depending on time and day); journey time: 15 minutes.

**By car:** Leave the A9, which skirts the south side of the city, from the north at Sortie Est and take the D66, avenue Pierre Mendès-France, to the centre. From the south, leave at Sortie Sud and at the Rond-Point des Prés d'Arènes take avenue de Maurin. Driving in the centre can be a nightmare. As well as being busy, it is difficult to negotiate, as much of the central area, signposted Centre Historique or L'Ecusson, is

**City Tourist
Information** *30 allée
Jean de Lattre de Tassigny,
Esplanade Comédie; tel: 04
67 60 60 60; email:
contact@ot-montpellier.fr;
www.ot-montpellier.fr. Open
daily all year.* Coach parking
at *Moulin de l'Evêque, 78
avenue du Pirée.*

pedestrianised. Moreover, the new Antigone area, which stretches like a spur off the east side of the centre, is both difficult to locate and worse to get into, especially from the south and west, due to its one-way streets and restricted entry. The important thing to bear in mind is that boulevard d'Antigone and boulevard de L'Aéroport International run along the north side of it and allée du Nouveau Monde, avenue Samuel de Champlain and avenue Jacques Cartier along the south side. They are linked by rue Léon Blum.

**By train:** rue Jules Ferry. Reservations: *tel: 36 35.*

**Parking:** Though there are parking meters on the streets around the Centre Historique, the underground car park at place de la Comédie allows more time for sightseeing. There are also several car parks around the Antigone, but be warned: to get to them, you have to crack the one-way almost-bus-only street layout, which even the locals find difficult.

**ⓘ City Card Montpellier** The tourist office sells the City Card, which allows free bus and tram travel and entry to most tourist and cultural venues over 1, 2 or 3 days, including a guided tour of the historical centre and a visit to the gardens of Château de Flaugergues.

**Public transport:** The Centre Historique is easily walkable from the Antigone area through Le Polygone shopping mall, though it's not so straightforward finding your way back again. **Le Tramway**, the city's latest pride and joy, runs east–west over 15km, with distinctive deep blue air-conditioned trams (*www.tram-way.com*). A second line, running north–south, opens in 2012. **Petibus** is a minibus service on a circular route every 6 minutes Monday–Saturday around the Centre Historique and out to the Antigone. Normal buses go further afield; **TAM** *tel: 04 67 22 87 87*. Single-journey fares include changes. Services to the local beaches including Carnon-Plage, La Grande Motte and Palavas-les-Flots depart from the bus station in rue Jules Ferry, which is linked by escalators to the railway station in place Auguste-Gibert.

There are taxi ranks beside place de la Comédie and outside the train station, 24-hour call: *tel: 04 67 03 20 00, 04 67 58 10 10*.

Nearly 50 **Vélomagg** bike 'stations', where you can pick up a hire-bike for a half- or whole day, are located around the city centre, including at the tourist office – handy for sightseeing or even a trip to the seaside; *tel: 04 67 22 87 82*.

Guided tours in French start from the tourist office (*twice daily Jun–Sept; Wed & Sat–Sun Oct–May*). From the esplanade Charles de Gaulle, the Petit Train (road-train) sets off on a tour of the town every 45 minutes from 1400; *tel: 06 63 46 63 48*.

# Sights

### Antigone
Only the French could have dared to sanction such a startling new quarter only a few steps away from the Centre Historique. As the name suggests, this is classical Greece and Rome re-created in a postmodern development of apartments, offices, hotels and shops. It was conceived in 1980 by a Catalan architect, Ricardo Bofill, to provide housing on a site vacated by the army. Whether you get to it on foot through Le Polygone shopping mall or approach it from the side, it always comes as a surprise. The tall, beige, pseudo-classical buildings face wide, circular, symmetrically tiled piazzas. Avenues of trees, window boxes and giant pots trailing with geraniums add softness, but the area, which is pedestrian-only, has yet to really come alive, probably because *le tout Montpellier* is out gossiping on the place de la Comédie.

### Arc de Triomphe
This grand triumphal arch at the Porte de Peyrou was erected in honour of Louis XIV in 1691. Bas-reliefs around it depict the major events during his reign, including the building of the Canal du Midi, the capture of Naumur and, something that he might with hindsight prefer history to forget, the revocation of the Edict of Nantes, which made Protestantism illegal.

**Musée Atger** *2 rue de l'Ecole de Médecine; tel: 04 67 41 76 40. Open Mon, Wed & Fri afternoons Sept–Jul, except Christmas. Admission free.*

**Musée de la Pharmacie** *15 avenue Charles Flahault; tel: 04 67 54 80 62. Open Tue & Fri mornings all year. Admission free.*

**Jardin des Plantes** *boulevard Henri IV; tel: 04 67 63 43 22; email: jdplantes@univ-montpl.fr; www.jardindesplantes.univ-montpl.fr. Open Tue–Sun all year. Admission free.*

**Musée du Vieux Montpellier** *Hôtel de Varenne, 2 place Pétrarque; tel: 04 67 66 02 94. Open Tue–Sat all year. Admission free.*

**Musée Fabre** *€€ 39 boulevard Bonne Nouvelle; tel: 04 67 14 83 00; email: musee.fabre@montpellier-agglo.com; www.montpellier-agglo.com. Open daily all year.*

**Below**
Montpellier's Antigone district

### Cathédrale St-Pierre

The city's cathedral was started in the 14th century but not completed until the 19th. Its most striking feature is an immense Gothic porch with two large pillars, though they are somewhat out of proportion to the rest of the building.

### Faculté de Médecine

The city's medical school occupies former abbey buildings, much enlarged and renovated. It was founded in 1220 and claims to be the oldest in the world. Rabelais, the 16th-century French satirist, was one of its most famous graduates. Its **Musée Atger** displays over 500 drawings collected by Jean-François Atger in the 18th century. Other university faculties also have specialist museums, including the **Musée de la Pharmacie** in avenue Charles Flahault.

### Jardin des Plantes

France's oldest botanic garden was planted in 1593 to enable the medical school students to study medicinal plants. A *Phillyrea latifolia* tree dating from that time is among its treasures. Statues of eminent botanists grace paths leading to an orangery, conservatories and ponds.

### Musée du Vieux Montpellier

The museum of old Montpellier in the Hôtel de Varenne conjures up images of the city as it used to be, through pictures, old maps and furniture. On its top floor, the small **Musée du Fougau**, run by volunteers, displays traditional costumes, old sewing machines and local crafts.

### Musée Fabre

Facing the Esplanade, the Musée Fabre is the city's main art gallery and pride of Montpellier. It houses one of the finest art collections in all France. Over 800 works are displayed in an area covering over

**Musée de l'Histoire de Montpellier** € place Jean Jaurès; tel: 04 67 54 33 16. Open Tue–Sat all year. Admission free for visitors on a guided tour from the Office de Tourisme.

**Musée Languedocien** €€ 7 rue Jacques Coeur; tel: 04 67 52 93 03. Open Mon–Sat all year.

**Musée du Fougau** € Hôtel de Varenne, 2 place Pétrarque; tel: 04 67 84 31 58. Open Wed–Thur afternoons all year.

9,200sq metres. The gallery has undergone 3 years' refurbishment, modernisation and building work and now has a modern purpose-built extension in addition to the original buildings, a fine mansion that was once a Jesuit college and the Hôtel de Massilian. The Fabre Museum is the home of works by François-Xavier Fabre and French and Italian artists of the 16th to 19th centuries. Bequests have added Dutch and Flemish masterpieces and a collection of 19th-century works featuring Eugène Delacroix, Jean Auguste Ingres, Raoul Dufy and Gustave Courbet. New sections of the Fabre display works from the graphic arts collections that number 3,500 drawings and 900 engravings, and ceramics and sculptures. The renovated Fabre Museum has introduced new services including a multimedia gallery, creative workshops, an auditorium, a bookshop and a restaurant.

### Musée Languedocien

Housed in a carefully restored 15th-century mansion, the Musée Languedocien displays prehistoric objects and classical artefacts from ancient Rome, Greece and Egypt.

### Place de la Canourgue

Surrounded by grand mansions, this handsome square was once the centre of the city. Its fountain with a unicorn was built in the 1760s to distribute water around the town from the nearby St-Clément Aqueduct.

### Place de la Comédie

This enormous square laid out in the 18th century is the heart of the city, despite being on the edge of the Centre Historique. The Comédie theatre with its fancy stucco façade, built in 1889, is at one end. In the centre is the ornately sculpted Fontaine les Trois-Grâces depicting – as you might not expect from its name – three male bathers. The square is known locally as l'Oeuf, after its egg-shaped central roundabout which traffic used to race around until it was pedestrianised.

### Promenade du Peyrou

The promenade's two tiers of terraces were built at the beginning of the 18th century at the city's highest point. Their purpose was to provide a suitably impressive setting for a commemorative equestrian statue of Louis XIV, which was eventually placed there in 1718. Due to several misadventures, including toppling off a boat into the River Garonne, it had taken 20 years to arrive, and was then destroyed during the revolution. The present statue is a 150-year-old replica. In the 1760s, the promenade acquired the splendid Château d'Eau, a water tower which is truly a mini-castle with pillars, arches and carved pediments. It was built for the St-Clément Aqueduct, which is itself a grand affair, inspired by the Roman Pont du Gard.

From the top terrace you get a splendid view over the city and countryside with the sea and foothills of the Cévennes in the distance.

# Shopping

The old streets in the Centre Historique are delightful for shopping, thanks to the many small boutiques which have opened in the ground floors of the ancient buildings. Those in rue de l'Ancien-Courrier occupy a former abbey and have vaulted ceilings. Their wares are equally appealing, as in **Bérénice**, a hat shop for men and women at 7 rue Jean Moulin; and **Pomme de Reinette**, 33 rue de l'Aiguillerie, which is crammed with toys old and new. The modern **Polygone** shopping mall is filled with chain stores as well as **Galeries Lafayette** and **Inno**. There's a daily covered food market at place Castellane and an open-air market on the Plan Cabannes along boulevard Gambetta. On Saturdays, a flea market occupies the arches of the old aqueduct along the boulevard des Arceaux.

# Entertainment

Because of the city's warm climate and large number of students, much of its evening entertainment consists simply of strolling the old streets, sitting at cafés and watching street performers such as buskers and jugglers. Place de la Comédie, which has the distinction of being the largest traffic-free square in France, gets packed out on summer evenings.

Entertainment of a more formal kind is provided by ten theatres, notably opera at **l'Opéra-Comédie**, place de la Comédie, and **Opéra Berlioz** in the Corum building. Box office for both: *tel: 04 67 60 19 99; email: location@opera-montpellier.com; www.opera-montpellier.com*

For multiplex cinemas, head east from the town centre along avenue Pierre Mendès-France.

Nightclubs include **Le Cotton Club**, which specialises in 30s and 70s music (*129 avenue de Palavas; tel: 04 67 65 45 25*).

Annual events include: **Spring Theatre Festival**, le Printemps des Comédiens (*tel: 04 67 63 66 67*), and **Dance Festival** (*tel: 04 67 60 83 60*), both in June. **Festival de Radio France et de Montpellier** is a 3-week music festival in mid-July featuring young performers, including free jazz concerts (*tel: 04 67 61 66 81*). The tourist office website has up-to-date details at *www.ot-montpellier.fr*

# Accommodation and food

There are hotels in all price ranges. Several are situated in the streets around the railway station such as rue de la République, rue de Verdun and rue Maguelone. The newest are in the Antigone area.

**Hôtel du Palais €** *3 rue du Palais des Guilhem; tel: 04 67 60 47 38; email: hoteldupalais2@wanadoo.fr; www.hoteldupalais-montpellier.fr. Open all year.* An inexpensive small hotel in the heart of the Centre Historique. Pets allowed.

**Hôtel Mercure Centre €€** *218 rue du Bastion Ventadour; tel: 04 67 99 89 89; email: h3043@accor.com; www.mercure.com. Open all year.* Handily situated modern hotel within a short walking distance of the Antigone area or place de la Comédie and the old quarter.

**New Hôtel du Midi €€** *22 boulevard Victor Hugo; tel: 04 67 92 69 61; email: montpelliermidi@new-hotel.com; www.new-hotel.com. Open all year.* Though occupying a grand 19th-century building (only steps from the place de la Comédie), it has smart new rooms, all air-conditioned.

**Pullman Montpellier Antigone €€€** *1 rue des Pertuisanes; tel: 04 67 99 72 72; email: H1294@accor.com; www.pullmanhotels.com. Open all year.* Modern in design and facilities. Well placed between Le Polygone and Antigone, it is next door to an underground garage. The rooftop terrace with a restaurant and pool has one of the best views in town.

As a university town, Montpellier abounds in inexpensive good-quality eating places. You are never far away from a restaurant or café in the old squares and streets of the Centre Historique. They come in all price ranges and their ancient surroundings make them very atmospheric.

**Le Bistrot St-Côme €** *2 place Saint-Côme; tel: 04 67 60 75 24. Open daily all year.* One of the best of the small restaurants in the old quarter. In summer, its tables spread on to the small square beside St-Côme church.

**Café du Théâtre €** *3 place de la Comédie; tel: 04 67 66 06 55. Open daily all year to 0200.* Offers an inexpensive *plat du jour* (dish of the day) as well as snacks. Its best feature is its prime position for watching the world go by.

**Below**
Fresh, local produce is always easy to find

**Cellier Morel** € *27 rue de l'Aiguillerie; tel: 04 67 66 46 36; www.celliermorel.com. Open Mon–Sat all year.* A small but smart restaurant serving quality fare ranging from lobster cous cous to Lozère specialities such as *aligot* (potato mashed with cheese).

**Les Bains** €€ *6 rue Richelieu; tel: 04 67 60 70 87. Open Mon–Sat all year.* Occupies a leafy courtyard and has small arcaded rooms which functioned for 200 years as public baths until they closed in 1963. A *salon-de-thé* in the afternoons, it becomes a fashionable restaurant serving local specialities at moderate prices in the evenings.

**La Diligence** €€ *2 place Pétrarque; tel: 04 67 66 12 21; www.la-diligence.com. Open Mon–Sat all year.* A smart little restaurant in a vaulted building, typical of the many atmospheric eateries which lurk in the narrow streets of the Centre Historique.

# Suggested walk

**Length:** 2.5km.

**Duration:** 1 hour.

After lingering at a café on the **PLACE DE LA COMEDIE ❶**, stroll under the plane trees along the **Esplanade Charles-de-Gaulle**. This wide promenade, laid out in the 18th century, is bordered by flowerbeds and fountains. It leads to the **Corum** building (Palais des Congrès Opéra), a bunker-like 1980s addition in concrete and pink granite (from Finland) which houses the Opéra Berlioz, a conference centre and exhibition rooms. From the terrace (*open daily all year*), the dazzling white spire of the **Eglise Ste-Anne** stands out in the distance over the rooftops.

Rue Girard and rue des Augustins on the west side lead immediately into a different world, the **Centre Historique**. Locals call it *lou clapas* (the rubble) but it is signposted **L'Ecusson** because of its coat-of-arms shape formed by the boulevards which surrounded its maze of old narrow streets. The whole area, with its many old churches and Renaissance *hôtels particuliers* (mansions) built in cream stone, is a delight – the true spirit of Montpellier.

Making your way towards the **CATHEDRALE ST-PIERRE ❷**, perhaps down the hilly rue de l'Université and turning along rue de Candolle, you will see informative plaques on the most important of the 17th- and 18th-century mansions with their decorative stonework and wrought-iron balustrades. A glimpse through any of the sturdy wooden doorways which happen to be open is likely to reveal an intimate courtyard. The area was rebuilt after the destruction of virtually all the earlier buildings during various religious wars. Interesting little shops and restaurants now occupy many of the ground floors.

## Les Folies Montpelliéraines

Scattered in the countryside around Montpellier, anything from 3km to 16km from the city centre, are its *folies*. These are not the buildings usually referred to as 'follies', but elegant family mansions. Indeed, the rest of France would call them *châteaux*. They were built in the 18th century by local aristocrats and wealthy bourgeois citizens, particularly bankers, as country houses where they could retreat during the hot summer months. Most have pretty gardens adorned with statuettes and fountains. At least 30 are still surrounded by their original vineyards, though the city's suburbs have encroached on some. A number can be visited, including several now owned by the city such as **Château d'O** and **Château la Mosson** (details from the tourist office). Others are still private homes whose owners often act as hosts to visitors. Moderate entry charges provide much-needed funds towards their upkeep.

**Place St-Pierre**, with the cathedral and **FACULTE DE MEDECINE** ❸ beside it, is one of many small squares where you can while away the time in a café or restaurant. From the square, narrow streets and cobbled alleys lead uphill past **PLACE DE LA CANOURGUE** ❹ to the **ARC DE TRIOMPHE** ❺ on the edge of the Centre Historique. The **PROMENADE DU PEYROU** is across the busy boulevard Prof Valleton.

Turning back along the broad rue Foch, a right turn into rue du Petit Scel takes you to the oldest part of the city, the **Ancien Courrier** district. Rue de l'Ancien Courrier, which leads back towards place de la Comédie, is particularly worth strolling along because of its interesting old façades and courtyards.

### Also worth exploring

🏰 **Château de Flaugergues €€**
*1744 avenue Albert Einstein; tel: 04 99 52 66 37; email: contact@flaugergues.com; www.flaugergues.com. Open daily Jun–Sept; Mon–Sat Oct–May.*

**Château de la Mogère**
*€ 2235 route de Vauguières; tel: 04 67 65 72 01. Open daily afternoons Jun–Sept; Sat–Sun Oct–May.*

Château de Flaugergues, Château de la Mogère and Château d'Assas are three very different examples of the *folies* (*see box above*) in the countryside around Montpellier. **Flaugergues**, a 15-minute drive east from the city centre, is one of the oldest. An unassuming, early 18th-century mansion in cream stone set in a symmetrical French garden beside informal gardens and woodland, it is the home of the de Colbert family. Count Henri de Colbert, his wife Brigitte or one of their children show visitors round. Vineyards which were first cultivated by the Romans surround it. Inside, the walls of the extravagant staircase, which occupies a quarter of the entire interior, are covered in Brussels tapestries and family portraits. The lived-in rooms contain a variety of family treasures including some fine antique furniture. The count's highly regarded wines are on sale in the winery's cellars in an adjoining courtyard.

**Château de la Mogère** nestles in a little piece of parkland among the fields close to the airport exit from the A9 autoroute, 4km east of the city centre. The château is open for visits in the afternoons during

**Château d'Assas**
€€ Assas; tel: 04 67
59 61 60. Open by
appointment.

the summer, when it is not in use for wedding receptions and other events.

The castle-like **Château d'Assas**, built in 1759, is 12km north of the city in Assas on the D109 beyond Castelnau. It is the home of Madame Demangel who owns a collection of musical instruments, including an 18th-century harpsichord. Another treasure is a small decoratively painted domestic organ positif dating from 1737. Concerts are staged in the château occasionally. Also look for an unusual collection of model steam engines. The grounds are landscaped with French- and English-style gardens. The château gives its name to the finest wine produced in the village's vineyards, which can be bought at Vignerons du Pic, *285 avenue de Ste-Croix; tel: 04 67 59 62 55; www.vigneronsdupic.com. Open Mon–Sat all year.*

# Grottes and cirques

## Ratings

| | |
|---|---|
| Caves | ●●●●● |
| Geology | ●●●●● |
| Scenery | ●●●●○ |
| Villages | ●●●●○ |
| Food | ●●●○○ |
| Historical sights | ●●●○○ |
| Children | ●●○○○ |
| Outdoor activities | ●●○○○ |

The word cirque (natural amphitheatre of rocks) will have a new significance after you travel this route up the valley of the River Hérault. It includes two very different cirques. The deep wide bowl at Navacelles is surely one of the most spectacular pieces of countryside in France, whereas the cluster of massive eroded dolomite rocks at Mourèze is more like a crowded ghost town.

The route also visits some of the caves (*grottes*) that lie under the rugged white limestone hills and plateaux. Patched with yellow gorse, these hills are divided up by the surprisingly green waters of the Hérault and its tributaries.

Rural as the countryside feels once you leave the main roads, it is by no means remote, particularly now that the new A75 autoroute speeds motorists through it, and it is punctuated with small towns where pavement cafés spill out invitingly on to shaded squares.

## ANIANE

**ⓘ Aniane Tourist Information** *Mairie Chapelle des Pénitents; tel: 04 67 57 01 42; email: com.aniane@gmail.com; www.ville-aniane.wanadoo.fr. Open Mon–Sat all year.*

The roots of this busy little town go back to 792 when St Benoît founded a Benedictine monastery here. Many of the tall old houses along the straight narrow streets in the old quarter have fancy stonework and wrought-iron balconies, a reminder of the town's importance in the Middle Ages when it was on the ancient salt route north of the Mediterranean lagoons.

## CIRQUE DE NAVACELLES

This 280m-deep basin in the mountains, 1.5km across, is one of the most spectacular natural wonders that Europe has to offer, especially for motorists. The road winds down the sides, looking like a thin thread on the grey limestone hillsides which are patched with scrubby bushes and yellow gorse. The River Vis meanders

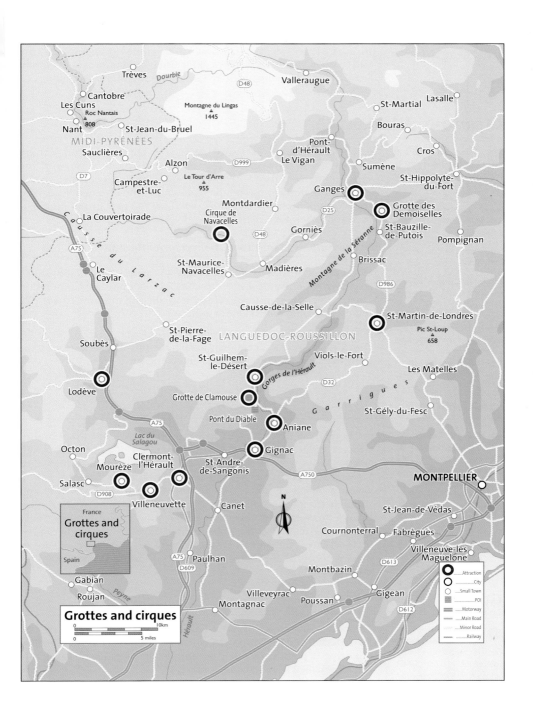

Trèves
*Dourbie*
(D48)
Valleraugue

Cantobre
Les Cuns
Roc Nantais
St-Martial
Lasalle

Nant
808
St-Jean-du-Bruel
Bouras

Montagne du Lingas
1445
Cros

MIDI-PYRÉNÉES

Sauclières
Pont
d'Hérault
Le Vigan
Sumène

St-Hippolyte-
du-Fort

(D7)
Alzon
(D999)

Campestre-
et-Luc
Le Tour d'Arre
955
Ganges

Grotte des
Demoiselles

Montdardier
(D25)

La Couvertoirade
Cirque de
Navacelles
St-Bauzille-
de-Putois
Pompignan

(A75)
(D48)
Gorniès

Le
Caylar
St-Maurice-
Navacelles
Madières
Brissac

Montagne de la Séranne
(D986)

Causse-de-la-Selle
St-Martin-de-Londres

St-Pierre-
de-la-Fage
LANGUEDOC-ROUSSILLON
Pic St-Loup
658

Soubès

St-Guilhem-
le-Désert
Viols-le-Fort
Les Matelles

*Gorges de l'Hérault*
(D32)

Lodève
Grotte de Clamouse

Pont du Diable
Aniane
*Garrigues*
St-Gély-du-Fesc

(A75)

*Lac du
Salagou*
Gignac

Octon
Clermont-
l'Hérault
St-Andre-
de-Sangonis
(A750)
MONTPELLIER

Mourèze
Salasc

(D908)
Villeneuvette
Canet
St-Jean-de-Védas

France
**Grottes and
cirques**
Cournonterral
Fabrègues

Spain
(A75)
Paulhan
(D613)
Villeneuve-lès-
Maguelone

(D609)

Gabian
Montbazin

Roujan
*Peyne*
Gigean

Villeveyrac
Poussan
(D612)

Montagnac

**Grottes and cirques**

0 ——— 10km
0 ——— 5 miles

*Hérault*

○ ....... Attraction
◎ ....... City
○ ....... Small Town
■ ....... POI
▬▬ ..... Motorway
━━ ..... Main Road
── ..... Minor Road
┄┄ ..... Railway

through the cirque, crossed by a single-arched bridge in the tiny village of St-Maurice-Navacelles, which nestles almost at the bottom. Stop here for refreshment and to take in the awesome surroundings.

# CLERMONT L'HERAULT

**Clermont l'Hérault Tourist Information**
place Jean Jaurès; tel: 04 67 96 23 86; email: tourisme@cc-clermontais.fr; www.cc-clermontais.fr. Open daily Jul–Aug; Mon–Sat Sept–Jun.

There is a market on Wed mornings.

**Huilerie Coopérative**
avenue Président Wilson; tel: 04 67 96 10 36; email: olidoc@wanadoo.fr; www.olidoc.com. Open Mon–Sat all year. Sells olive oil made on the premises from olives supplied by over 200 local producers.

Clermont l'Hérault is overlooked by the ruins of its huge 10th-century castle whose ramparts and towers provide splendid views of the surrounding countryside. Eglise St-Paul, which was fortified in the 15th century to help defend the town during the Hundred Years War, has a beautiful blue and red rose window, the best in the Midi, but unfortunately it is partially obscured by the organ pipes.

## Accommodation and food in Clermont l'Hérault

**Hôtel du Terminus €€** *11 allée Roger Salengro; tel: 04 67 88 45 00; email: leterminus@wanadoo.fr. Open all year.* Former railway hotel on quiet leafy avenue in town centre, now smartly modernised with 22 rooms, including some in a rear annexe.

**Restaurant les Remparts €€** *3 place de la République; tel: 04 67 96 33 81. Open Tue–Sun all year.* Traditional restaurant with shaded terrace by the lively marketplace. Try *tarticlette*, its speciality flan.

# GANGES

**Ganges Tourist Information** Plan de l'Ormeau; tel: 04 67 73 00 56; email: contact@ot-cevennes.com; www.ot-cevennes.com. Open daily Jul–Aug; Tue–Sat Sept–Jun.

Set beside the River Hérault below a bowl of wooded mountains, Ganges made its fortune during the reign of Louis XIV when silk stockings were in vogue. Several factories still make high-class hosiery, though nylon has replaced both artificial and real silk. A walking trail leads round the points of interest in the centre and through the *chemins de traverses*, a network of covered alleys (like Lyon's more famous *traboules*) which now look disappointingly scruffy. The murder of the Marquise de Ganges by her brother-in-law in 1667 shook the French aristocracy and gave the town a place in literary history as it inspired the Marquis de Sade to write a 500-page novel based on it.

# GIGNAC

**Gignac Tourist Information** place du Général Claparède (Hôtel de Laurès); tel: 04 67 57 58 83; email: oti.gignac@wanadoo.fr. Open Mon–Fri all year.

The fortress-like tower of Notre-Dame-de-Grâce church overlooks the River Hérault and the town's pleasant waterside promenade and marina. Canoeing is popular on the river and details of canoe or kayak hire can be obtained from the tourist office.

# GROTTE DE CLAMOUSE

**Grotte de Clamouse €€€**
route de St-Guilhem-le-Désert, St-Jean-de-Fos; tel: 04 67 57 71 05; email: grotte@clamouse.com; www.grottedeclamouse.com. Open daily Mar–mid-Nov for 75-minute guided tours.

Although this beautiful cave with outstanding crystal formations was not explored until the exceptionally dry summer of 1945, the poignant story of the local family whose son worked as a shepherd on the plateau above is much older. One day he discovered that a carved stick he had thrown into a swallow hole (fissure) above it had emerged far below from a spring where his mother collected water. Afterwards he regularly sent things to his parents down the hole. But, alas, one day she found his body there; he had fallen into it and drowned. Its name means 'howling' in the local dialect.

# GROTTE DES DEMOISELLES

**Grotte des Demoiselles €€** In the village of St-Bauzille-de-Putois; tel: 04 67 73 70 02; email: grotte@demoiselles.fr; www.demoiselles.com. One-hour guided tours daily all year.

Walkways lead around this enormous cave (120m long, 80m wide and 50m high) discovered in 1770 and explored by E-A Martel in 1884. The high natural columns inside give it a church-like quality. One of the most extraordinary formations is a virgin and child stalagmite.

# LODEVE

**Lodève Tourist Information** 7 place de la République; tel: 04 67 88 86 44; email: tourisme@lodevoisetlarzac.fr; www.lodeve.com. Open daily all year.

**Gobelins workshops €€**
avenue du Général de Gaulle; arrange one-hour guided tours on Thur–Fri by appointment through the tourist office.

**Musée de Lodève €€**
Hôtel du Cardinal-de-Fieury, square Georges Auric; tel: 04 67 88 86 10; email: museelodeve@lodeve.com. Open Tue–Sat all year.

The scenically positioned town of Lodève lies at the foot of hills where the rivers Lergue and Soulondres meet. It flourished in the 13th century thanks to wool from the sheep reared in the hills to the north. One of its bishops had developed the cloth trade, having installed a mill to make paper from rags. Though the industry closed down in 1960, **Gobelins** tapestries are now made there, mainly copies of antique designs for official buildings. Uranium mining is another new industry and the local deposits amount to a quarter of France's reserves. The Cathédrale St-Fulcran is an imposing Gothic building with a splendid rose window. **Musée de Lodève**, once the cardinal's palace, covers the town's history since Roman times and also palaeontology including huge fossilised dinosaur footprints.

## Food in Lodève

**Le Petit Sommelier €** 3 place de la République; tel: 04 67 44 05 39. Open Tue–Sun all year. Old lace-curtained restaurant whose menus offer a wide choice of local specialities.

# MOUREZE

The main reason for visiting this smart little village of pink pastel houses is its extraordinary **Cirque**, a 2km-wide amphitheatre covered in huge eroded boulders, some the size of buildings, with bushes and sandy paths in between. It is a 5-minute walk (signed) from the main street. The ruins of an old castle perch above it at the top of a sheer cliff.

# ST-GUILHEM-LE-DESERT

ⓘ **St-Guilhem-le-Désert Tourist Information** 2 rue de la Font du Portal; tel: 04 67 57 44 33; email: ot-saintguilhem-valleeherault.com; www.saintguilhem-valleeherault.fr. Open daily all year. Guided walks.

ⓗ **L'Abbaye de Gellone** Guided visits every afternoon Jun–Sept.

This medieval village, spread up the narrow Verdus Gorge between green hillsides, deserves the many visitors it attracts. Small houses in beige stone, now with craft and souvenir shops occupying their ground floors, line the two narrow lanes leading up to its 11th-century monastery church, **l'Abbaye de Gellone**. This massive building is rather plain and austere inside, apart from a striking marble altar and decorative organ. Its main treasure is a fragment of Christ's Cross given to Guilhem by his lifelong friend Charlemagne. He had been one of Charlemagne's most devoted warriors but left his service around 800 to build the monastery and become a monk. His relics, housed in the crypt, are carried with the fragment of the Cross in procession through the streets in May.

### Accommodation in St-Guilhem-le-Désert

**Hostellerie St-Benoît €€** route St-Guilhem; tel: 04 67 57 71 63; email: info@hostellerie.saint-benoit.com; www.hostellerie-saint-benoit.com. Open Mar–Nov. Thirty-room hotel with garden, pool and children's playground, on the edge of the village.

# ST-MARTIN-DE-LONDRES

ⓘ **St-Martin-de-Londres Tourist Information** place de la Mairie; tel: 04 67 55 09 59; email: contact@tourismed.com; www.tourismed.com. Open daily Jul–Aug; Tue–Sat mornings Sept–Jun.

With its arcaded triangular square and 17th-century mansions, St-Martin-de-Londres (no connection with London) is an attractive but surprisingly un-touristy little town. The monks of St-Guilhem-le-Désert built the simple Romanesque church with its arcaded tower in the 12th century, though the interior has been considerably modified since.

# VILLENEUVETTE

In 1677, Louis XIV decreed that this small cloth factory, 3km southwest of Clermont l'Hérault, could become a 'Manufacture Royale' of flags. With royal subsidies and his chancellor Colbert ensuring that

**ⓘ Villeneuvette Tourist Information**
*Mairie; tel: 04 67 96 23 96; email: villeneuvettemairie@ libertysurf.fr. Open Mon–Fri all year. Guided tours of the village by appointment. Park in the car park in front of the entrance as only residents' cars are allowed inside.*

**☾ Hôtel de la Source**
**€€** *Maision de Manufacture; tel: 04 67 96 05 07; email: info@hoteldelasource.com; www.hoteldelasource.com. Open Apr–Sept. Well-appointed family-run hotel with 13 rooms in former factory houses. Large garden, pool, tennis, children's playground.*

high standards were maintained, it thrived and the workforce rose to 800. Many of them lived on the site in a 'model' village of terrace houses built for them around a small cobbled square. Since the factory closed in 1954 other residents have moved in and the village is now being preserved as an example of industrial heritage.

# Suggested tour

**Total distance:** 135km plus 38km each way between Montpellier and Gignac. The detour to St-Martin-de-Londres adds 24km and the detour to the Cirque de Navacelles adds 23km.

**Time:** 5 hours' driving. Allow at least a day for the main route, two with detours. Those with limited time should concentrate on St-Guilhem-le-Désert and the Cirque de Navacelles.

**Links to other tours:** From Ganges, the D999 leads northwest to Le Vigan (*see page 231*), 17km away or northeast to St-Hippolyte-du-Fort (*see page 232*), 17km away. From Lodève, the N9 leads north to La Couvertoirade (*see page 239*), 26km away. From Clermont l'Hérault, the N9 leads south to Pézenas (*see page 274*), 20km away.

Starting from **GIGNAC ❶** (38km west of Montpellier on the A750), head north on the D32 to **ANIANE ❷**. On the far side of Aniane, turn left on to the D27, which shortly passes the **Pont du Diable** where St Guilhem is said to have thrown the Devil into the River Hérault. Built by Benedictine monks in the 11th century, it is believed to be France's oldest bridge, though widened later. From it you get a good view up the narrow **Gorges de l'Hérault** where the river flows below steep white cliffs. The **GROTTE DE CLAMOUSE ❸** is on the left just after the bridge. The D4 then continues up the gorge to the village of **ST-GUILHEM-LE-DESERT ❹**.

**Detour:** To visit **ST-MARTIN-DE-LONDRES ❺**, turn right off the D4 at Causse-de-la-Selle on to the D122 (12km).

Beyond Causse-de-la-Selle the D4 drops back down to the River Hérault on its way to **Brissac**. Ruined ramparts stand guard over this ancient village framed by the 500m-high Roc Blanc. Its park, laid out at the foot of the village in the 17th century, is a pleasant spot to stroll and savour the rugged scenery. From Brissac, take the D108, which crosses the Hérault into **St-Bauzille-de-Putois**. Turn left on to the D986 (towards Ganges), but soon afterwards take the side road on the right to the **GROTTE DES DEMOISELLES ❻** at the foot of towering white cliffs. From there, go to **GANGES ❼**, which lies in a bowl of wooded hills. Leave it on the D25, which runs southwest through **Gorniès** where the scenery becomes wild and rugged across the lonely Montagne de la Séranne. Then beyond **Madières** the road drops steeply down to **St-Maurice-Navacelles**.

**La Calade** € *place de l'Eglise, Octon; tel: 04 67 96 19 21; email: lacalade-octon@wanadoo.fr; www.la-calade.monsite. wanadoo.fr. Open Mar–Dec.* Thick stone walls give this old house near the Lac du Salagou plenty of character. Seven rooms, large terrace restaurant.

**Auberge les Norias** €€ *254 avenue des Deux Ponts, Cazilhac, near Ganges; tel: 04 67 73 55 90; email: lesnorias@wanadoo.fr; www.les-norias.fr. Open Apr–mid-Nov.* Smart 11-room hotel in former spinning mill beside River Hérault. The owner-chef provides gourmet cuisine. Flower-decked outdoor restaurant in summer.

**Hotel Auberge de la Cascade** €€ *Cirque de Navacelles; tel 04 67 81 50 95. Hotel and restaurant open Apr–Oct.* 15th-century building with five rooms dramatically situated by a waterfall in the village at the bottom of the cirque.

**Detour:** From St-Maurice-Navacelles, the D130 climbs steeply north along a ridge, with beautiful views across the Larzac plain, to the spectacular **CIRQUE DE NAVACELLES** ❽, 8km away. The drive down to the floor of the cirque and up out again extends for 7km.

Continue southwest from St-Maurice-Navacelles on the D25 to join the A75 into **LODEVE** ❾. Leave the town on the A75, turning off it after 5km at junction 54 to take the D148 past the **Lac du Salagou** to **Octon** and **Salasc**. This is literally red-earth country – La Ruffe – as the soil is an amazingly dark-rust colour (due to high amounts of bauxite). Next the D8 takes you through a valley of rocks to **MOUREZE** ❿ and its cirque on the way to Clermont l'Hérault. Fork right just beyond Mourèze (keeping the river on your left) and then turn left on to the D908 to visit **VILLENEUVETTE** ⓫, which is on the left shortly before **CLERMONT L'HERAULT** ⓬. Beyond Clermont l'Hérault the D908 and A750 return you to Gignac, crossing the **Pont de Gignac** shortly before the town. This majestic 175m-long, three-arch 17th-century bridge is considered to be the best of its date in France.

## Getting out of the car

At the top of St-Guilhem-le-Désert, a marked path leads along the **rue du Bout-du-Monde** ('road of the end-of-the-world') through the valley and then zigzags sharply up the mountainside. You get a splendid view of the village's red roofs as well as a panorama over the white cliffs and ridges of the mountains all around which gets ever more spectacular the higher you go. Fragments of a ruined castle, the **Château du Géant**, dating from 807, are perched on a high rock. Long ago the path was part of a pilgrimage route to Spain. Beyond St-Guilhem-le-Désert the gorge widens slightly. The D4 then climbs away from the River Hérault towards **Causse-de-la-Selle**.

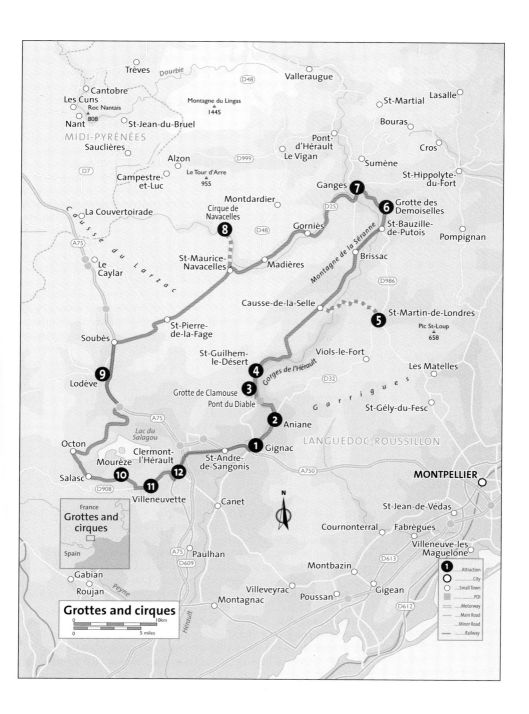

# The Corniche des Cévennes

## Ratings

| | |
|---|---|
| National parks | ●●●●● |
| Scenery | ●●●●● |
| Mountains | ●●●●○ |
| History | ●●●○○ |
| Museums | ●●●○○ |
| Nature | ●●●○○ |
| Restaurants | ●●●○○ |
| Trains | ●●●○○ |

The Corniche des Cévennes is a glorious top-of-the-world road that sweeps along the spine of the mountains. To the north, the peaks of Mont Lozère spread out like a relief map. You reach the corniche up a hairpin-bending road, thrilling to drive, at St-Laurent-de-Trèves beneath Mont Aigoual, the highest peak in the Cévennes National Park.

But this is not a route to travel just for scenery. Little towns along it such as Le Vigan, St-Jean, Anduze and St-Hippolyte all have a rich history and plenty of good restaurants serving local specialities including *pelardon* (goats' cheese), young lamb, chestnut sauces and home-made charcuterie.

In winter there is likely to be snow on the passes and you may need chains or snow tyres (look out for the warning signs); otherwise the roads are commendably good.

## ANDUZE

**ⓘ Anduze Tourist Information** *Plan de Brie; tel: 04 66 61 98 17; email: anduze@ot-anduze.fr; www.ot-anduze.fr. Open daily Jun–Sept; Mon–Sat Oct–May.*

**ⓜ Musée de la Musique €€** *4 route d'Alès; tel: 06 81 33 26 71; email: contact@musee-musique.com; www.musee-musique.com. Open by appointment only.*

This attractive medieval town of narrow streets and quaint little squares nestles at the foot of a massive white rock, near the River Gardon. It has lived through more turbulent times than most places in the area. Only the clock tower, complete with sundial, remains from the 14th-century fortifications which were enlarged and strengthened in 1622 by the Protestant leader, the Duc de Rohan, when the town was at the heart of local resistance to Catholicism. A century later it was at the centre of the Camisard uprising (*see page 31*). Eventually, it settled down and was much improved by the building of the embankment which protected it from flash floods.

Vines, orchards, mulberries, distilleries and particularly pottery have all brought it prosperity. It became famous throughout France for its giant glazed vases after some were installed in the orangery at Versailles. Today it continues to produce garden pots in all sizes and colours. The **Musée de la Musique** provides a

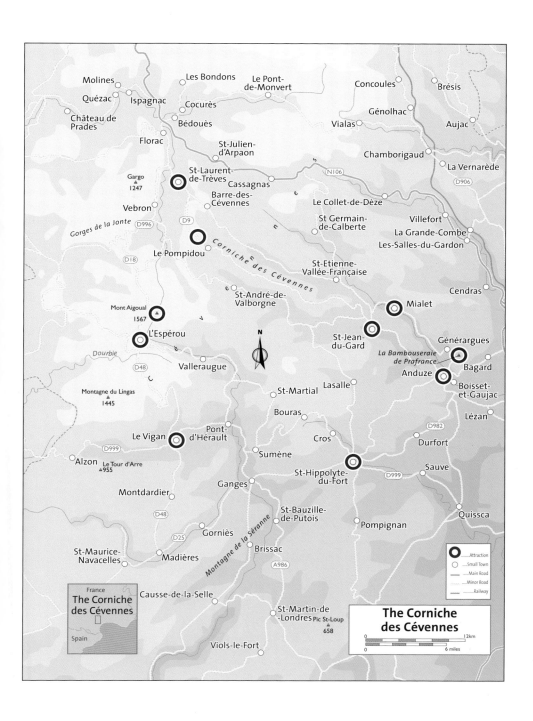

The Corniche des Cévennes

**Poterie de la Madeleine** *At Tornac (4km south on the D982); tel: 04 66 61 63 44; www.poterie.com.* Pottery workshop and sales counter.

musical tour through 1,400 historic instruments from around the world.

## CORNICHE DES CEVENNES

We have King Louis XIV to thank for this remarkable road which winds along the high ridge between two rivers – both called Gardon. He had it built in haste at the beginning of the 18th century to enable his troops to penetrate the Cévennes more easily and quash the Camisard uprising. Pines, oaks, chestnuts and mulberry bushes cover the steep valley sides and the few scattered farmhouses and cottages are built on terraces to catch the sun. Their attics were once used for breeding silkworms.

## LA BAMBOUSERAIE DE PRAFRANCE

**La Bambouseraie de Prafrance** €€ *tel: 04 66 61 70 47; www.bambouseraie.fr. Open daily Mar–mid-Nov.*

The botanic garden at Générargues includes Europe's only forest of giant bamboo trees. It also has a water garden, 19th-century tropical greenhouses and an Asian village.

# L'Esperou

ℹ️ **Maison de l'Aigoual**
*Col de la Serreyrède on the D986 north of the village; tel: 04 67 82 64 67. Open daily all year. Information on the Cévennes National Park and sells local produce.*

**L'Espérou Tourist Information**
*In Valleraugue, 19km down the valley; tel: 04 67 82 25 10; www.aigoual-cevennes.com. Open daily all year. Information on the Cévennes National Park also available.*

Surrounded by forests and high mountain pastures, the village of L'Espérou is an exhilarating base for walking in summer and skiing in winter. Its remote setting made it ideal as the base for the Aigoual-Cévennes Resistance groups during World War II.

## Accommodation and food in L'Espérou

**Hôtel du Parc €€** *carrefour des Hommes de la Route; tel: 04 67 82 60 05; email: hotelduparc-besperou@dbmail.com. Open Jan–Nov.* Tranquil family-run hotel with ten rooms, sun terrace and garden. Restaurant specialises in regional dishes.

# Le Vigan

ℹ️ **Le Vigan Tourist Information** *place du Marché; tel: 04 67 81 01 72; email: contact@cevennes-meridionales.com; www.cevennes-meridionales.com. Open daily Jul–Aug; Mon–Sat Sept–Jun.*

◐ **Hotel Mas de la Prairie €€** *avenue Sergent Triaire; tel: 04 67 81 80 80; email: contact@masdelaprairie.com; www.masdelaprairie.fr. Open Apr–Oct.* Comfortable 25-room hotel, charmingly furnished, with outdoor pool and sun terrace.

Le Vigan is a prosperous and relaxed little town enjoying a sunny position on the south-facing slopes of Mont Aigoual. Set in the lush Arre Valley, its prosperity grew from spinning silk; this led to making

**Left**
View from the Corniche des Cévennes over the village of Le Pompidou

**Right**
Le Vigan war memorial

**Musée Cévenol €**
*rue des Calquières;*
*tel: 04 67 81 06 86. Open*
*Wed–Mon Jul–Aug;*
*Wed–Sun Sept–Jun.*

hosiery which continues today. The **Musée Cévenol**, in an old spinning mill beside a soaring 12th-century bridge over the River Arre, provides an excellent introduction to the Cévennes, covering everything from the food and wine to traditional crafts such as basketwork, gold panning, glass-blowing and tin mining. There are life-size reconstructions of workshops and a typical cottage.

## MIALET

**Musée du Désert**
*€€ Mas Soubeyran;*
*tel: 04 66 85 02 72; email:*
*musee@museedudesert.com;*
*www.museedudesert.com.*
*Open daily Apr–Nov.*

The **Musée du Désert** in this small village occupies the Mas Soubeyran, the old house where one of the leading Camisards was born. It explains the movement's history through displays which include full-size reconstructions showing how they hid and lived during the 'desert' years (1685–1787) when Protestantism was banned.

## MONT AIGOUAL

**Mont Aigoual observatory**
*tel: 04 67 82 60 01; email:*
*infos@aigoual.asso.fr;*
*www.aigoual.asso.fr.*
*Open daily May–Sept.*

France's meteorological office has an **observatory**, built in 1887, at the top of this mountain (1,567m) which enjoys one of the finest panoramas in Europe, extending in fine weather as far as the Mediterranean, Pyrenees and Alps. Overlooking the Gard, Hérault and Tarn valleys, the observatory is perfectly positioned to record what is happening to the wind and weather. An exhibition inside explains the history of weather forecasting and the methods used today.

## ST-HIPPOLYTE-DU-FORT

**St-Hippolyte-du-Fort Tourist Information** *place des Enfants de Troupe; tel: 04 66 77 91 65; www. cevennes-garrigue-tourisme.com. Open Mon–Sat Jul–Aug; Mon–Fri Sept–Jun.*

Market *Tue & Fri.*

**Musée de la Soie**
*€€ place du 8 Mai;*
*tel: 04 66 77 66 47; email:*
*museedelasoie@hotmail.com;*
*www.museedelasoie-cevennes.com. Open daily Jul–Aug; Tue–Sun Sept–Oct & Apr–Jun.*

This little town has an extraordinary mixture of specialities including no fewer than 23 decorative sundials and 13 fountains. It also makes shoes and has a silk museum, **Musée de la Soie**, which depicts the history of silk production in the Cévennes. The museum occupies the old barracks built for Louis XIV's soldiers when they constructed the Corniche des Cévennes. Visitors see how silkworms make corms of silk and how it is spun into thread then made into fabric. Silk items are on sale in its shop.

### Accommodation and food in St-Hippolyte-du-Fort

**Le Kim Oanh €** *27 rue du Plan; tel: 04 66 77 91 55. Open daily all year.* Small restaurant with painted façade beside the market square. Its terrace tables are handily placed for watching boules games while you eat. Good-value Asian fare.

**Auberge Cigaloise €€** *route de Nîmes; tel: 04 66 77 64 59; email: aubergecigaloise@orange.fr; www.aubergecigaloise.fr. Open all year.* Ten-room family-run hotel with garden, pool and playground. Car park.

## Reafforestation

In 1875, Georges Fabres, head warden of the French Rivers Authority and Forestry Commission, initiated a reafforestation programme in the Cévennes, having seen the devastation caused by floods once land had been stripped bare. He won considerable support by showing that the sand clogging up the port at Bordeaux had been washed down from the slopes of the Aigoual, the area's highest peak.

Up to then, thousands of trees were being cut down every year to create more pastures or by glass-makers to provide charcoal for their furnaces. Sheep contributed to the problem too, by nibbling young shoots on their way between pastures. As a result, whenever rain fell very heavily – the area is subject to violent storms – torrents of water surged unchecked into the valleys.

Now, following the planting of thousands of seedlings, extensive areas have been reafforested, particularly with cedar, fir, pine and spruce, contributing greatly to both the safety and beauty of the landscape.

Fabres, a formidable man, also initiated the building of the observatory on Mont Aigoual in 1887.

**Below**
Cévennes forest

# St-Jean-du-Gard

**St-Jean-du-Gard Tourist Information** *place Rabaut St-Etienne; tel: 04 66 85 32 11; email: otsi.st.jeandugard@free.fr; www.otsi.st.jeandugard. free.fr. Open daily Jul–Aug; Mon–Sat Sept–Jun.*

**Musée des Vallées Cévenoles** € 95 *grand-rue; tel: 04 66 85 10 48; email: valceven@ wanadoo.fr. Open daily all year.*

**Atlantide Parc** €€€ *avenue de la Résistance; tel: 04 66 85 40 53. Open daily Jun–Aug; Tue–Sun Sept–Nov & Apr–May.*

There is a *weekly market* on Tue; night markets on Thur in Jul–Aug; and a **Cheese fair** in Jun.

Surrounded by orchards, St-Jean-du-Gard has a distinctly southern feel with tall houses lining narrow streets and a large riverside square shaded by plane trees. The pretty six-arch humpback bridge over the River Gardon is a reconstruction of the original built in 1754, which was swept away by floods in 1958. The **Musée des Vallées Cévenoles**, occupying a 17th-century inn, devotes one room to the local silk industry, showing how it became an important cottage industry in the area at the beginning of the 18th century. The museum also has a section devoted to chestnuts, which for centuries were ground into flour to make bread. As a result the chestnut was known as the 'tree of life' until the silk industry started and mulberry cultivation became more important.

Tropical fish including piranhas and sharks (which can be fed) swim in the exotic aquarium at **Atlantide Parc**, where there is also an artificial river and waterfall.

## Accommodation and food in St-Jean-du-Gard

**Auberge du Peras** €€ *route de Nîmes; tel: 04 66 85 35 94; email: aubergeduperas@free.fr. Open Mar–mid-Nov.* Twelve-room family-run hotel in an old stone building on the edge of town with a garden and car park. Hire bicycles here.

# St-Laurent-de-Treves

The claw footprints indented in the flat rocks on the high windy headland above the village were left by dinosaurs 190 million years ago when the area was covered by a lake.

# Suggested tour

**Total distance:** 175km. The detour to the Barre des Cévennes adds 6km, the detour to Mialet adds 18km and the detour to the Bambouseraie de Prafrance botanic garden at Générargues adds 6km.

**Time:** 5 hours' driving. Allow at least a day for the main route, more with detours. Those with limited time should concentrate on the Corniche des Cévennes.

**Links to other tours:** From Le Vigan, the D999 leads southeast to Ganges (*see page 222*), 17km away, or west to La Couvertoirade (*see page 239*), 39km away. From L'Espérou, the D986 leads northwest to Meyrueis (*see page 251*), 27km away. From St-Laurent-de-Trèves, the

**Sentier de Barre-
des-Cévennes** leaflet
at the information kiosk on
the edge of the village.

**Château du Rey**
€€€ Le Rey, Pont-
d'Hérault; tel: 04 67 82 40
06; email: contact@
chateaudurey.fr;
www.chateau-du-rey.com.
Open Apr–Aug. Much-
restored 13th-century
castle, now a comfortable
12-room hotel. Vaulted
restaurant, the
**Abeuradou** (€€ tel: 04
67 82 49 32). Two-hectare
grounds with pool and
helicopter pad. Fishing
available.

D983 and D907 lead north to Florac (*see page 260*), 10km away.
From Anduze, the D910 leads northeast to Alès (*see page 258*), 16km
away. From St-Hippolyte-du-Fort, the D999 leads southwest to Ganges
(*see page 222*), 17km away.

Starting from **LE VIGAN** ❶, take the D48, which quickly begins to twist
and climb into the mountains through forests, around sheer rock faces
and across ravines where water cascades down. There are two passes to
cross, the Col du Minier (1,373m) and then, just beyond **L'ESPEROU**
❷, the Col de la Séreyrède (1,299m) where you reach the
Mediterranean–Atlantic watershed. This used to be on a wide trail – the
Draille du Languedoc – which shepherds used for their transhumance
when 25,000 sheep were driven each year between their summer
pastures in the mountains and winter shelter in the valley. Now they are
taken to and fro by lorry. Continue north on the D18 over the Col de
Prat Peyrot (1,380m) where you can expect plenty of snow in winter
and congestion from skiers and their cars. Shortly beyond it, you
pass close to the summit of **MONT AIGOUAL** ❸ (1,567m), signposted
to the right.

Having continued north on the D18 and then the D996 (towards
Florac) along the broad valley below the Causse Méjean, turn right
5km before Florac at the junction with the D983. This takes you south
round hairpin bends to **ST-LAURENT-DE-TREVES** ❹ and the Col du
Rey (992m) just beyond it.

**Detour:** At the Col du Rey, turn left on to the D983 to **Barre des
Cévennes** (3km). As part of the **Ecomusée de la Cévenne**, a 4km
walking trail, one of five in the national park, has been mapped out
around this typical Cévenol village on a hillside halfway between
valley and plateau. A descriptive leaflet covers not only its old
buildings but also the landscape and local flora and fauna.

The **CORNICHE DES CEVENNES** ❺ begins at the Col du Rey as the D9
crosses a spectacular windswept plateau, Le Can de l'Hospitalet.
Continue south past viewpoints and over the Col des Faïsses (1,026m)
and the Col de Solpérière (1,010m) to the small village of **Le Pompidou**.
Further on, after crossing the Col L'Exil (704m) and Col de St-Pierre
(597m), you reach **ST-JEAN-DU-GARD** ❻.

**Detour:** At St-Jean-du-Gard, turn left on to the D50 to visit **MIALET**
❼ (9km).

**Detour: LA BAMBOUSERAIE DE PRAFRANCE** ❽ botanic garden at
**Générargues** is on the D129, 3km north of Anduze (*see below*).

Continuing southeast from St-Jean-du-Gard towards **ANDUZE** ❾,
look out for the derelict spinning mill at the junction with the D57. In
the 18th century, the area's mulberry bushes, on which silkworms
feed, became so valuable that they were nicknamed the *arbres d'or*
(trees of gold).

From Anduze, the D133 leads to **ST-HIPPOLYTE-DU-FORT** ❿, then follow the D169, D153, D11 and D999 to return to Le Vigan, passing through Cros, Bouras, Sumène and Pont-d'Hérault.

## Getting out of the car

**Train à Vapeur des Cévennes**
*tel: 04 66 60 59 00; email: contact@citev.com; www.citev.com.*
Runs between Anduze, La Bambouseraie de Prafrance and St-Jean-du-Gard, *daily May–Oct.*

Views from the top of Mont Aigoual (which are best in winter) are breathtaking. On a clear day you can see across a quarter of France. But the very best time of all to be there is to see sunrise, particularly in the autumn.

The **Train à Vapeur des Cévennes**, sometimes pulled by a steam locomotive, runs on a 13km line between St-Jean-du-Gard and Anduze along the Gardon Valley. The 40-minute journey provides wonderful views (some carriages are open). The train makes a stop at Générargues just before Anduze for passengers who want to visit the **BAMBOUSERAIE DE PRAFRANCE** ❽.

# Templars, plateaux and cheese

## Ratings

| | |
|---|---|
| Scenery | ●●●●● |
| Museums | ●●●●○ |
| Villages | ●●●●○ |
| Walking | ●●●●○ |
| Food | ●●●○○ |
| Geology | ●●●○○ |
| History | ●●●○○ |
| Wildlife | ●●●○○ |

The Causse du Larzac is one of the Cévennes' four great limestone plateaux. On these high expanses where sheep graze and birds of prey wheel overhead, little disturbs the tranquillity except the wind. Side by side, literally, with this wild landscape are dramatic gorges, such as the Canyon de la Dourbie, where rivers have carved their tortuous way through the soft rock. The contrast provides a rich variety along this route. The many signposted footpaths will tempt you out of the car to savour the surroundings even more.

Although the area is less well known than many in France, the name of one of its villages – Roquefort – is famous all over the world. It has been producing its creamy blue-veined cheese for centuries. Also unique are the fortified villages of La Couvertoirade and St-Jean-d'Alcas, both interesting mini-versions of Carcassonne. But it is the most modern of structures, the spectacular Millau Viaduct, which has brought the area new-found fame.

## CANTOBRE

The name of this quaint village derives from *quant obra*, meaning 'what a masterpiece'. Its old stone houses are built into a rocky outcrop high above the rivers Dourbie and Trévézel. The walk up to the little church and cemetery at the top is well worth the effort for the beautiful view down into the valley on either side. Rock plants grow in profusion and thistles hang on most of the front doors – the local way to forecast the weather (the thistles close up when rain is imminent).

## CHAOS-DE-MONTPELLIER-LE-VIEUX

This group of craggy stone columns spreads over 1.5sq km among oak and pine trees north of La Roque-Ste-Marguerite. It was given its name (meaning 'ruined city') by shepherds who brought their flocks up from the Languedoc plain to summer pastures there, though they feared the shapes were linked with the Devil.

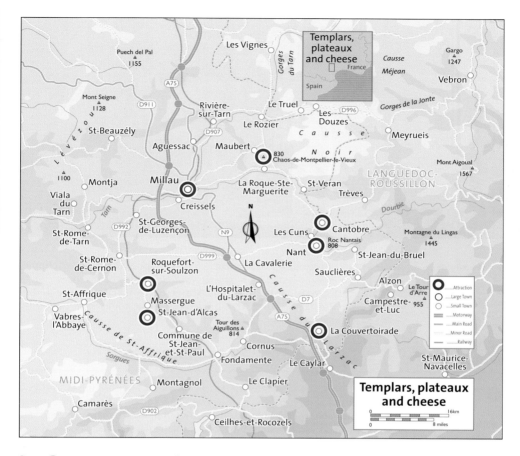

Templars, plateaus and cheese

# LA COUVERTOIRADE

**La Couvertoirade
Tourist
Information** *Mairie;
tel: 05 65 58 55 59; email:
tourisme@lacouvertoirade.com;
www.lacouvertoirade.com.
Open Mon–Fri all year; also
daily Jul–Aug at the car park.
Entrance to La Couvertoirade,
including 20-minute video, €.
Three guided visits daily in
English Jul–Aug.*

Situated in the middle of the Causse du Larzac is La Couvertoirade, a miniature Carcassonne. Completely surrounded by high ramparts, it has a castle, church and tiny cemetery. It was built by the Templars in 1158 as a staging post for pilgrims on the old Roman road across the *causse*, though the forbidding grey-stone walls were a later addition by the Knights of St John in the 15th century. Unlike Carcassonne, La Couvertoirade has never been smartened up, though a few of the buildings have been restored and craft workers have taken up residence in several of them.

The entrance is through an arched gateway beneath a square tower. In summer, the narrow streets and handful of shops and cafés throng with visitors. You can walk round the ramparts and look down on the main street, rue Droite, which is lined with attractive

**Musée de la Traction Animale**
€€ *L'Hôtel de la Scipione; tel: 05 65 62 26 85. Open daily all year (guided walks only).*

little 17th-century houses. Eglise St-Christophe, the fortified church, with a tiny old cemetery next to it, formed part of the defences.

Nearby, outside the walls, the **Musée de la Traction Animale** has 60 old carriages. Most were horse-drawn but some were pulled by oxen, dogs or goats.

# MILLAU

**Millau Tourist Information**
*1 place du Beffroi; tel: 05 65 60 02 42; email: office.tourisme.millau@ wanadoo.fr; www.ot-millau.fr. Open daily all year.* Millau has become famous for its 100km circular walk along the Gorges du Tarn, annually, *last Sat in Sept.*

**Belfry** *rue Droite. Open daily mid-Jun–Sept.*

**Fouilles de la Graufesenque** €€ *chemin de Graufesenque, across the Tarn; tel: 05 65 60 11 37. Open Tue–Sun all year.*

This little town, where the rivers Tarn and Dourbie meet, enjoys a beautiful setting in a majestic bowl of mountains. Its red roofs blend comfortably with them and the surrounding cherry orchards. The wide streets and squares, shaded by lines of plane trees, have a good selection of shops, particularly for leather gloves, bags and coats. The oldest quarter centres on the arcaded place du Maréchal-Foch, which has the Romanesque Eglise Notre-Dame-de-l'Espinasse in one corner. Named after a thorn which it was reputed to possess from Christ's crown, the church attracted pilgrims from far and wide during the Middle Ages. It has a fine set of modern stained-glass windows by Claude Baillo. A curiosity on the west side of the square is a stone slab, once part of the town's stocks, with the warning *Gara que faras*, meaning 'watch what you are doing'. The imposing **belfry** in rue Droite is all that remains of the old town hall. The best way to explore the town is by following the guided walk past 18 sights marked by plaques explaining their history.

The town's prosperity dates back to AD 1 when it was called Condatomagus – 'the market where the rivers meet' – and was one of the main pottery-making centres in the Roman Empire. More than 500 potters produced shiny bright red pots of all shapes and sizes which were exported throughout Europe and the Middle East. The pottery site by the river, **Fouilles de la Graufesenque**, has recently

**Above**
La Couvertoirade

**Musée de Millau €€**
*place Maréchal-Foch; tel: 05 65 60 01 08. Open daily May–Sept; Mon–Sat Oct–Apr.*

**Causse Gantier**
*5 boulevard des Gantières; tel: 05 65 60 03 05; email: infos@causse-gantier.fr; www.causse-gantier.fr. One of the oldest glove-making workshops in Millau, now operating in modern purpose-built premises. Watch leather gloves being made using traditional methods. These gloves are destined for fashion houses and luxury boutiques around the world. You can buy gloves in a shop in the workshop complex. Open to visitors Mon–Sat. Admission free but advanced reservation advised.*

**Le Viaduc de Millau** *The Millau Viaduct Information Centre is located on the D992, the road out of Millau towards Albi; www.leviaducdemillau.com. Open daily all year. The centre is free and has displays and videos telling the story of the construction of the viaduct and a shop for souvenirs. The Millau tourist office (tel: 05 65 60 02 42) can arrange guided tours by bus including the viewing point at the north end of the viaduct.*

Markets are held on *Wed & Fri. Local specialities are young lamb, trenels (haggis of tripe), flaune (orange-flavoured flan made with ewes' milk) and plump cherries.*

been excavated, revealing a huge number of pots and providing important information about life in Roman times.

The vaulted cellars of the **Musée de Millau** display a well-preserved collection of tools and pottery from the site. An equally enthralling section is devoted to fossils and dinosaur remains – including skeletons and footprints – which have been found in the area, once covered by the sea. One room is set out as a glove-making workshop with old sewing machines and patterns – another aspect of the town's past. Gloves have been made there for over 800 years, a by-product from the huge numbers of sheep reared on the plateaux for cheese-making. For centuries the town councillors never appeared on ceremonial occasions without gloves. Haute-couture gloves are exported all over the world.

### Le Viaduc de Millau

The Millau Viaduct is the highest bridge in the world and a masterpiece of civil engineering. It is 2.5km long and spans the Tarn Valley between two plateaux, the Causse du Larzac and the Causse Rouge, with the roadway held in place by steel cables suspended from pylons on top of seven concrete pillars set in the valley floor. The viaduct carries the A75/E11 *Méridienne* autoroute, one of France's main north–south routes. For decades, traffic heading to the south of France and Barcelona in Spain was forced to drop down into the Tarn Valley, causing congestion in the town of Millau, especially in the summer. Le Viaduc de Millau was designed by the renowned British architect Lord Norman Foster and built by the Eiffage group, an amalgamation of companies including the one that built the Eiffel Tower in Paris. In some conditions travellers get an impression of driving above the clouds. The viaduct dominates the Tarn Valley west of Millau and has become a tourist attraction in its own right; it is viewed with pride by local people and there is a great trade in pictorial souvenirs in the town. A visitor centre has opened beneath the bridge, and a motorway rest area, Aire du Viaduc, has been established to give access to a panoramic viewing point at the north end of the viaduct. There is a toll to cross the viaduct and to reach the Aire (*€7.85 for cars in Jul–Aug; €6.10 Sept–Jun*).

## Accommodation and food in Millau

**Mercure Millau €€** *place de la Tine; tel: 05 65 59 29 00; email: H5614@accor.com; www.accorhotels.com. Open all year.* A modern high-rise building, this 109-room hotel is close to the main square, with good views from the higher floors.

**Restaurant La Braconne €€** *7 place Maréchal-Foch; tel: 05 65 60 30 93. Open daily all year.* In this 13th-century stone building with a vaulted ceiling, grills seasoned with local herbs are cooked in front of you on an open fire.

# NANT

**Nant Tourist Information** *Chapelle des Pénitents, place du Clause; tel: 05 65 62 24 21; email: contact@ot-nant.fr; www.ot-nant.fr. Open daily Jun–Aug; Mon–Sat Sept–May.*

**Hôtel des Voyageurs** € *place St-Jacques; tel: 05 65 62 26 88.* Family-owned hotel with 14 rooms and garden, just off the main square, and a restaurant, Le Ménestrel.

The Roc Nantais, a massive tower-like rock (808m), juts out dramatically from the hilltop opposite this old market town at the head of the Dourbie Gorge. The town's origins date back to the 7th century when Benedictine monks drained the broad swampy valley in order to plant vineyards. The St-Pierre church, a rather austere building with an octagonal tower and spire, survives from their huge monastery. In the square, the Vieille Halle, a small market hall with arches, roofed with *lauzes* (limestone slabs) typical of the area, was also part of it. A plaque on the side commemorates nine local Resistance heroes shot by the Germans in August 1944. The best view of the high 14th-century arched river bridge, Pont de la Prade, is from beside the tall cross near the square.

# ROQUEFORT-SUR-SOULZON

**Roquefort-sur-Soulzon Tourist Information** *avenue de Lauras; tel: 05 65 58 56 00; email: info@roquefort.com; www.roquefort.com. Open daily Jul–Aug; Mon–Sat Sept–Oct & Apr–Jun; Mon–Fri Nov–Mar.*

**Caves de Roquefort Société** € *avenue François Galtier; tel: 05 65 58 54 38; www.roquefort-societe.com. Open for guided tours of the cellars daily.*

**Fromagerie Papillon** *rue de la Fontaine; tel: 05 65 58 50 08; www.roquefort-papillon.com. Open for free guided tours of the cellars daily.*

**Hôtel Le Combalou** €€ *avenue de Lauras; tel: 05 65 59 91 70. Open all year.* Fifteen basic rooms and a restaurant where Roquefort cheese omelette and steak in Roquefort cheese sauce feature on the menu.

The single main street of this drab little town (though it enjoys splendid views over the Grands Causses) at the foot of the Combalou plateau always seems to be full of huge cheese lorries manoeuvring to and fro, a reminder that it is the home of the world-famous Roquefort. As early as 1407, Charles VI granted the cheese its own brand name, an *appellation d'origine*, which has been protected by law ever since. Two cheese producers, **Caves de Roquefort Société** and **Fromagerie Papillon**, offer guided visits (including videos) to their caves which resemble the crypts of a church. Wear warm clothing!

## Roquefort cheese

Made from unpasteurised ewes' milk, this world-famous cheese is injected with *Penicillium roquefortii* mould cultivated on breadcrumbs which produces its characteristic – and tasty – blue veins. Early connoisseurs are said to have included Pliny and Charlemagne. The limestone caves under the Combalou plateau at the side of the town play a crucial role in its production as their temperature (7–9°C/45–48°F) and humidity remain constant all year. Air circulates through long fissures in the rock. The round cheeses are left there on oak shelves to mature for at least three months. A website in English tells the story of the cheese: *www.fromages.com/usa/roqueleg.htm*

# St-Jean-d'Alcas

**ⓘ St-Jean-d'Alcas Tourist Information** *Mairie; tel: 05 65 97 61 07; email: si-stjeanstpaul@orange.fr. Jul–Aug information kiosk in the fort. Guided tour of the village available.*

This tiny fortified village, a mini-version of La Courvertoirade (*see page 239*), was built in the 15th century by Cistercian nuns as a safe haven during the Hundred Years War. Symmetrically laid out – the Cistercians' abbeys were built in a similarly tidy style – and totally enclosed by ramparts, it has undergone highly commended restorations.

## Suggested tour

**Total distance:** 115km. The detour to St-Jean-du-Bruel adds 14km, the detour to Cantobre adds 3km and the detour to the Chaos-de-Montpellier-le-Vieux adds 18km.

**Time:** 3 hours' driving. Allow most of a day for the main route, at least a day with detours. Those with limited time should concentrate on Millau and Roquefort-sur-Soulzon, or for scenery the Canyon de la Dourbie.

**Right**
Roquefort-sur-Soulzon

**Links to other tours:** From Millau, the N9 and D907 lead northeast to Le Rozier (*see page 251*), 22km away. From Roquefort, the D999 leads southwest to St-Sernin-sur-Rance (*see page 186*), 45km away. From La Couvertoirade, the D55 and N9 lead to Lodève (*see page 223*), 26km away, and the D999 leads east to Le Vigan (*see page 231*), 39km away.

Starting from **MILLAU** ❶, drive southwest through **Creissels** on the D992 and under the 2.5km-long viaduct, designed by British architect Norman Foster and opened in 2004, which soars 270m above the valley, carrying the A75 autoroute past Millau. The D992 runs high above the River Tarn with wonderful views over the flat brown hills of the Causses. Then swinging south, you cross the River Cernon and accompany a scenic railway line through a wooded valley. Four kilometres beyond **St-Rome-de-Cernon**, turn left on to the D23 and climb up to **ROQUEFORT-SUR-SOULZON** ❷.

From Roquefort-sur-Soulzon, the D93 makes its way around the edge of the **Causse du Larzac** through **Massergue** to **ST-JEAN-D'ALCAS** ❸ where sheep graze below wooded cliffs on hillsides which merge into flat hedgeless fields – a truly rural landscape. The road continues on its quiet way to **Commune de St-Jean-et-St-Paul** and **Fondamente** where you take the D7 to **Cornus**. Pop into the post office for information on this little town, which huddles at the foot of the Larzac plateau under an 80m-high cliff.

Continue on the D7 beyond Cornus and then go over the A75 autoroute towards **LA COUVERTOIRADE** ❹ on the D185. On this stretch the *causse* is a wild unspoilt landscape apart from the incongruous autoroute. The rocky red soil is dotted with boulders and

**Left**
Millau

**Right**
Cornus

**Hôtel Midi-Papillon** € *St-Jean-du-Bruel; tel: 05 65 62 26 04; www.hotel-midi-papillon.com. Open Easter–mid-Nov.*
A 19-room hotel owned and run by four generations of the Papillon family.

**Relais des Gorges** €
*La Roque-Ste-Marguerite; tel: 05 65 59 14 10. Open all year.* Cosy ten-room hotel splendidly positioned in an isolated spot beside the River Dourbie north of the village. Fishing nearby. *Open daily Mar–Oct.*

**Château de Creissels** €€
*route de St-Affrique, Creissels; tel: 05 65 60 16 59; email: chateau-de-creissels@wanadoo.fr; www. chateau-de-creissels.com. Open mid-Mar–mid-Nov.*
Twelfth-century château with modern extension, overlooking the village on the River Tarn. Family run with 31 rooms, most with terrace or balcony. Restaurant €€; *tel: 05 65 60 31 79, in former guard-room.* Dinner on covered terrace in summer. Large garden.

splashed with patches of yellow broom and hardy green box bushes. From La Couvertoirade, the D55 leads north across the *causse* and then through soft hillsides of beech trees to **NANT** ❺ where the **Roc Nantais** towers up on the right. This section is the 'Garden of Aveyron' where apple and plum orchards thrive in the broad river valley. Look out on the south side for the ruins of the **Château d'Algues**.

**Detour:** The small town of **St-Jean-du-Bruel**, 7km east of Nant on the D999, is popular as a base for exploring the area. It has an ancient humpback bridge over the River Dourbie and a 200-year-old covered market. Barrels for harvesting grapes are made in the town.

From Nant, continue north along the D991 as it winds along the broad **Dourbie Valley** past the small 12th-century church at **Les Cuns** and below Cantobre.

**Detour:** To visit **CANTOBRE** ❻, turn right off the D991 (5km north of Nant) on to the D145 (1.5km).

Beyond Cantobre, the Dourbie Valley changes into the **Canyon de la Dourbie**, a deep but wide gorge in the limestone rocks between the **Causse du Larzac** and **Causse Noir**. The steep wooded slopes on either side are topped with cliffs where weirdly shaped pillars of rock jut out above the trees. Later you get a superb view of **St-Veran**, a tiny hamlet built into a cliff top with a tower that was once part of a castle. After crossing the River Dourbie just after St-Veran, the D991 runs along its north bank as the river turns west through **La Roque-Ste-Marguerite**. This terraced village nestles at the foot of a Romanesque chapel and the circular tower of a 17th-century castle.

**Detour:** This weird **CHAOS-DE-MONTPELLIER-LE-VIEUX** ❼ area of eroded columns is a 9km drive north from La Roque-Ste-Marguerite through **Maubert**.

After La Roque-Ste-Marguerite, the route continues along the D991 beside the Dourbie, finally entering Millau across the Tarn.

**Left**
The Chaos-de-Montpellier-
le-Vieux

## Getting out of the car

The **Sentier des Echelles** is a 6km path around the **Plateau du Combalou**, a 791m-high plateau above the village of Roquefort-sur-Soulzon. The views are panoramic as you gradually climb to the top of cliffs where grassy footpaths lead past curiously shaped rock formations and a ruined chapel. The trail leads back through the village past the **Combalou caves** where Roquefort's inimitable cheese is matured.

The **Tour d'Aiguilhon**, a 815m-high viewpoint over the Larzac plateau, reached along a 1.5km footpath from Cornus, is just one of several rewarding walks in this area.

# Great plateaux and gorges

## Ratings

| | |
|---|---|
| Gorges | ●●●●● |
| Scenery | ●●●●● |
| Villages | ●●●●○ |
| Caves | ●●●○○ |
| Churches | ●●●○○ |
| Food | ●●●○○ |
| Walking | ●●●○○ |
| History | ●●○○○ |

This route around the Causse Méjean in the Cévennes includes one of the most famous stretches of river in France, the Gorges du Tarn. But the Tarn is not the only river to have gouged its way through the limestone to create a deep, winding canyon. The Jonte's gorge, along the southern side of the Causse, is just as scenic – and less busy.

Equally spectacular in a very different way are the famous caves under the plateau, notably L'Aven Armand and Grotte de Dargilan. In the sky, birds of prey wheel around, including vultures which have been successfully reintroduced to the area.

The driving is not for the faint-hearted as the roads twist tightly around cliffsides hugging the rivers or climb steeply up on to the Causse above. The little towns and villages along the way make welcome ports of call.

## CHATEAU DE PRADES

**Château de Prades**
*Not open to the public.*

This grand castle, occupying a commanding position just above the River Tarn 6km east of Ste-Enimie, was built by the bishops of Mende in the 13th century to guard access to the gorges and Ste-Enimie abbey just downstream. Its high-vaulted rooms and imposing stone fireplaces reflect the wealth of the area at the time.

## GORGES DE LA JONTE

**Hôtel-Restaurant de la Jonte** € *Les Douzes; tel: 05 65 62 60 52. Open Mar–Nov. Small roadside hotel facing the river in the spectacular Gorges de la Jonte. Thirty-six rooms.*

After rising on Mont Aigoual, the River Jonte is swollen by two smaller rivers, the Bétuzon and Brèze. It then cuts a deep wooded course between orange-tinged limestone cliffs for 21km from Meyrueis to Le Rozier, with the road below the Causse Méjean on the north side and the Causse Noir on the south side. For some of the way, there are two levels of cliffs, the Terrasses du Truel. As the river nears the Tarn at Le Rozier, the gorge becomes increasingly narrow. All the way, the road twists on a shelf along the cliffside, mostly high above the river.

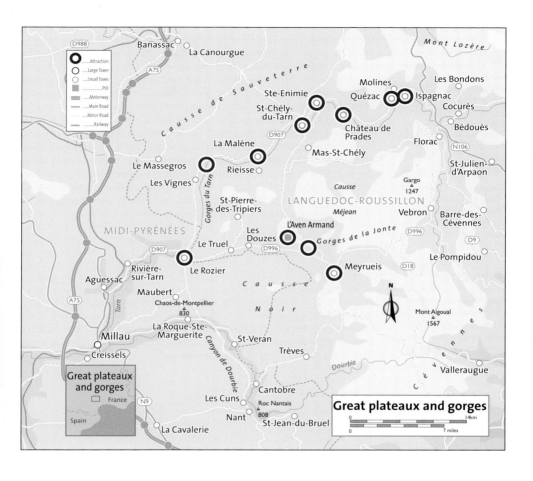

## Louis Armand

When Edouard-Alfred Martel, the famous speleologist, began exploring the extraordinary underground world hidden beneath the Causse Méjean, one of his main helpers was Louis Armand, a local locksmith. Farmers told Martel about what they called l'aven, a deep crevice or swallow hole in the rock. When Armand climbed down it in 1897, he found it was 75m deep and had a huge chamber at the bottom. Eventually, in 1927 it was opened to the public, having been named – at Martel's insistence – after Armand. Recently, it has been relit with imaginative illuminations that highlight the most impressive formations.

# GORGES DU TARN

**ⓘ Gorges du Tarn Tourist Information**
*route des Gorges du Tarn, Rivière-sur-Tarn; tel: 05 65 59 74 28; email: ot-gorgesdutarn@wanadoo.fr; www.ot-gorgesdutarn.com. Open daily Jul–Aug; Mon–Fri Sept–Jun.*

**Ⓑ Société Coopérative des Bateliers des Gorges du Tarn** € Boat trips with the Tarn Gorges local ferrymen; *tel: 04 66 48 51 10; email: lesbateliers@gorgesdutarn.com*

From its source on Mont Lozère, the River Tarn flows west towards the Grands Causses where it cuts its way through the limestone plateaux. The Gorges du Tarn, one of the most spectacular in France, starts past Quézac and continues for 50km to Le Rozier, running between orange cliffs and steep wooded hillsides below the Caussed de Sauveterre (to the north) and Causse Méjean. The river is fed by 40 springs which burst from underground, tumbling into it as waterfalls. Villages are few and far between as the water level can vary dramatically and unpredictably. Those which have developed in the valley's wider stretches now thrive on tourism – canoeing, potholing and rock climbing are popular pursuits – and also industriously cultivate their orchards and vineyards.

During the French Revolution, when the nobility were being cruelly pursued, many left their homes and hid in caves in the gorge.

# ISPAGNAC

**ⓘ Ispagnac Tourist Information** *Le Pavilion; tel: 04 66 45 01 14; email: otsi@mescevennes.com; www.mescevennes.com. Open Mon–Sat all year.*

Ispagnac is a go-ahead little town, popular as a touring base and offering a range of river activities. The sheltered slopes around it are covered in orchards, vineyards and strawberry fields. The delightful 11th-century church in yellow stone beside a shaded square has a fine rose window and octagonal bell tower.

# LA MALENE

**ⓘ Parc National des Cévennes Information Centre** *Tel: 04 66 48 50 77; www.les.cevennes.free.fr. Open Mon–Sat mid-Jun–mid-Sept. Out of season call the tourist office at Ste-Enimie; tel: 04 66 48 53 44.*

This scenic riverside village used to be an important watering point for sheep on their way to the Sauveterre and Méjean *causses* (plateaux). From medieval times to the French Revolution, it was the seat of the powerful barons of Montesquieu whose 16th-century castle is now a hotel. The Falise de la Barre, the black stains on the cliffs above, are said to be from the smoke of a house full of walnuts when the whole village was set on fire during the revolution.

# L'AVEN ARMAND

**ⓗ L'Aven Armand** €€€ *Meyrueis; tel: 04 66 45 61 31; email: contact@aven-armand.com; www.aven-armand.com. Open daily for 45-minute guided tours mid-Mar–Nov.*

In an area which abounds in underground marvels, this is definitely one not to miss. About 11km northwest of Meyrueis, it is one of the most spectacular caves in Europe, containing a forest of colourful rocks shaped like cypress and palm trees with massive branches and delicate leaves. You view them at the end of the 200m-long entrance tunnel, which opens out on to the vast cavern, 60m wide, 100m long and 45m high.

# LE ROZIER

ℹ **Le Rozier Tourist Information**
tel: 05 65 62 60 89; email: ot.lerozier@orange.fr; www.officedetourisme-gorgesdutarn.com. Open daily Jul–Aug; Mon–Fri Sept–Jun.

🏛 **Château de Peyrelade €**
tel: 05 65 59 74 28. Open daily Jun–Aug; rest of year by appointment.

Spread along the River Jonte just before it flows into the Tarn, the village is dwarfed by the cliffs of the Causse Méjean and the Causse Noir. An ancient bridge over the Jonte leads to Peyreléau, a quaint hillside village whose ruined castle, the **Château de Peyrelade**, which is built into the rock, occupies a commanding position above the gorges. Autumn is a particularly good time to be in the area when game from the *causses* is in season. Truffles are also a local speciality.

## Accommodation and food in Le Rozier

**Grand Hôtel des Voyageurs €€** *tel: 05 65 62 60 09; email: salguesvialasylvie@club-internet.fr; www.grandhoteldesvoyageurs.fr. Open Apr–Sept.* Comfortable 20-room hotel in the main street where E-A Martel stayed in 1888 while mapping nearby caves. Fully modernised. Menus include local specialities such as tripe and lamb.

# MEYRUEIS

ℹ **Meyrueis Tourist Information** Tour de l'Horloge; tel: 04 66 45 60 33; email: office.tourisme. meyrueis@wanadoo.fr; www.meyrueis-office-tourisme.com. Open daily Easter–Nov; Mon–Fri Dec–Easter.

Three small rivers, the Bétuzon, Brèze and Jonte, join together here before heading down the Gorges de la Jonte. The town is 706m high so you can enjoy clear mountain air as you stroll along the riverside promenades under plane trees or pause at a terrace bar. Its clock tower was once part of the town's fortifications and there are several elegant Renaissance buildings lurking along the narrow streets, as well as an attractive covered market hall by the river.

## Accommodation and food in Meyrueis

**Château des Ayres €€€** *tel: 04 66 45 60 10; email: chateau-d-ayres@ wanadoo.fr; www.hotel-restaurant-meyrueis.com. Restaurant open mid-Mar–mid-Dec.* Benedictine monastery, now a 29-room hotel with garden, pool and tennis.

# QUEZAC

ℹ **Quézac Tourist Information** In Ispagnac; tel: 04 66 45 01 14; www.mescevenues.com. Open Mon–Sat all year.

The village, situated on the left bank of the Tarn, pipes its famous mineral water from a spring on the opposite side to a large bottling plant on the edge of Ispagnac. The bridge across the Tarn was built 500 years ago at the express wish of Pope Urban V, who lived in the Lozère. He wanted pilgrims to be able to come to the sanctuary he had founded on the spot where a statue of the Virgin Mary had been discovered in 1050. Pilgrims still come to the church there.

# ST-CHELY-DU-TARN

Son-et-lumière performances are staged in summer in front of the **Chapelle du Clémaret**.

Across a pretty stone bridge on the left bank of the river, this ancient hamlet and its small 12th-century chapel, **Chapelle du Clémaret**, nestle picturesquely where two waterfalls cascade down. Its tiny square overlooking the river still has an old walk-in communal bread oven. Narrow alleys lead off it past stone cottages.

## Accommodation and food in St-Chély-du-Tarn

**Auberge de la Cascade €€** *tel: 04 66 48 52 82; email: aubergecascade@wanadoo.fr; www.aubergecascade.com. Open mid-Mar–mid-Nov.* Old stone building with 27 rooms, modern comforts and a pool in a timeless little village in the Tarn Gorge.

# STE-ENIMIE

**Ste-Enimie Tourist Information** *Next to the Mairie; tel: 04 66 48 53 44; email: contact@gorgesdutarn.net; www.gorgesdutarn.net. Open daily Jul–Aug; Mon–Sat Sept–Oct & Easter–Jun.*

**Musée Le Vieux Logis €** *tel: 04 66 31 69 20; email: vieuxsteenimie@yahoo.fr. Open daily mid-Jun–mid-Sept for guided tours; rest of year by appointment.*

Everyone who has driven up the twisting Gorges du Tarn arrives at this village with a certain relief. Suddenly there are shops and bars! But it's hard to believe now that such a small place, which stretches up from the river in terraces, used to be an important trading centre. The centre is a medieval grid of steep narrow streets and pale stone buildings roofed in round grey slates. In the small 12th-century chapel, colourful modern ceramics by Henri Constans tell the story of Enimie, a 7th-century saint whose discovery of the Burle spring nearby cured her of leprosy. The **Musée Le Vieux Logis** shows what life used to be like in the area.

## Accommodation and food in Ste-Enimie

**Auberge du Moulin €€** *rue de la Combe; tel: 04 66 48 53 08; www.aubergedumoulin.free.fr. Open Apr–mid-Nov.* Old converted mill in pink stone by the River Tarn, just across the road from the town's medieval village. Ten rooms and homely restaurant.

### Sainte Enimie

Sainte Enimie was a beautiful 7th-century princess who developed leprosy after her father, the king of Merovingia, insisted she marry one of his barons. Searching desperately for a cure, she was led by an angel to the Source de Burle, a spring fed by rainwater from the Causse de Sauveterre. She jumped in and was immediately cured, but as soon as she tried to return home the leprosy returned. Recognising that her cure must be a sign from God, she set up home in a cave beside the spring and stayed in it to do good works.

**Above**
Le Rozier

**Château de la Caze €€€** *Near Ste-Enimie; tel: 04 66 48 51 01; email: chateau.caze@orange.fr; www.chateaudelacaze.com. Open Apr–mid-Nov.* Former castle, complete with towers, dating back to the 15th century and romantically situated on the riverbank in the Tarn Gorge, 5km north of La Malène on the D907. Garden with swimming pool. Also noted for its cuisine.

# Suggested tour

**Total distance:** 125km. The detour to L'Aven Armand cave adds 22km, the detour to Roc des Hourtous and Roc de Serre adds 26km and the detour to St-Chély-du-Tarn adds 1km.

**Time:** 4 hours' driving. Allow a day for the main route, more with detours. Those with limited time should concentrate on the Gorges de la Jonte and the Gorges du Tarn.

**Links to other tours:** At Florac, this route touches the 'Heart of the Cévennes' route (*see page 262*). From Florac, the D907 leads south to St-Laurent-de-Trèves (*see page 234*), 10km away. From Le Rozier, the D907 leads southwest to Millau (*see page 240*), 22km away. From Meyrueis, the D986 leads southeast to L'Espérou (*see page 231*), 27km away.

**Below**
Gorges du Tarn

Climb out of **Florac** up to the **Causse Méjean** on the D16 (signposted Les Vignes). This is one of the most exciting roads in the region as it twists in steep hairpin bends around the cliffsides, providing a magnificent panorama over the Cévennes and Mont Lozère with Florac spread out below along the valley bottom. Sunset is the most dramatic time of all to drive up it. The plateau at the top, a desolate expanse of rough grass, box bushes and strangely shaped white boulders, is over 1,000m high. Grazed in summer by sheep, it is dotted by the occasional farmhouse. A wide variety of birds inhabit the crags, particularly birds of prey such as kestrels, hen harriers and golden eagles. Drive across the *causse* (21km) to the junction with the D986. Turn left there to drop down towards **MEYRUEIS** ❶.

**Detour: L'AVEN ARMAND** ❷ cave is signed to the right 9km after the D16/D986 junction. Take the 2km road to it.

Continue into Meyrueis where the route turns back on itself to go west along the D996 through the 21km-long **GORGES DE LA JONTE** ❸. As the gorge becomes increasingly impressive downstream, with pillars of rock jutting up on the skyline above the steep hillsides of pines and beeches, this is definitely the better way to drive along it rather than going in the other direction. Halfway along you pass through **Les Douzes**, a pretty riverside village with a bell tower and hillside cemetery, and then come to **Le Truel**.

Continuing the route towards **LE ROZIER** ❹, look out just after Le Truel for signs to the **Belvédère des Vautours** where two viewing platforms enable you to see over both sides of the gorge. You might also catch sight of vultures wheeling over the crags of the *causses* above, as protected nesting sites have led to their reintroduction to the area. At Le Rozier, the River Jonte flows into the Tarn, which you cross to follow the D907 north along the **GORGES DU TARN** ❺. The valley widens a little at **Les Vignes**, a starting point for rafting, and bends dramatically below the Cirque des Baumes before reaching **LA MALENE** ❻.

**Detour:** Across the river from La Malène, a steep narrow road climbs to the Col de Rieisse (946m) on the D16 (8km). Three kilometres beyond the Col, turn right to **Rieisse**. Beyond it, two cliff-top viewing points, the **Roc des Hourtous** (1km to the left) and the **Roc de Serre** (1km to the right), both enjoy superb views of the gorge.

**Detour:** Eight kilometres beyond La Malène, a bridge over the Tarn leads straight into **ST-CHELY-DU-TARN** ❼ on the opposite bank.

**Below**
Gorges de la Jonte

Twisting and turning along the Gorges du Tarn, the D907 continues to **STE-ENIMIE** ❽.

From Ste-Enimie, continue along the gorge past the **CHATEAU DE PRADES** ❾. Two kilometres after it, you will see the ruins of Castelbouc castle on a steep rock overhanging the village which huddles below it. The gorge officially ends just beyond it where the river and road bend very sharply left between the plateaux, but the scenery remains similar. Continue to **Molines**, **QUEZAC** ❿ (just across the river) and **ISPAGNAC** ⓫. From there, take the N106 south, still beside the Tarn, to return to Florac.

## Getting out of the car

To walk around the **Arcs de St-Pierre**, an area of extraordinary rock formations, turn right off the D996 at Le Truel on to the unnumbered road which climbs steeply up hairpin bends towards

**St-Pierre-des-Tripiers**. After 3km, the rocks are signposted off to the left. The Arcs themselves (a 10-minute walk from the road) are three big natural arches. Other dramatically eroded rocks, within a further 10-minute walk which passes the remains of a prehistoric village, include the Grande Place, an amphitheatre with a 10m-high column in the centre.

To see the **Burle spring**, take the footpath behind the Gîtes St-Vincent at the top of Ste-Enimie. The walk takes about 25 minutes each way or you can get there by driving 3km along the D986 towards Mende. Two rocks are hollowed out like chairs at the entrance to L'Hermitage de Ste-Enimie, the cave where Enimie is said to have lived. Inside is a tiny chapel. The view is magnificent, extending over both the town and the Tarn.

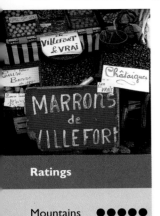

# The heart of the Cévennes

From the less-than-lovely tower blocks of Alès, this route soon climbs northwest into the mountains, becoming more and more remote all the way. Along the edge of the Montagne du Bourges the road is impressively speedy, as it now bypasses most of the villages, though it would be a shame to hurry through such majestic scenery. After the route turns east, however, it twists and turns so much that there is no chance of hurrying through the villages that nestle in the rural valleys below Mont Lozère. Idyllic now as holiday retreats, many were the scene of bitter skirmishes 400 years ago between Catholics and Protestants.

Mont Lozère itself, vividly splashed with yellow gorse all summer, can only be truly discovered on foot. Fortunately, its rugged hillsides are criss-crossed with ancient sheep trails which now make wonderful paths.

## ALES

**❶ Alès Tourist Information** *place de l'Hôtel de Ville; tel: 04 66 52 32 15; email: tourisme@ville-ales.fr; www.ville-ales.fr. Open daily Jul–Aug; Mon–Sat Sept–Jun.*

**◍** The modern Marché de l'Abbaye market hall (*open Mon–Sat mornings*) specialises in local produce, notably honey and mushrooms.

Try to ignore the tower blocks on the outskirts of this former mining town – the last mine closed in 1986 – as you head for the centre. Its wide boulevards, close to the broad River Gardon, have the biggest selection of shops in the area. Not surprisingly, the town's main points of interest concern mining. The **Mine-Témoin** €€€ (*chemin de la Cité, Ste-Marie, Rochebelle (3km west beyond the Rochebelle bridge over the River Gardon); tel: 04 66 30 45 15; email: mine.temoin@orange.fr; www.mine-temoin.fr. Guided tours, lasting 1 hour 20 minutes. Open daily Feb–Nov*), a disused colliery with 650m of shafts hollowed out of the hillside, vividly depicts the history of mining in the region. Benedictine monks first extracted coal there in the 13th century. Wear a sweater as the temperature remains a constant 13–15°C (55–59°F).

The **Musée Minéralogique** €€ (*6 avenue de Clavières, attached to the Ecole des Mines; tel: 04 66 78 51 69; www.ema.fr. Open Mon–Fri mid-Jun–mid-Sept; mid-Sept–mid-Jun by appointment*) at the mine engineering school has one of Europe's finest collections of minerals,

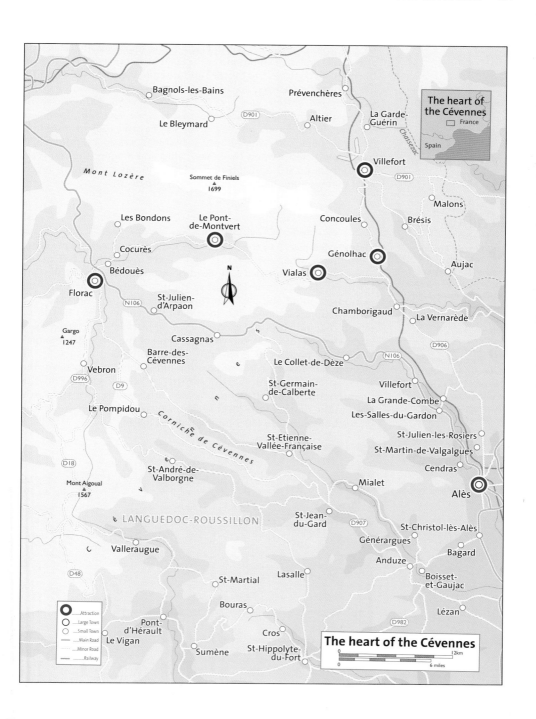

The heart of the Cévennes

France
Spain

Bagnols-les-Bains
Prévenchères
La Garde-Guérin
Altier
Le Bleymard
D901
Villefort
Malons
Mont Lozère
Sommet de Finiels
1699
Concoules
Brésis
Les Bondons
Le Pont-de-Montvert
Cocurès
Génolhac
Aujac
Bédouès
Vialas
Florac
St-Julien-d'Arpaon
N106
Chamborigaud
La Vernarède
Gargo
1247
Cassagnas
Barre-des-Cévennes
D906
Vebron
Le Collet-de-Dèze
N106
D996
D9
St-Germain-de-Calberte
Villefort
Le Pompidou
La Grande-Combe
Corniche de Cévennes
Les-Salles-du-Gardon
St-Julien-les-Rosiers
St-Martin-de-Valgalgues
D18
St-Etienne-Vallée-Française
Cendras
St-André-de-Valborgne
Mont Aigoual
1567
Mialet
Alès
LANGUEDOC-ROUSSILLON
St-Jean-du-Gard
St-Christol-lès-Alès
D907
Générargues
Bagard
Vallereaugue
Anduze
D48
Lasalle
Boisset-et-Gaujac
St-Martial
Lézan
Bouras
D982
Pont-d'Hérault
Cros
The heart of the Cévennes
Le Vigan
St-Hippolyte-du-Fort
Sumène

0                    12km
0              6 miles

Attraction
Large Town
Small Town
Main Road
Minor Road
Railway

ranging from Australian opal to black quartz found locally. There are also fossils and an exhibition on the natural resources of the region. In complete contrast, the **Musée-Bibliothèque Pierre-André-Benoît €** (*33 montée des Lauriers, Rochebelle (take the Rochebelle bridge over the Gardon and follow the signs); tel: 04 66 86 98 69; email: museepab@wanadoo.fr; www.ville-ales.fr. Open Tue–Sun afternoons Mar–Jan*), in the former bishops' residence, has an excellent collection of contemporary art donated by M Benoît who was a local printer and painter. It includes works by Picasso, Miró and Braque. The 200-year-old Cathédrale St-Jean-Baptiste is a large gloomy building in much need of restoration but with interesting frescoes.

# FLORAC

**Florac Tourist Information** *33 avenue Jean Monestier; tel: 04 66 45 01 14; email: otsi@mescevennes.com; www.mescevennes.com. Open daily Jul–Aug; Mon–Sat Sept–Jun.*

**Château de Florac** *Parc National des Cévennes information centre; tel: 04 66 49 53 01; email: info@cevennes-6parcnational.fr; www.cevennes-6parcnational.fr, with Passagers du Paysage exhibition about the park €€. Open daily Jun–Aug; Mon–Fri Oct–May.*

*Thur morning market.*

Though well placed in the heart of the Causses as a touring or walking base, this is otherwise a rather plain little town. The **Château de Florac**, its much-modified 17th-century castle, is now used by the Parc National des Cévennes to house its information centre and an exhibition about the park. Previously, the building was used as a prison, military hospital and then bank. An earlier castle had to be rebuilt, like much of the town, following skirmishes between local lords when the area was known as the 'land of the Gévaudan tyrants'. The town's position is interesting geologically as it is sited at the meeting point of four formations: the limestone Causse Méjean, the schist of the Cévennes, the granite of Mont Lozère and the granite/schist of Mont Aigoual. A footpath starting near the castle leads to the source of the River Pêcher, which froths up from a spring on the Causse Méjean (30 minutes' walk each way).

# GENOLHAC

**Génolhac Tourist Information**
L'Arceau; tel: 04 66 61 18 32; email: ot-genolhac@wanadoo.fr; www.cevennes-montlozere.com. Open daily Jul–Aug; Tue–Sat Sept–Jun.

**Hotel Le Chalet €**
place de la Gare; tel: 04 66 61 11 08; email: bruno-vernhat@orange.fr. Open all year. Traditional 150-year-old bar-restaurant, popular with locals. Eight rooms.

This small old town of tall grey granite houses with warm red roofs has narrow streets often bridged by arches. Many of the buildings in the medieval centre were originally warehouses with living quarters above storage areas. If you wonder why some of them have stones sticking out in odd places from their otherwise plain walls, the explanation is that they were put there by the builder to show when he needed a drink. The owner would then put wine on them. Eglise St-Pierre has a *clocher-peigne*, a flat open stone belfry with two suspended bells, typical of the area. A plaque opposite the Hôtel du Mont Lozère marks the spot where a Resistance hero was gunned down by the Germans in June 1944.

## Bells

The area's bell towers are called *clochers de tourmente* – storm towers – because in bad weather they were rung continuously to help travellers find their way. Otherwise, their main use was to call people to Mass and let farmers working in the fields know the time.

Although holidaymakers find the mountains very attractive, the towers provide a constant reminder that when the cold *Tramontane* wind blows from the northwest, the area can be very bleak. The local people have always had a struggle to make a living on the rocky terrain and poor soil, hence the chilling phrase 'Mont Lozère, terre de misère' (land of misery).

**Left**
Château de Florac

# LE PONT-DE-MONTVERT

**Le Pont-de-Montvert Tourist Information** rue du Quai; tel: 04 66 45 81 94; email: montlozerecevennes.free.fr; www.cevennes-montlozere.com. Open daily Jul–Sept.

**Eco-Musée du Mont Lozère €** tel: 04 66 45 80 73; email: ecomusee@cevennes-parcnational.fr; www.mescevennes.com. Open daily Apr–Sept; Sat Oct–Mar. Combined admission with Ferme de Troubat, an old farmhouse, 6km east of the D998 at Troubat.

The old-fashioned village of Le Pont-de-Montvert, straddling the River Tarn and two of its tributaries, has a real mountain atmosphere and is a popular walking centre. The tower at one end of the old bridge over the Tarn once served as a tollbooth. In 1702, a Catholic abbot was flung off the bridge while trying to escape from local Protestants. His death sparked off the Camisard uprising, a bitter two-year struggle by local peasants to be allowed to worship as Protestants. The Maison du Mont Lozère, part of the **Eco-Musée du Mont Lozère**, houses an exhibition about the local landscape, its people and wildlife.

## Accommodation and food in Le Pont-de-Montvert

**Aux Sources du Tarn €** tel: 04 66 45 80 25; email: auxsourcesdutarn@wanadoo.fr; www.hotellozere.com. Open all year. Homely 19-room hotel beside the Tarn, popular with walkers. Advance reservations essential December–February.

# VIALAS

Vialas, a little hamlet of stone dwellings clustered around narrow streets, has a church and sweeping views across the valley. Typical of the area, its Protestant church has a sloping *lauze*-tiled roof and a bell.

## Accommodation and food in Vialas

**Chantoiseau €€** *tel: 04 66 41 00 02; www.chantoiseau-vialas.fr. Open Apr–Oct.* A 17th-century post house transformed into a charming five-room guesthouse (B&B only). A delightful place to stay, especially in summer thanks to its charming garden and swimming pool with panoramic views.

# VILLEFORT

Nestling beneath Mont Lozère in the Phalère Valley, Villefort makes a good holiday base, surrounded as it is by walking trails. The Lac de Villefort reservoir on its north side is popular for watersports.

## Accommodation and food in Villefort

**Hôtel Balme €** *place Portalet; tel: 04 66 46 80 14; email: hotelbalme@free.fr; www.hotelbalme.online.fr. Open mid-Feb–mid-Nov.* Traditional and elegant 16-room hotel run by chef-owner and his wife for over 30 years. High reputation for both hospitality and food. La Clède gastronomic restaurant. Garden and garage.

## Suggested tour

**Total distance:** 200km. The detour to the Belvédère des Bouzède adds 16km and the detour to La Garde-Guérin adds 12km.

**Time:** 6 hours' driving. Allow most of two days for the main route, two full days with detours. Those with limited time should concentrate on the stretch from Florac to Villefort.

**Links to other tours:** At Florac, this route touches the 'Great plateaux and gorges' route (*see page 254*). From Florac, the D907 leads to St-Laurent-de-Trèves (*see page 234*), 10km away. From Alès, the D910 leads to Anduze (*see page 228*), 16km away.

From **ALES** ❶ take the N106 northwest beside the River Gardon, bypassing the former mining town of **La Grand-Combe**, which contains little of interest. Beyond the Cambous dam (on the left), the road climbs along wooded mountainsides, still beside the river, over

**Robert Louis Stevenson Trail**
*Association sur le Chemin de R L Stevenson, Le Pont-de-Montvert; tel: 04 66 45 86 31; email: asso.stevenson@ libertysurf.fr; www.chemin-stevenson.org. Open Mon–Fri all year.*

passes and past villages such as **Cassagnas** and **St-Julien-d'Arpaon** to **FLORAC** ❷. On the far side of Florac, turn right on to the D998, a quiet winding road through peaceful countryside along the River Tarn valley. Here the scenery is pretty rather than grand. Sheep – sometimes black – graze in fields which give way to the rocky slopes and forests of Mont Lozère. Each village has its landmarks – a huge church surrounded by campsites in **Bédouès**, a sawmill in **Cocurès** and the ancient tollbooth beside the quaint stone bridge in **LE PONT-DE-MONTVERT** ❸. Now the road narrows, climbing through beech woods high above the river over the Col de la Croix de Berthel (1,088m). Approaching **VIALAS** ❹, the hillsides are patched with broom and heather among the boulders.

From Vialas, you pass through forests and over the Col de Valoussière (501m) on the way to **GENOLHAC** ❺.

**Detour:** Turn left out of Génolhac up an unnumbered road to the spectacular 1,235m-high **Belvédère des Bouzède** viewpoint (8km) where the views stretch like a relief map south over the Cévennes and east towards the Ardèche.

From Génolhac, the route goes north on the D906, twisting through woods. Beyond **Concoules**, the countryside opens out and you get wide mountain views to the east on the way to **VILLEFORT** ❻.

**Detour:** North of Villefort, the D906 continues past the town's reservoir to **La Garde-Guérin** (6km), a quaint medieval village whose narrow streets and simple stone houses seem to have changed very little over the centuries. During the Camisard uprising, it was fiercely attacked by Protestants. The ruined tower which stands guard over it

**Left**
Villefort

## Stevenson's travels in the Cévennes

When Robert Louis Stevenson's book *Travels with a Donkey in the Cévennes* was published in 1879, it put this remote area of France on the map.

The previous year he had taken himself to Le Monastier because he wanted to get away and decide on his feelings for Fanny Osbourne – whom he later married. Having bought a donkey, Modestine, he set off on 22 September to walk south via Le Pont-de-Montvert (which reminded him of the Killiecrankie Pass in Scotland) and Florac to St-Jean-du-Gard. The 220km journey took him only 12 days.

On the way he drew small sketches in his diary (now at Yale University in America), with notes such as 'The road lay under chestnuts and though I saw a hamlet or two below me in the vale and many lone houses of the chestnut farmers, it was a very solitary march all afternoon'. Later he added background information about the Camisards to turn it into a book for which he was paid 30 francs – though he thought it worth at least 50 francs.

The R L Stevenson Association's leaflet (available from local tourist offices) has lists of places to stay and eat along the route and where to hire a mountain bike, horse – or donkey.

## The Voie Régordane

The Régordane long-distance path, GR72, runs north–south along the crests of the Cévennes through La Garde-Guérin, Villefort, Génolhac and Alès. It is part of an ancient route between the Auvergne and the Mediterranean which pilgrims used on their way to Rome in the Middle Ages. Originally, it was probably formed by shepherds driving flocks between the valleys and the plateaux during the traditional transhumance in spring and autumn. In Roman times, it was the only route between the Languedoc and the Auvergne. When Marseilles developed as a port, it would have been busy with mule carts, but with the construction of the railways, it once again became a quiet country track.

**Hôtel Lou Cante Perdrix €€**
*Le Château, La Vernarède (between the D29 and the D906, 5km east of Chamborigaud); tel: 04 66 61 50 30; email: lou.cante.perdrix@wanadoo.fr; www.canteperdrix.fr. Open Feb–Dec.* Fifteen-room hotel in a 200-year-old mansion with garden, pool and tennis. Bicycles for hire. The name means 'partridge field' in the local dialect.

provides good views over the Gorges du Chassezac – though the steps up to the tower are steep.

From Villefort, the route turns east (towards Les Vans) on the D901 over the Col Mas de l'Air (846m). Two kilometres beyond the Col, turn right on to the D155 through **Malons** to join the D51 at **Brésis**. This quiet rural road through trees and along stone terraces has a wonderful view of Mont Lozère with its gentle hilltops spread out above wooded slopes. Enjoy the remoteness as you continue on the narrow D51 through **Aujac**, overlooked by a hilltop castle, then wind down through the forest above the River Cèze to **Bessèges**, a distinctly industrial town. Cross the river, turning immediately right on to the D29 to **Chamborigaud**. Now the remoteness has gone but there are still good views as the D906 takes you back to Alès.

### Getting out of the car

For a flavour of Mont Lozère, take the **Sentier de Gourdouse**, a rocky footpath which climbs north from Vialas into the hills below granite ridges. Listen for the sound of cowbells competing with the roar of mountain streams and look out for wild pansies and orchids.

### Also worth exploring

France's second-largest collection of prehistoric standing stones (after Carnac in Brittany) is on the Mont Lozère plateau north of Florac. Turn left off the D998 at Cocurès and go through Les Bondons to the junction with the D35 (9km from Cocurès). Turn left again and the stones, which include 21 menhirs and a dolmen, are signed shortly afterwards on the left.

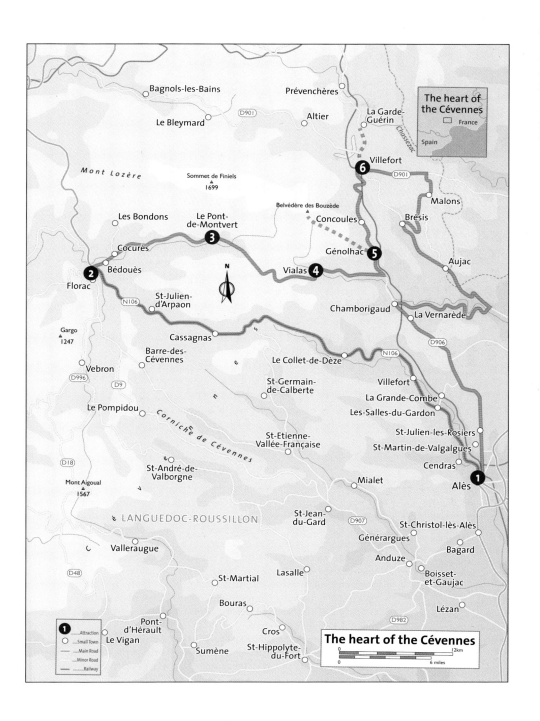

The heart of the Cévennes

Bagnols-les-Bains
Prévenchères
Le Bleymard
D901
Altier
La Garde-Guérin
Villefort
6
D901
Malons
Brésis
Mont Lozère
Sommet de Finiels
1699
Belvédère des Bouzède
Concoules
Génolhac
5
Aujac
Les Bondons
Le Pont-de-Montvert
3
Cocurès
Bédouès
Vialas
4
Florac
2
St-Julien-d'Arpaon
N106
Chamborigaud
La Vernarède
Gargo
1247
Cassagnas
D906
Barre-des-Cévennes
Le Collet-de-Dèze
N106
Vebron
D996
D9
St-Germain-de-Calberte
Villefort
Le Pompidou
La Grande-Combe
Les-Salles-du-Gardon
St-Etienne-Vallée-Française
St-Julien-les-Rosiers
St-Martin-de-Valgalgues
D18
St-André-de-Valborgne
Mialet
Cendras
Mont Aigoual
1567
Alès
1
LANGUEDOC-ROUSSILLON
St-Jean-du-Gard
D907
St-Christol-lès-Alès
Générargues
Bagard
Vallerauge
Anduze
D48
Lasalle
Boisset-et-Gaujac
St-Martial
Lézan
Bouras
Pont-d'Hérault
Cros
D982
Le Vigan
Sumène
St-Hippolyte-du-Fort

The heart of the Cévennes
0        12km
0    6 miles

1 Attraction
O Small Town
Main Road
Minor Road
Railway

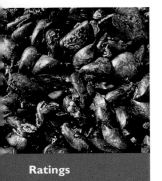

# The coastal resorts south from Montpellier

## Ratings

| | |
|---|---|
| Beaches | ●●●●● |
| Naturism | ●●●●● |
| Children | ●●●●○ |
| Coastal villages/ towns | ●●●●○ |
| Wildlife | ●●●●○ |
| Entertainment | ●●●○○ |
| Food | ●●●○○ |
| Outdoor activities | ●●●○○ |

Along this route you will discover the essence of the Languedoc-Roussillon coast with its long sandy beaches and lagoons. Until the 1960s, comparatively few holidaymakers went there. Sète was the only town of any importance, though Palavas, an old fishing village, had been attracting visitors from Montpellier since the railway arrived a hundred years ago.

Purpose-built resorts arrived when the French government initiated an ambitious programme of tourist development in 1963. Le Cap d'Agde headland and beaches were transformed by the building of smart marinas and apartment/villa complexes stylishly laid out with gardens and promenades.

Shallow lagoons – *étangs* – lie just inland along much of the coast, separated from the sea by narrow sandbars. The calm semi-salt water of the Bassin de Thau has proved ideal for the cultivation of shellfish, while delicate pink flamingos have long been at home on the quieter lagoons around Palavas-les-Flots.

## AGDE

**ⓘ Agde Tourist Information** *Rond point du Bon Accueil; tel: 04 67 01 04 04; email: contact@capdagde.com; www.en.capdagde.com. Open daily all year.*

**ⓗ Cathédrale St-Etienne** *Open only for Mass. Guided visits only, bookable at tourist office, except when concerts are held on its Baroque organ.*

The ancient little town of Agde spreads along the River Hérault just before it reaches the sea. It was once the largest port on the Languedoc coast, having first been developed by the ancient Greeks in 500 BC. However, the river silted up centuries ago and now only pleasure craft and small fishing boats line its narrow quays, overlooked by rows of former merchants' houses. Many of the buildings in the town centre are made of sombre-looking local black basalt, hence the town's nickname – 'La Ville Noire' (Black Town). They include the dour 12th-century **Cathédrale St-Etienne** whose sturdy tower and slit windows make it look like a fortress.

The **Musée Agathois Espace Molière**, housed in a quaint 17th-century building, formerly a hospital, vividly presents the town's history through pottery, paintings, costumes and reconstructions of interiors of local houses. It also has a splendid array of ancient

The coastal resorts south from Montpellier

**Musée Agathois Espace Molière €**
5 rue de la Fraternité;
tel: 04 67 94 82 51; email:
dau.darret@libertysurf.fr.
Open daily all year.

Jousting tournaments
in Jul–Aug.

wooden shields used in jousting tournaments which are still a colourful feature of the town's summer entertainment on the river.

Agde is well endowed with places to eat, particularly along the narrow riverside terraces where you can bask in the evening sun and watch the comings and goings on the water as you dine.

## Accommodation and food in Agde

**Hôtel Le Donjon €€** place Jean Jaurès; tel: 04 67 94 12 32; email: hotelledonjon@wanadoo.fr; www.hotelagde.com. Open Nov–Jan. Inexpensive 20-room hotel with plenty of character and a pool. In the old town centre, only steps away from the shops and restaurants.

# BASSIN DE THAU

**Musée de l'Etang de Thau** € *quai du Port de Pêche, Bouzigues; tel: 04 67 78 33 57; email: musee.etang.thau@ libertysurf.fr; www.bouzigues.fr. Open daily all year.*

**Below**
Le Cap d'Agde

This lagoon, the largest of many along the Languedoc coast, is separated from the sea by a 20km-long sandbar, the Isthume des Onglous. The villagers on its northern shore, who used to make their living from fishing, have now turned to oyster and mussel farming. The water ripples around the poles and garlands of nets used in their cultivation. Bouzigues is the main oyster centre, and the lagoon's oysters are known as *huitres de Bouzigues*. An oyster fair is held here in mid-August, and the **Musée de l'Etang de Thau** on the quay of Bouzigues' small fishing harbour traces the history of shellfish breeding.

# FRONTIGNAN

ℹ **Frontignan Tourist Information** *avenue des Etangs; tel: 04 67 18 31 60; www.tourisme-frontignan.com. Open daily Jul–Aug; Mon–Sat Sept & Apr–Jun; Mon–Fri Oct–Mar.*

Muscat, the highly reputed local wine, is the best reason for seeking out Frontignan, which is surrounded by vineyards in an otherwise industrial area between the sea and the *garrigue* – hilly scrubland. The sweet fortified wine can be tasted in various cellars.

# LE CAP D'AGDE

ℹ **Le Cap d'Agde Tourist Information** *Rond-Point du Bon Accueil; tel: 04 67 01 04 04; email: contact@capdagde.com; www.en.capdagde.com. Open daily all year.*

**Naturist information** *Service d'Accueil du Quartier Naturiste, Rond-point du Bagnas; tel: 04 67 26 00 26; www.agdenaturisme.com. Open Mon–Fri Apr–Sept.*

🔟 **Aqualand €€** *In Richelieu quarter; tel: 04 67 26 85 94; www.aqualand.fr. Open daily Jun–Sept.*

○ Festival of the Sea in *Jul.*

◑ **Hôtel Eve €€€** *Impasse Saissan; tel: 04 67 26 71 70; email: info@hoteleve.com; www.hoteleve.com. Open Apr–Sept. Naturist hotel with 48 rooms.*

Developed in the 1960s around a headland, this purpose-built town could scarcely be more different from its ancient sister, 3km away. Broad avenues bordered by gardens of colourful oleanders lead to clusters of pink and ochre villas and apartments beside a large marina and 14km of sandy beaches.

On summer evenings, a constant flow of visitors parade up and down in front of the restaurants, bars and souvenir shops surrounding the quays. Singers and groups compete to entice customers into their bars – and the party atmosphere continues well into the night. Other revellers head for the Ile des Loisirs, which offers a choice of over two dozen nightclubs, a funfair and a casino.

By day, the town seems to have a club for every pursuit – tennis, golf, squash, horse riding, scrabble, bridge, snooker, etc. You can take a boat trip round the harbour, snorkel along an underwater trail or have a course of thalassotherapy. To keep children happy, **Aqualand**, the water park, has slides and a wave pool. There are beachclubs and daily children's shows too.

Le Cap d'Agde's famous Quartier Naturiste, Europe's largest naturist village, has accommodation for 20,000 people. It has its own shops, restaurants, marina and a hotel beside a wide beach. Day visits (nudity optional) are permitted for a small charge. The beach is excellent but you must be prepared to take all your clothes off.

# MAGUELONE

🔁 **Maguelone** is a 30-minute walk from the car park at the end of rue Maguelone in Palavas-les-Flots. From June to September you have to park there and walk or take the free road-train.

The history of the isolated **cathedral** at Maguelone is no less remarkable than its breathtaking location at the end of a sandbar. Remains found there have been traced back almost 2,000 years. Together with a palace it was built by Bishop Arnaud in the 11th century and became very important when several popes sought refuge there during quarrels between Church and State. The whole estate

**Cathedral** *Tel: 04 67 69 75 87. Open daily all year; organ concerts on Sat evening Jul–Aug.*

later fell into ruin and changed hands several times during the construction of the Rhône–Sète Canal beside it. The former cathedral, whose thick walls and small windows make it seem more like a castle than a church, dates back to the 15th century. It was bought and restored in the middle of the 19th century by Frédéric Fabrège.

# MARSEILLAN

**Marseillan Noilly Prat** *Tel: 04 67 77 75 19; www.noillyprat.com. Open daily May–Sept.* Free guided tours ending with a tasting. You can also buy the product.

Hard as it is to imagine today, Marseillan was situated on the coast in Roman times when it was an important port of call for shipping between Agde and Sète. Later drifting sand caused the Bassin de Thau to form behind a sandbar. Now it is an unassuming fishing port on the Bassin de Thau. It has achieved worldwide fame thanks to **Noilly Prat**, an aromatic vermouth aperitif made from the local wine. After being left to age in oak vats for a year in quayside cellars, it is transferred to open casks and left for another year. The small quantity which evaporates is said to be fit for angels. Finally it is mixed with fruit alcohol, herbs and *mistelle* (grape juice).

**Right**
Marseillan: the Noilly Prat cellars

# MARSEILLAN-PLAGE

**ⓘ Marseillan-Plage Tourist Information**
*avenue de la Méditérranée;*
*tel: 04 67 21 82 43;*
*www.ville-marseillan.fr. Open*
*daily Apr–Sept; Mon–Sat*
*Oct–Mar.*

**ⓐ** A local festival with traditional music takes place halfway through Lent.

**🍴 Côté Sud €€**
*18 quai Antonin Gros;*
*tel: 04 67 01 72 42.*
*Open Wed–Mon all year.*
*Small restaurant on the*
*quayside, strong on fish.*

This small seaside resort with the usual selection of campsites, beach shops and holiday homes is situated on a sandy beach which stretches for miles in both directions. Altogether the sandbar, backed by dunes, goes all the way from Cap d'Agde to Sète – a distance of 20km. The stretch of beach on the west side of the resort is reserved for naturists, joining up with the one at Cap d'Agde. To avoid paying to get an all-over tan on the naturist beach, park your car in one of the roads behind the dunes in Marseillan-Plage and walk there (2km).

# MEZE

**ⓘ Mèze Tourist Information** *8 rue*
*P A Massaloup, Mèze;*
*tel: 04 67 43 93 08;*
*email: tourisme.ccnbt@*
*orange.fr; www.ville-meze.fr.*
*Open daily Jul–Aug; Mon–Sat*
*Sept–Jun.*

**ⓐ** Jazz festival in Jul.

The charming old town of Mèze, with its narrow streets, has an attractive harbour on the Bassin de Thau where fishing boats and yachts line up. Stalls along the waterfront sell freshly gathered oysters, clams and mussels. **Station de Lagunage**, the lagoon's research station (2km west of Mèze), has an aquarium of tropical fish as well as displays, films and photographs about the local shellfish industry (*tel: 04 67 46 64 94; email: visites@ecosites.fr; visits by appointment only*).

# PALAVAS-LES-FLOTS

**ⓘ Palavas-les-Flots Tourist Information** *place de la Méditérranée; tel: 04 67 07 73 34; email: tourisme@ palavaslesflots.com; www.palavaslesflots.com. Open daily all year.*

**🍴 Redoute de Ballestras €€**
*Tel: 04 67 68 56 41.*
*Open Tue–Sun afternoons all year.*

This lively little resort, much loved by families for its 7km-long sandy beach, is on the narrow band of land between the Etang de Pérols lagoon and the sea. Unlike most resorts along the Languedoc-Roussillon coast, it is no latter-day tourist development. Having started out as a fishing community, it became popular for a day out with people from nearby Montpellier when the railway (now closed) arrived in 1872. The way they flocked in on the 'Petit Train de Palavas' with their shrimping nets and picnics was later immortalised by a local cartoonist, Albert Dubout. A collection of his work is housed in an old fort, the **Redoute de Ballestras**, which is a landmark on the edge of the Etang de Pérols. It was built in 1743 to protect local fishermen from pirates. When the threat subsided, it became a water tower until being converted into a museum to house the Dubout cartoons.

**Jousting tournaments** in Jul–Aug.

**Rôtisserie Palavas**
€€ 5 rue de l'Eglise;
tel: 04 67 68 52 12. Open Wed–Mon all year. Seafood restaurant.

On the west side of the busy old fishing port, there is now a large marina for yachts and cruisers. Its seafood restaurants, which buy direct from the fishermen, are as popular for a night out with people from Montpellier as they are for holidaymakers. Throughout the summer, street entertainment and open-air concerts are staged. The casino is another attraction for many.

# Pezenas

**Pézenas Tourist Information** place Gambetta; tel: 04 67 98 36 40; email: accueil-pezenas@otpvh.fr; www.pezenas-tourisme.fr. Open daily all year. Guided tours available.

**Musée Vulliod-St-Germain €**
3 rue Albert-Allais;
tel: 04 67 98 90 59.
Open Tue–Sun all year.

The town stages several colourful events during the year, including pre-Lent carnival processions.

For 250 years this small town was the seat of the governors of Languedoc. During the 16th and 17th centuries, its royal court rivalled that of Versailles. The *vielle ville* (old quarter) has not changed much since those illustrious times when aristocrats built fine mansions with ornate doorways and balconies. Leading artists and musicians of the day came to entertain the court. Molière made his name as a playwright there, putting on several plays with his own theatre company. He stayed at the **Maison du Barbier Cély**, now the tourist office, and staged the plays at the **Hôtel Alphonse** (now a private house), which is one of the best-preserved buildings from that period. It has a decorative portico and two tiers of loggias.

**Musée Vulliod-St-Germain**, in the 16th-century Hôtel de St-Germain, devotes a room to Molière memorabilia. There are Aubusson tapestries and an audiovisual on the town's history, particularly its Molière connections.

In cake shops, watch out for *petits pâtés* – little pies – the town's speciality. They look like cotton reels and are stuffed with sweet spice, glacé lemon and minced meat. Restaurants serve them for dessert.

## Food in Pézenas

**Côté Sud** €€ 12 place du 14 Juillet; tel: 04 67 09 41 74. Open Tue–Sun all year. Small lively brasserie on the edge of the old town with imaginative menus featuring local specialities such as *petits pâtés*.

### Petits pâtés de Pézenas

In 1768, Lord Clive of India spent the winter at Larzac castle near Pézenas, hoping the mild weather would be good for his health. He was accompanied by his Indian cooks, who passed on the recipe for these little pies to local bakers. Several continue to make them by hand and restaurants proudly serve them for dessert. Incidentally, they're also made in Market Drayton, Lord Clive's home town in England (now 'twinned' with Pézenas), where they are known as Clive Pies.

# SETE

Sète is the oldest and most interesting town along this part of the coast, thanks to its canal-side restaurants, small speciality shops and sandy beach. It is also an important fishing and industrial port. The port was developed 300 years ago as part of the grand Canal du Midi project. This included building the town itself on the sides of Mont St-Clair, a rocky 183m-high outcrop with the sea on one side and the Bassin de Thau on the other.

Narrow streets spread steeply up the hillside from the Canal Royal where pastel-coloured Italianate buildings line the busy quays. A row of restaurants and bars makes this one of the liveliest places along the coast for eating out.

The climb up Mont St-Clair is strenuous but it is definitely more interesting to walk (at least 15 minutes) than drive. The views from the top are splendid. The complex port is laid out below you and, on a clear day, the Cévennes and Pyrenees mountains are visible in the distance. **Chapelle Notre-Dame-de-la-Salette** behind the terrace is delightful. This small chapel with elaborate mosaic decorations was built in 1864 on the site of a medieval hermitage and is a centre for pilgrimages; the most important are in September and October. On the way, you will be tempted to linger in the pâtisseries, *épiceries* and other small shops, particularly in rue Gambetta and rue Jean Jaurès.

On the sea side, the formidable **Fort Richelieu** was built in 1744 after a two-day occupation by the English. The sailors' cemetery, Cimetière Marin, just below it, is the subject of a moving poem by Paul Valéry, who was born in the town and buried there in 1945. The local history museum, **Musée Paul Valéry**, has sections devoted to him and another local personality, the singer Georges Brassens. Below it the defences which Vauban constructed, Fort St-Pierre, have been

**Above**
The Canal Royal in Sète

Jousting
tournaments,
dating back to 1666 when
the port was built, take
place on the Grand Canal
during the Sète Festival
season in *Jul–Aug*, which
also includes plays, music
and dancing.

transformed into the 1,500-seat open-air Théâtre de la Mer where plays are staged from mid-June to mid-August.

## Accommodation and food in Sète

**La Calanque €** *17 quai Gal Durand; tel: 04 67 74 28 37; email: info@restaurantlacalanque.com; www.restaurantlacalanque.com. Open daily all year.* Quayside restaurant where you can watch the world go by as you eat such Sète specialities as *tièles* (fish and tomato pies) or stuffed mussels.

**La Conga €€** *Plage de la Corniche; tel: 04 67 53 02 57; email: contact@conga.fr; www.conga.fr. Open all year.* Small hotel in quiet location near the beach. Nineteen rooms.

**Grand Hôtel €€€** *17 quai de Lattre-de-Tassigny; tel: 04 67 74 71 77; email: info@legrandhotelsete.com; www.legrandhotelsete.com. Open all year.* Imposing old 45-room hotel with modernised facilities overlooking the canal. Garage and car park.

**Below**
Water plays a large part in life
in the south

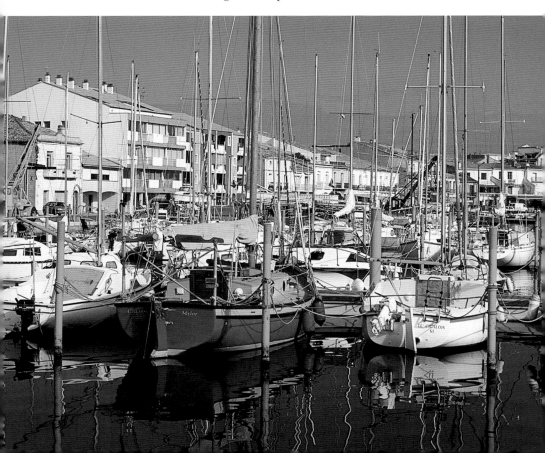

# VILLENEUVE-LES-MAGUELONE

**Mas d'Andos €**
*route de Mireval
(D116); tel: 04 67 69 58
44. Open daily Jul–Aug for
guided visits (40 minutes) at
1700; Sun Sept–Jun.*

A comparatively recent addition to this ancient village is an ostrich farm, the **Mas d'Andos**. Visitors can see how the 500 birds are reared and buy decorative eggshells, feathers and ostrich sausage.

## Accommodation and food in the coastal resorts area

Though there are plenty of small hotels to be found in the area, self-catering dominates the purpose-built resorts like Cap d'Agde, which has a huge choice of holiday apartments and villas. The area has many campsites too; some have chalets to rent for those who do not have their own caravan or tent. Pre-erected tents can be booked through several British tour operators. **Hérault area** hotel reservations: *tel: 04 67 67 71 71; www.herault-tourisme.com*

# Suggested tour

**Total distance:** 135km. The detour to Maguelone adds 8km and the detour to Pézenas adds 40km.

**Time:** 4 hours' driving. Allow at least a day for the main route, more with detours. Those with limited time should concentrate on the stretch between Sète and Agde.

**Links to other tours:** From Agde, the D612 leads to Béziers (*see page 200*), 23km away. From Pézenas, the N9 also leads to Béziers, 22km away, or to Clermont l'Herault (*see page 222*), 20km away.

*Joutes nautiques*

Jousting tournaments provide colourful entertainment during summer, particularly at Sète and Agde. Two jousters dressed in splendid costumes stand facing each other on *tintaines* – small platforms – in rowing boats, one red, one blue, propelled by teams of ten oarsmen. The one who dislodges the other with his 3m-long, three-pronged lance is the winner – and of course there is much cheering and jeering whenever one or the other falls into the water.

This is a mainly flat route of good, well-signposted roads. However, it covers peak holiday territory and is near Montpellier so the roads get very busy in high season. Leave Montpellier on the D986 to **PALAVAS-LES-FLOTS** ❶. This takes you between the Pérols and Arnel lagoons, home to hundreds of pink flamingos which stand picturesquely in groups preening themselves, foraging for fish or asleep on one leg. Those with grey/white feathers are the youngest. The shallow lagoons also attract many seabirds so you are unlikely to want to hurry along their tranquil shorelines.

## Getting out of the car

**Detour:** Eucalyptus trees, cedars and pines shade the former cathedral, a small castle-like building in cream stone, at **MAGUELONE** ❷, 4km southwest from Palavas-les-Flots. You walk to it along a spit of land between the sea and L'Etang de l'Arnel.

From Palavas-les-Flots, return on the D986 to join the D185, which goes past **VILLENEUVE-LES-MAGUELONE** ❸. Interestingly, a causeway road used to lead direct from Maguelone to Villeneuve-lès-Maguelone until the 1700s when the Rhône–Sète Canal was built, cutting it in two. The D612 leading to Sète is not an attractive road, though a visit to the Muscat cellars in **FRONTIGNAN** ❹ *(just north of it; tel: 04 67 48 93 20. Open daily all year)* can provide a welcome distraction. Note, however, that it's very easy to speed past the turning by mistake. There are two routes around **SETE** ❺ and **Mont St-Clair**, either south along the scenic corniche beside the sea or to the north across canals and past the railway station. The D612 then continues to **MARSEILLAN-PLAGE** ❻ beside the railway line along a long straight sandbar with water on both sides. The **BASSIN DE THAU** ❼ lagoon is mostly hidden behind trees, while dunes obscure the sea. The road system around **LE CAP D'AGDE** ❽ (just south of the D612) is confusing and the only way to reach either the marinas or the beaches is to park and walk. Watch for signs to the various *Plages*, or for the central marina follow 'Capitainerie du Centre-Port'. The naturist village is signed *Naturisme*. The old town of **AGDE** ❾ is 4km inland on the north side of the D612 beside the River Hérault.

**Detour:** To visit **PEZENAS** ❿, leave Agde on the D13 (20km).

From Agde, the route goes north on the D51 through **MARSEILLAN** ⓫ until it meets the D613, which goes to **MEZE** ⓬ and **Bouzigues** on the way back to Montpellier. At **Poussan**, you have the option of joining the A9 autoroute to Montpellier. This is only slightly faster but enables you to skirt the south side of the city. If you continue on the N113, it is worth taking a right-hand turn at **Gigean** up to **St-Félix-de-Montceau**, the ruins of a Benedictine abbey on a hilltop. The view is superb and the countryside smells sweetly of herbs and pines.

🌙 **Camping Californie Plage €**
*Côte Ouest, Vias Plage; tel: 04 67 21 64 69; email: californie.plage@wanadoo.fr; www.californie-plage.fr.* Secluded beachside campsite under trees with swimming pool, restaurant and shop. Caravans for rent by the week.

## Also worth exploring

To take time off on the beach, a further alternative is to turn south off the D912 for **Vias Plage**. This is one of several small resorts in the

**La Maison des Vins du Languedoc €€**
*Mas Saporta (beside the D986/D189 junction just south of Montpellier); tel: 04 67 06 88 66; www. coteaux-languedoc.com. Open Mon–Sat all year.* Restaurant serving regional specialities with own wine cellars selling local Coteaux du Languedoc wines.

area, all popular with families as they have well-equipped campsites. For walking, there is the shady towpath of the Canal du Midi which runs parallel to the coast all the way from Portiragnes-Plage to Agde. Boat excursions on the Canal (*Tue–Sat Jul–Aug*) start from **Agde**, **Marseillan** and **Portiragnes-Plage**, operated by **Bateaux du Soleil** (*tel: 04 67 94 08 79; www.bateaux-du-soleil.com*). Alternatively, you can hire a self-drive cruiser for weekend or one-week trips (*Mar–Oct*) from **Le Boat**'s base at **Port Cassafières** in **Portiragnes** (*tel: 04 67 90 91 70; www.leboat.co.uk*).

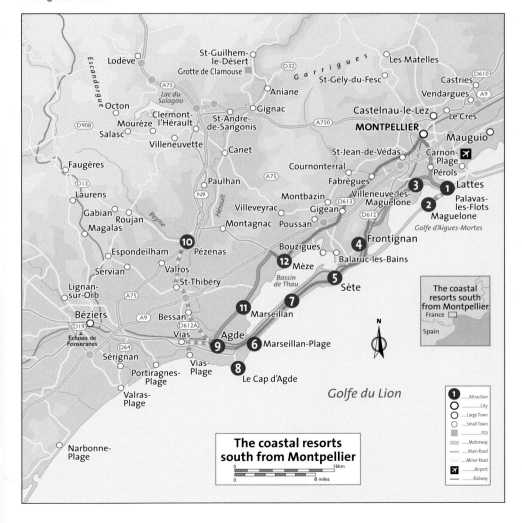

The coastal resorts south from Montpellier

# Language

Although English is spoken in most tourist locations, it is courteous to attempt to speak some French. The effort is generally appreciated, and may even elicit a reply in perfect English! The following is a very brief list of some useful words and phrases, with approximate pronunciation guides. For drivers' vocabulary, see page 26. The *Thomas Cook European 12-Language Phrasebook* (£5.99) lists more than 300 travel phrases in French (and in 11 other European languages).

- **Hello/Goodbye**
  Bonjour/Au revoir *Bawngzhoor/Ohrervwahr*
- **Good evening/Good night**
  Bonsoir/Bonne nuit *Bawngswahr/Bon nwee*
- **Yes/No**
  Oui/Non *Wee/Nawng*
- **Please/Thank you (very much)**
  S'il vous plaît/Merci (beaucoup) *Seelvooplay/Mehrsee (bohkoo)*
- **Excuse me, can you help me, please?**
  Excusez-moi, vous pouvez m'aider, s'il vous plaît? *Ekskewzaymwah, voo poovay mahyday, seelvooplay?*
- **Do you speak English?**
  Vous parlez anglais? *Voo pahrlay ahnglay?*
- **I'm sorry, I don't understand.**
  Pardon, je ne comprends pas. *Pahrdawng, zher ner kawngprawng pah.*
- **I am looking for the tourist information office.**
  Je cherche l'office de tourisme. *Zher shaersh lohfeece de tooreezm.*
- **Do you have a map of the town/area?**
  Avez-vous une carte de la ville/région? *Ahvehvoo ewn cart der lah veel/rehzhawng?*
- **Do you have a list of hotels?**
  Vous avez une liste d'hôtels? *Voozahveh ewn leesst dohtehl?*
- **Do you have any rooms free?**
  Vous avez des chambres disponibles? *Voozahveh deh shahngbr deesspohneebl?*
- **I would like to reserve a single/double room with/without bath/shower.**
  Je voudrais réserver une chambre pour une personne/pour deux personnes avec/sans salle de bain/douche. *Zher voodray rehsehrveh ewn shahngbr poor ewn pehrson/poor der pehrson avek/sawns sal der banne/doosh.*

- **I would like Bed & Breakfast/(room and) half board/(room and) full board.**
  Je voudrais le petit-déjeuner/la demi-pension/la pension complète. *Zher voodray ler pewtee-dehjewneh/lah dermee-pahngsyawng/lah pahngsyawng kawngplait.*
- **How much is it per night?**
  Quel est le prix pour une nuit? *Khel eh ler pree poor ewn nuwy?*
- **I would like to stay for . . . nights.**
  Je voudrais rester . . . nuits. *Zher voodray resteh . . . newyh.*
- **Do you accept traveller's cheques/credit cards?**
  Vous acceptez les chèques de voyages/les cartes de crédit? *Vooz aksepteh leh sheck der vwoyazh/leh kart der krehdee?*
- **I would like a table for two.**
  Je voudrais une table pour deux personnes. *Zher voodray ewn tabl poor der pehrson.*
- **I would like a cup of/two cups of/another coffee/tea.**
  Je voudrais une tasse de/deux tasses de/encore une tasse de café/thé. *Zher voodray ewn tahss der/der tahss der/oncaw ewn tahss der kafeh/teh.*
- **I would like a bottle/glass/two glasses of mineral water/red wine/white wine, please.**
  Je voudrais une bouteille/un verre/deux verres d'eau minérale/de vin rouge/de vin blanc, s'il vous plaît. *Zher voodray ewn bootayy/ang vair/der vair doh mynehral/der vang roozh/der vang blahng, seelvooplay.*
- **Could I have it well-cooked/medium/rare, please?**
  Je le voudrais bien cuit/à point/saignant, s'il vous plaît. *Zher ler voodray beeang kwee/ah pwahng/saynyang, seelvooplay.*
- **May I have the bill, please?**
  L'addition, s'il vous plaît? *Laddyssyawng, seelvooplay.*
- **Where is the toilet (restroom), please?**
  Où sont les toilettes, s'il vous plaît? *Oo sawng leh twahlaitt, seelvooplay?*
- **How much does it/this cost?**
  Quel est le prix? *Kehl eh ler pree?*
- **A (half-)kilo of . . . please.**
  Un (demi-) kilo de . . . s'il vous plaît. *Ang (dermee)keelo der . . . seelvooplay.*

# Index

# Acknowledgements

**Project management:** Cambridge Publishing Management Limited
**Project editor:** Karen Beaulah
**Series design:** Fox Design
**Cover design:** Liz Lyons Design
**Layout:** Cambridge Publishing Management Limited
**Map work:** PCGraphics (UK) Limited
**Repro and image setting:** PDQ Digital Media Solutions Ltd/Cambridge Publishing
Management Limited

We would like to thank Image Select International/Chris Fairclough Colour Library for the
photographs used in this book, to whom the copyright belongs, with the exception of the
following:

**Dreamstime.com** (pages 113 Cynoclub and 134 Davidmartyn);
**Gillian Thomas/John Harrison** (pages 21, 138, 140, 150, 152, 154, 157, 159, 183, 196 and 198);
**Wikimedia Commons** (page 193 Zewan);
**World Pictures** (pages 36, 130, 137 and 200).

# Feedback form

We're committed to providing the very best up-to-date information in our travel guides and constantly strive to make them as useful as they can be. You can help us to improve future editions by letting us have your feedback. Just take a few minutes to complete and return this form to us.

**When did you buy this book?** ..............................................................................................
..............................................................................................................................................

**Where did you buy it? (Please give town/city and, if possible, name of retailer)**
..............................................................................................................................................
..............................................................................................................................................

**When did you/do you intend to travel in Languedoc and Southwest France?** ......................
..............................................................................................................................................

**For how long (approx)?** ........................................................................................................

**How many people in your party?** ........................................................................................

**Which cities, national parks and other locations did you/do you intend mainly to visit?**
..............................................................................................................................................
..............................................................................................................................................
..............................................................................................................................................
..............................................................................................................................................

**Did you/will you:**
❏ Make all your travel arrangements independently?
❏ Travel on a fly-drive package?
Please give brief details: ........................................................................................................
..............................................................................................................................................

**Did you/do you intend to use this book:**
❏ For planning your trip?          ❏ Both?
❏ During the trip itself?

**Did you/do you intend also to purchase any of the following travel publications for your trip?**
A road map/atlas (please specify) ..........................................................................................
Other guidebooks (please specify) ........................................................................................

**Have you used any other Thomas Cook guidebooks in the past? If so, which?**

...........................................................................................................................................
...........................................................................................................................................

Please rate the following features of *driving guides Languedoc & Southwest France* for their value to you (circle VU for 'very useful', U for 'useful', NU for 'little or no use'):

| | | | |
|---|---|---|---|
| The *Travel facts* section on pages 12–21 | VU | U | NU |
| The *Driver's guide* section on pages 22–27 | VU | U | NU |
| The *Highlights* on pages 38–39 | VU | U | NU |
| The recommended driving routes throughout the book | VU | U | NU |
| Information on towns and cities, national parks, etc | VU | U | NU |
| The maps of towns and cities, parks, etc | VU | U | NU |

Please use this space to tell us about any features that in your opinion could be changed, improved, or added in future editions of the book, or any other comments you would like to make concerning the book:

...........................................................................................................................................
...........................................................................................................................................
...........................................................................................................................................
...........................................................................................................................................
...........................................................................................................................................
...........................................................................................................................................
...........................................................................................................................................
...........................................................................................................................................

**Your age category:**      ❏ 21–30    ❏ 31–40    ❏ 41–50    ❏ over 50

Your name: Mr/Mrs/Miss/Ms ..............................................................................................
(First name or initials) .......................................................................................................
(Last name) .......................................................................................................................

Your full address: (Please include postal or zip code)

...........................................................................................................................................
...........................................................................................................................................
...........................................................................................................................................
...........................................................................................................................................
...........................................................................................................................................

Your daytime telephone number: ......................................................................................

**Please detach this page and send it to: driving guides Series Editor,**
**Thomas Cook Publishing, PO Box 227, Coningsby Road, Peterborough PE3 8SB.**

**Alternatively, you can email us at: *books@thomascook.com***